THE LIBRARY
North Devon District Hospital
Raleigh Park, Barnstaple
Devon EX31 4JB
Tel: 01271 - 322363
library@ndevon.swest.nhs.uk
Return on or before the last date stamped below.

Valuing

Other books from M&K include:

A Pre-Reader for the Foundation Degree in Health and Social Care Practice
ISBN: 9781905539680

The Primary Care Guide to Mental Health
ISBN: 9781905539109

Nurses and Their Patients:
Informing practice through psychodynamic insights
ISBN: 9781905539314

Perinatal Mental Health: A clinical guide
ISBN: 9781905539499

Preventing and Reducing Aggression & Violence in Health and Social Care:
A holistic approach
ISBN: 9781905539574

My Health, My Faith, My Culture: A guide for healthcare practitioners
ISBN: 9781905539802

Research Issues in Health and Social Care
ISBN: 9781905539208

Identification and Treatment of Alcohol Dependency
ISBN: 9781905539161

Valuing People
with a
Learning Disability

Steve Mee

Valuing People with a Learning Disability

Steve Mee

ISBN: 978-1-905539-66-6

First published 2012

British Library Cataloguing in Publication Data

A catalogue record for this book is available from the British Library

Notice

Clinical practice and medical knowledge constantly evolve. Standard safety precautions must be followed, but, as knowledge is broadened by research, changes in practice, treatment and drug therapy may become necessary or appropriate. Readers must check the most current product information provided by the manufacturer of each drug to be administered and verify the dosages and correct administration, as well as contraindications. It is the responsibility of the practitioner, utilising the experience and knowledge of the patient, to determine dosages and the best treatment for each individual patient. Any brands mentioned in this book are as examples only and are not endorsed by the publisher. Neither the publisher nor the authors assume any liability for any injury and/or damage to persons or property arising from this publication.

To contact M&K Publishing write to:

M&K Update Ltd · The Old Bakery · St. John's Street

Keswick · Cumbria CA12 5AS

Tel: 01768 773030 · Fax: 01768 781099

publishing@mkupdate.co.uk

www.mkupdate.co.uk

Designed and typeset by Mary Blood

Printed in England H&H Reeds, Penrith

Contents

The 'stories' that appear in each chapter are listed below each chapter.

Chapter 4: Metaphor and Attribution 39

Chapter 5: Impression Management 49

Chapter 6: Schemas, Social Representation and Stereotypes 67

Acknowledgements

The question 'what do you mean by valuing?' was first asked by Roger Clough, my PhD supervisor. I thank him for never letting it drop, despite my impatience. I thank Carol Thomas for the simple suggestion 'write a book that your students would like' when I had no idea of what to do with a PhD.

Thank you to Dennis Howlett who provided invaluable support as a critical friend. I only wish I had been able to reciprocate properly. Thanks to Dick Follows for allowing the use of his research and for critiquing the chapter on communication.

I also want to acknowledge the many seminal theorists mentioned in this book. The phrase 'standing on the shoulders of giants' may be a cliché but it certainly applies to this fascinating area of study. Some true luminaries have crafted these theories and I hope I have done them justice in this book.

As an inveterate collector of stories, I am indebted to those people with a learning difficulty whose narratives fill these pages. Some of these stories fill us all with horror and I only hope that the act of telling them will help to ensure that they never happen again.

Thanks also to the students and colleagues who have contributed their accounts to my collection. Apologies to those (especially past students) who have heard many of these stories before.

Thanks to the University of Cumbria for their support and for sustaining the right to continue scholarly pursuits at a time when all academic institutions are under financial pressure and have to justify the use of resources. Thanks to my colleagues in the Learning Disability Teaching Team for supporting my ideas. Thanks as well to Phil Ratcliffe for the idea of the theme continuum.

Thanks to the people from my publishers, M&K Update, who have enabled me to get this book to print. These are Mike Roberts (publisher), Kelly Davis (editor), Mary Blood (designer) and Felicity Watts (proofreader and indexer).

Thank you to Hazel for her patience and her unerring critical eye.

To Hazel and Kate

The purpose of this book

■ Water torture

A woman with a learning disability who lived in supported care had been forced out of bed following a verbal confrontation with her support staff. This confrontation escalated to the point at which the staff restrained her in an illegal manner. This woman was then forced into the shower fully clothed, after which she was made to stand outside, where the temperature was near to freezing. She lay on the floor shivering uncontrollably. When she was allowed inside, she appeared to be in the early stages of hypothermia.

(BBC 3)

This incident was reported in 2011 on a *Panorama* programme entitled 'Undercover Care: The Abuse Exposed', broadcast on 31 May 2011. The woman involved had allegedly been subjected to assault and mistreatment.

This book asks the question, 'What do we mean by valuing people with a learning disability?' The 'Water torture' story appears to be a clear example of *de*-valuing people with a learning disability. It is probably safe to assume that, for most people, 'valuing' means the exact opposite to the behaviour described in this story. The programme narrative suggested that one particular man was the instigator and perpetrator of this mistreatment. Other members of the support staff were described as being scared of him and were reported to have gone along with what was happening. It would be possible to see this as just one example of mistreatment, which in no way reflects the standards within that service or the wider life experience of people with learning disabilities. This incident could be seen as an anomaly (or one-off incident) arising from the actions of one rogue member of the 'care' staff.

Castlebeck is the service provider at the centre of this exposé and their website contains a clear statement about the service they intend to provide:

The aim is to enable people to define and achieve the kind of life and relationships that work for them with the outcome being the quality of life for that individual…

Their website also has statements about the support plans they offer:

> Person-centred plans help us discover and encourage the individual's wants, wishes, dreams, ambitions and so on and make sure that 'clinical' plans don't take up his or her whole time. Person-centred plans address the need for us to listen to people and their expectations and make sure we also monitor their progress in terms of quality of life.

> We aim to focus on what progress means for the individual and will produce a plan that states exactly how we will support each person, the standards and outcomes to be achieved and who will deliver each aspect of the plan. This will also identify the resources we need to provide for each person's needs.

These statements probably describe what most of us involved with services to people with a learning disability would recognise as clear intentions to 'value' those with a learning disability. Yet in the 'Water torture' story above, there is a huge gulf between stated intentions and the alleged reality. At one end of a 'valuing' spectrum, there is the intention to listen and work towards an individual's dreams. At the other end of the spectrum, we have allegations of systematic abuse and even torture. What has happened here?

Was the abuse described in the *Panorama* programme an anomaly? Or was it an example of something altogether darker and more pervasive? It certainly did not appear to be an example of things getting temporarily out of hand, as the programme reported systematic abuse over a long period at this home. It told a story of the staff team apparently colluding in this mistreatment, of managers being reported as 'turning a blind eye', of the care organisation responsible allegedly ignoring a whistleblower, of the inspectors evidently finding nothing wrong (despite also apparently being contacted by the whistleblower), and of the devastated parents of the victim stating on the programme that they had not believed her when she told them of her mistreatment. It appears that the individual said to have instigated this mistreatment was not the only one who devalued this woman. Perhaps the other staff, the managers, the care organisation, the commissioners, the inspectors and her carers could all be viewed as 'guilty'.

We might also question the attitudes of policy makers who are at present cutting public resources for disabled people, and then we might ask about all the people who voted in a government with a mandate to make these cuts. The list of 'culprits' is damning and wide-ranging. It includes 'care' staff, parents, the 'care' organisation, the inspectorate, the electorate and the government. This specific abuse took place in a wider context, which allowed it to continue. At an individual level, those of us who are practitioners can probably all recall times when we 'turned a blind eye' to sub-standard treatment – albeit far less abusive than that reported in the 'Water torture' example. How might *we* have appeared if there had been undercover filming of those things to which we turned a blind eye?

A report from the Equality and Human Rights Commission (EHRC 2011, p. 26) indicates that abuse of people with disabilities is widespread and not confined to supported living:

> **In March 2002, a 30-year-old woman with learning disabilities was admitted to Borders General Hospital in Scotland with multiple injuries as a result of sustained physical and sexual assaults. The abuse had been carried out at home and was perpetrated by three men, one of whom was her carer. The woman had made allegations against one of the perpetrators as a child but agencies decided her mother could protect her. When her mother died, he was allowed to become her carer, making her sleep on a carpet in the hall at his home. He began taking the woman's benefit money, deprived her of food and liquid and made her sit in the dark for long periods. Together with two friends he forced her to strip, shaved her head, sexually assaulted her and repeatedly stamped on her face and body. They also threw the woman over a fence, handcuffed her to a door and set fire to her clothing.**

Added to the list of 'culprits' we now have support agencies that apparently allowed this woman to be 'cared for' by someone she had already made allegations against.

Not all abuse is as shocking as that described in the vignettes above. Here is an example that some readers may recognise as a fairly typical encounter.

▪ Behave

> An adult with a learning disability wanted to go to the shops to buy a DVD. He needed staff support to negotiate traffic safely. He had been promised that he could do this activity the day before but it had not happened. As he feared being let down again, he asked the support staff several times whether he would be able to get the DVD after lunch. The staff replied, *'If you don't stop fussing you won't be going at all, so behave.'*

This is clearly not severe abuse but it is still abuse. The Equality and Human Rights Commission report (EHRC 2011, p. 5) made the following point:

> **The really serious cases catch the headlines. But what about the constant drip, drip, nag, nag of the so-called 'low-level' harassment that many disabled people face on a daily basis? It ruins their lives. They don't have the confidence to go out. It undermines their ability to be part of society. It makes them behave differently.**

The man in 'Behave' had the right to visit his local town to buy a DVD. The staff member assumed an authority he did not actually have, to deny him that right. In this particular case, there was no apparent misdemeanour. The staff member was abusing power on a whim.

The same report (EHRC 2011, p. 163) goes on to describe systematic and widespread abuse and harassment of many people with a disability. It concludes:

> Our inquiry learnt much from both its investigation into 10 cases and the evidence that disability-related harassment is a widespread problem which has a significant impact on the day-to-day lives of disabled people. We found that the extent of harassment remains largely hidden, its seriousness rarely acknowledged, its link to the victim's disability not investigated...

The same thing is happening in all these stories and the Equality and Human Rights Commission report suggests it is widespread. Through several layers of society, from government through local organisations to individuals, there has been a collective 'devaluing'. At best it illustrates casual and unconscious disregard, but at worst we can see callous, conscious, systematic and sustained abuse. It would appear that the woman in 'Water torture' was not valued at any level. Yet these events all took place in a world in which the 'mission statement' from the service provider and government policy quite clearly defined what they consider to be 'valuing' treatment of people with a learning disability.

Several recent reports have highlighted similar issues.

● A joint investigation into the provision of services for people with learning disabilities at Cornwall Partnership NHS Trust (Healthcare Commission 2006, p. 5) highlighted abuse in care services in Cornwall and concluded:

> Some individuals, as the trust has acknowledged, have suffered abuse including physical, emotional and environmental abuse. The trust's own investigations at Budock Hospital have shown that some people using its services have had to endure years of abusive practices and some have suffered real injury as a result.

● An investigation into the service for people with learning disabilities provided by Sutton and Merton Primary Care Trust (Healthcare Commission 2007, p. 3) commented:

> The investigation team examined 15 serious incidents that occurred in the learning disability service between December 2002 and November 2005. These were incidents of sexual and physical abuse including one incident when a woman with learning disabilities was raped.

● 'Death By Indifference' (Mencap 2007, p. 5) reported on the way people with a learning disability are often excluded from access to healthcare, quoting Allan (the father of Mark, who died in August 2003 of bronchopneumonia):

> We believe that Mark died unnecessarily. Throughout his life, we encountered medical professionals who had no idea how to deal with people with a learning disability or what it is like to be a parent of someone with a learning disability – to know their suffering, to see their distress. If only they would listen...

- An independent inquiry (DOH 2008, p. 18), known as 'The Michaels Report', looked into the lack of healthcare for people with a learning disability and described the following example:

  I work with a client with learning disabilities who has a cataract and challenging behaviour. The GP refuses to treat on the basis that 'He can see out of his other eye'.

The examples discussed so far are relatively recent cases of significant devaluing of people with a learning disability. However, there is a long history of similar shocking exposés of abuse. Many of these cases have resulted in reports that have gone on to underpin policy change. For example, in the 1960s the conditions in long-stay hospitals for people with a learning disability were brought to public attention by a series of press reports of serious mistreatment. The *News of the World* exposed conditions in Ely Hospital in Wales in 1968. The Ely Report led to the Howe Report (1969), which in turn led to the White Paper 'Better Services for the Mentally Handicapped' (DHSS 1971).

The Seebohm Report (Home Office 1968) had led to the setting up of locally controlled, politically accountable social services. The building of the new hostels was based on the guidelines contained within 'Local Authority Building Note no. 2' (DHSS 1973). In 1974 the Secretary of State, Barbara Castle, set up the National Development Group and the National Development Team. She also commissioned the Jay Committee Report (1979), which suggested that hospital care was inappropriate for most people with a learning disability. In 1971 the Campaign for the Mentally Handicapped (CMH) was established to campaign for the rights of people with a learning disability in general and the closure of the long-stay hospitals in particular.

What do we mean by 'valuing'?

The discussion so far has largely focused on the abuse that people with a learning disability frequently experience. In other words, the focus has been on ***de***-valuing. There are problems in using words such as 'valuing' and 'devaluing' to aid understanding of the day-to-day experiences of people with a learning disability. These terms are in common currency in the world of learning disability. Of course the term 'valuing' appears in the titles of the most significant recent government directives, 'Valuing People' (DOH 2001) and 'Valuing People Now' (DOH 2009).

The word 'value' actually has two main meanings:

1 'To assess or estimate the worth, merit or desirability of…'

2 'To have a high regard for, especially in respect of worth, usefulness, merit etc.'
  (Collins 1994).

The first definition is a verb and implies neither negative nor positive outcome. In other words, a consequence of 'assessing or estimating the worth' of something could be to ascribe either negative or positive value. In this sense of the word it would be possible, for example, to 'value' a person and come to the conclusion that they were worthless. The second dictionary definition is closer to what is probably intended when the word is used in learning disability services: 'to have high regard for.' However, simply to 'have high regard' is a passive state, in which one has already decided the worth of something. It will therefore be argued later in this book that the first definition offers an important consideration. To 'assess or estimate' suggests an active state in which one uses mental effort to reach a conclusion. The cognitive processes by which one reaches a conclusion underpin Chapters 4 to 6, and the external forces that impact on these processes are considered in Chapters 7 to 9.

'Valuing People Now' (DOH 2009, p. 10) sets out a vision for the life experiences deemed most desirable for people with a learning disability:

> **The vision remains as set out in Valuing People in 2001: that all people with a learning disability are people first with the right to lead their lives like any others, with the same opportunities and responsibilities, and to be treated with the same dignity and respect. They and their families and carers are entitled to the same aspirations and life chances as other citizens.**

This appears to be a reasonable definition of valuing people with a learning disability, and most people who work in services supporting people with a learning disability would probably agree with it. Many would probably see the ideas expressed in this statement as the very basis of their job, possibly even the axiomatic basis of all services.

Any self-respecting support service for people with a learning disability will claim that it 'values' the people it supports, and many mission statements will make that claim explicit. A recent publication includes a chapter entitled 'Values Based Support' (Richardson 2011). This publication (Atherton & Crickmore 2011) includes a section entitled 'Implementing Values Based Support', which comprises seven chapters.

In everyday discourse in support services certain abstract words become reified – to reify is 'to consider an abstract idea or concept real or concrete' (Collins 1994). Terms such as 'community', 'care', 'empowerment', 'choice' and 'valuing' are taken out of common language and given assumed concrete meanings. These terms are all considered desirable aims at present and so services (itself a reified term) will describe what they *do* as being 'valuing'. The following quotation from the 'Valuing People' White Paper (DOH 2001, p. 1) makes a link between 'valuing' and 'doing':

> **What's also a real cause for concern and anxiety is that many parents of learning disabled children face difficulties in finding the right care, health services, education and leisure opportunities for their sons and daughters. At best, they**

can feel obstacles are constantly put in their way by society. At worst, they can feel abandoned by the rest of us.

We have to change this situation if we are to achieve our goal of a modern society in which everyone is valued and has the chance to play their full part.

Richardson (2011, p. 57) suggests that dignity is 'the fundamental value from which all other values follow'. He considers it essential that services to people with a learning disability should be values based. It could, however, be argued that all services are 'values based', whether or nor not they are predicated on dignity. Using the first dictionary definition outlined on p. 5 ('to assess or estimate the worth, merit or desirability of...'), it can be seen that it is possible to value people with a learning disability in a negative way, to come to the conclusion that they are worthless. A 'service' based on this value would still be 'values based', and this is more than a pedantic point. 'Values based' is sometimes seen as the opposite to, for example, 'based on financial concerns'. However, 'financial concerns' can also be seen as 'values based'. 'Valuing People' (DOH 2001, p. 1) makes an interesting reference to ensuring 'value for money from public investment in learning disability services'.

We could argue that 'value for money' is equally a value. We might argue that this is a 'morally lower' value than 'dignity' but it is a value nonetheless. Indeed, some neo-conservatives might argue that it is a higher value. Taking this idea of 'value' as 'value for money' one step further, we might argue that the following example is also a 'values led service', however abhorrent that 'value'.

■ Nazi nurse

In Nazi Germany it was legal to end the life of a person with a learning disability. One nurse described (Ebbinghaus 1987, p. 239, cited in Benedict & Kuhla 1999) how she actively administered a lethal dose of the drug used to take life:

When giving the dissolved medicine, I proceeded with a lot of compassion. I had told patients that they would have to take a cure. Of course I could tell these fairy tales only to those patients who were still in their right minds to the extent that they could understand it. I took them lovingly and stroked them when I gave the medicine. If, for example, a patient did not empty the entire cup because it was too bitter, I talked to her nicely, telling her that she had already drunk so much that she should drink the rest, otherwise her cure couldn't be finished. Some could be convinced to empty the cup completely... They were not to be tortured more than necessary...

In Nazi Germany, decisions on whether people's existence could be justified were based upon their productivity or past service to the nation. The nurse in this vignette was administering a lethal dose of medication to those deemed unworthy of life because of their negative impact on the economy. The 'value' upon which this practice was based is an extension of the economic notion of 'value for money'.

As described above, 'Valuing People' (DOH 2001) suggests that 'valuing' can be effectively demonstrated by actions, particularly the actions of giving people access to resources and removing obstacles. The following vignette suggests a separation between 'thinking' and 'doing' in valuing.

■ Hidden feelings

A learning disability nurse supports a man who is sectioned under the Mental Health Act. He has been convicted of sexual crimes against very small children. The nurse feels revulsion at this man's crimes and finds it very difficult to work with him in a non-judgemental way. In unguarded moments she thinks of him as a 'monster'. However, she has worked hard to put her feelings to the back of her mind and offer a 'professional' front to this man. She believes that she is good at this and the man considers her to be a friend.

This man's offences disgust the nurse but her actions are positive. This nurse appears to devalue the man in her thoughts but value him in her action. Does she therefore 'value' this man or not?

A further problem is that we can think more than one thing at once.

■ The cleaner (1)

A lecturer visited a student nurse on placement at a day centre. They found a quiet room in order to discuss the placement in private. A woman dressed in an overall and carrying polish and duster entered the room and started cleaning with her back to them. The lecturer felt frustrated at the disturbance to the meeting but thought that they were in the way. He apologised and said they would move so that the cleaner could get on. The woman turned to the lecturer and he then realised she had a learning disability. His instant feeling was one of, 'It doesn't matter, as she is not a real cleaner'. He was able to over-ride this initial feeling and he and the student excused themselves and left her to do her work. The lecturer later discovered that the woman was employed by Social Services to do the cleaning.

The lecturer had an immediate thought that the woman was not a 'real cleaner' and so could be seen to be devaluing her. However, he then realised what he had thought. In a conscious re-appraisal, he became aware that he had initially devalued her but was able (he hoped) to adjust his behaviour and 'value' her by leaving her to get on with the task. Within a very short space of time, perhaps one second, the lecturer had experienced a devaluing thought and then one that was more valuing. We might ask which was the 'truest' measure of the extent to which he valued the woman with a learning disability.

Another nurse who worked with a sex offender also had two very different thoughts about him, as described in the next story.

■ Revulsion

A nursing manager worked with a man detained under the Mental Health Act. The man's offences were against children and were sexual in nature. The manager said that her staff showed a positive attitude to this man, seeming to like him as a person. He sometimes punched and kicked staff if told he could not walk past the local school (a requirement of his detention under the Mental Health Act). Despite such attacks, the staff remained positive towards him. This manager shared the team view and was very fond of the man. However, she said that if she thought of this man when she was at home with her young children she felt a sense of revulsion and anger towards him. She never felt this at work.

In this case, the nurse experienced valuing and devaluing thoughts about the same person according to where she was and, significantly, what role she was fulfilling. As a *nurse*, she believed that she valued the man, but at times when she was performing the role of a *mother* she very strongly devalued him. Again, we might ask whether this nurse values the man and which is the truer measure of her feelings?

The following story came from a care-planning meeting for a man with a learning disability. Those of you who work in services supporting people with a learning disability have probably had similar discussions.

■ The pie man

A man with a learning disability lives in supported accommodation. He loves chips and pies and hates vegetables, fruit and salad. He is gaining weight and his GP has advised that his health is at significant risk. He dislikes low-fat alternatives and is very clear about what he wants to eat. He is able to tell you that if he continues eating this food he will 'have a heart attack'.

This man needs staff to support him when shopping, as he cannot manage his money. If the staff put pressure on him to buy healthy options he will reluctantly agree, as he has learnt that a good way to keep out of trouble is to agree with staff. However, once home, he will become distressed at mealtimes.

This is a story of everyday practice. It describes a typical decision that might be made in care planning for someone with a learning disability. Among other things, the planning meeting may well discuss:

- capacity
- best interest
- human rights
- professional responsibilities
- risk
- nutrition.

They will reach a multidisciplinary conclusion and consider it a 'professional' decision. In this particular case, the person with a learning disability agreed that staff would be able to have some control over his food and manage positive reinforcement when he complied. Many of us who have supported people with a learning disability in such areas will know that in many cases the same discussion will go on for many years, and the issue will remain.

In this example, unhealthy eating had been on the care planning agenda for 12 years and there was an ongoing conflict between the person's wish to eat unhealthily and the professionals' wish to enhance his health status. The team was split on this issue, some believing that the man had a right to eat himself to an early death if that decision was 'informed'. Meanwhile, others in the team thought professionals had the authority to over-ride that right in the name of 'the person's best interest'. In this meeting, and many other such meetings, it is possible to predict which members of the professional team will take which side in the debate. Some will tend to err on the side of the person making their own choices; others will err towards protection and risk avoidance.

Both approaches can be justified from a theoretical, legal and professional point of view. The people arguing from the 'rights' angle might quote the 'Valuing People' argument that 'Four key principles, Rights, Independence, Choice, Inclusion, lie at the heart of the Government's proposals' (DOH 2001, p. 3). These support staff are, after all, respecting rights and choice in allowing a person to choose to eat themselves into ill health. On the other hand, those who argue that enhancing the person's health is the priority might quote professional codes of conduct that emphasise best interest, informed choice and capacity.

Both sides would probably agree that it is essential to value the person with a learning disability. Because of this, and because each member of the group will have a natural tendency towards one side of the debate, the resulting decision is likely to be determined by which side of the argument is supported by the most vocal and powerful professionals. This then begs the question of what we mean by 'professional judgement'.

This book asks 'What do we mean by valuing?' In the 'Pie man' story, which outcome is most valuing? Is he more valued if his choice to eat himself to an early death is respected, or if his health is protected? If you, the reader, naturally tend towards the former then you might argue that valuing someone means respecting their choice. However, if you lean towards the latter, you might say that acting in someone's best interest is the most valuing outcome. It could also be argued that if the final decision results from whichever side has the most vocal and powerful advocates, neither decision truly values the person with a learning disability. He has had a decision imposed on him either way, and his true wishes and voice have been ignored. One term that is often used in such debates is 'informed choice'. A decision is made as to whether the person should be deemed competent to make a choice. This implies that the person has to meet a certain level of mental competence in order for their choice to be 'valued'.

So how do we make such decisions and is there a body of work to help us understand the relevant issues? This book will take similar stories of everyday practice and place them in the context of areas of theory that offer the potential for greater understanding. The question 'What do we mean by valuing?' will be asked in each section of the book.

Theory versus practice

The 'Pie man' story is a typical example of how those of us who work in services supporting people with a learning disability are required to do essentially practical things while also thinking in an abstract, theoretical way. It can be argued that it is this split that defines professional practice. However, this split can be problematic if it becomes a schism. How many times do we hear practitioners say something like 'it's all right in theory but in the real world…'?

At the other end of the scale, we have people who engage in theory who are defined as academics. They produce theory and publications but may become removed from the reality of practice. Burton & Chapman (2004) argue that this problem is compounded by the requirements of academia and publishing. The required style for journal publication makes the material less accessible to practitioners without a formal academic background. Furthermore, they say, the higher the status of the journal, the more inaccessible the information becomes to practitioners. Thus the academic conventions and pressures can be seen to actively alienate students and practitioners.

This schism is evident in professional courses in higher education. My own experience as a lecturer on a learning disability nursing course is that some students see the course as an obstacle to be overcome, rather than something with innate value for developing practice. Many of these students quickly forget the theory they have been taught, and tend to learn just enough to get them through an assessment. Once back in practice, their memory of the theory they have learned will be shadowy at best.

This book is an attempt to make theory accessible to practitioners and bridge the gulf that often exists between the two. Theory is of use only if it enables us to understand the everyday experiences of practice and so to improve our practice and have a positive impact on the lives of the people we claim to support. This book is based on my experience of teaching students who often have no natural inclination to engage with theory. This approach is based in practice, using stories as a bridge to theory.

Each area of theory is covered in a short chapter. The scope of the book means that each chapter can offer little more than an introduction to a particular area. In each case, the aim is to point the reader towards a body of theory that has the potential to help understanding of practice. I do not consider myself to be an expert in any one area; it is probable that you, the reader, may have a different view and interpretation of an area of theory. This is as it should be, and I would be pleased to hear from readers who have more expertise in any area.

Most importantly, this book asks the question 'What do we mean by valuing people with a learning disability?' From this initial question, flow two supplementary questions: firstly 'How does the process of valuing work?' and, in the final chapter, 'What needs to happen to ensure the valuing of people with a learning disability?'

The Power of Stories

■ Spiderman

> John is a boy who is on the autism spectrum. One day John's mother was talking on the telephone to a friend. She told her friend that a story had recently appeared in the newspapers, saying that since the tragedy of 9/11 the makers of *Spiderman* 1 had removed the World Trade Centre towers from the film, using computer technology. John overheard his mother and was very upset when she hung up.
>
> He asked his mother why she had lied. Mum assured him that it was true. He insisted it was not and took her to the TV and put on the *Spiderman* 1 video. He fast-forwarded the film to the exact point at which Spiderman emerges from the underground and scans the streets. The shot shows a close-up of his face and, for a fleeting moment, there is a reflection of the skyline in the black eyes on his mask. In that moment the twin towers can be seen in the reflection; the film-makers had missed it. John had found it immediately. It should be noted that he did not watch *Spiderman* in an obsessive way – it was just one of the films he had which he watched from time to time.

This story shows how people on the autistic spectrum can experience the world in a way that is incomprehensible to others. Tiny details that would typically go unnoticed can overwhelm people who are on the spectrum. In this case, the boy had noticed something apparently unremarkable and was able to recall that detail and find the exact point where it appeared in the film.

Stories can be seen to have particular power. Here is an example of how a story heard in an educational setting led directly to a change in practice. A woman with a learning disability and diagnosed with autism spectrum disorder (ASD) was thought to need three care staff most of the time because of her extremely challenging behaviour. The care plan included input from a range of specialists. The situation had remained static for a long time and the manager of this service felt 'stuck'.

On a course the manager heard the 'Spiderman' story and was struck by it. She knew the facts about hypersensitivity but the story helped her to realise the all-pervading nature of this difference, and how it applied all day, every day, every minute. Now she understood that sensory overload is not just overwhelming; it means every sense being drowned in detail, with no escape and no means of switching off. Some of that detail might cause overwhelming nausea, pain or some other unpleasant sensation. She wondered whether the woman she was supporting was experiencing the world in this way.

The manager decided to sit in the woman's chair for several hours, and try to see the world as she might. She reported that it was difficult to remain in this mindset, a different sort of 'discipline' to that usually suggested by research literature. It was like seeing the world for the first time. She noticed the noise of outside traffic, the clutter in the room, the decorations on the wall, the noise from the corridor, the slamming of doors, the way the staff chatted to each other, the bright contrasting colours of staff clothing, shiny dangling jewellery, the smell of garlic on the staff, the radio, and the list went on.

As a result, she drew up new guidelines. Staff should wear subdued pastel-coloured clothes, avoid eating garlic before coming on duty, and avoid chatting over the woman's head. The clutter was reduced and soundproof curtains were put up. The manager tried to change all the things that she had observed. She reported an immediate and drastic reduction in the challenging behaviour. The manager had known the facts about sensory difference for people with ASD and she had the motivation to improve a difficult situation. But hearing the 'Spiderman' story was the significant factor in getting her to make the cognitive leap required.

Recent reports (such as DOH 2008 and Equality and Human Rights Commission 2011) have used a small number of illustrative stories to demonstrate the ways in which abuse or neglect can take place. Certain stories have great power and Bolton (2006) argues that our lives are storied. When a memory is retrieved, it is in narrative form. We 'story' and 're-story' ourselves in the light of experience, as stories change in response to situations and narrative is constantly reformulated. Perception will determine which factors in this situation are incorporated into the narrative, and some stories will have more power than others.

In other words, we make sense of our experiences by creating a narrative that may, in turn, incorporate other stories. Heath & Heath (2007) suggest that some ideas 'stick' and others are lost quickly. Those that stick will usually include the 'core' of the idea, will be compact and will contain a surprise. The core of this story is that people on the autism spectrum experience the world in a way that is beyond most people's imagination. The story is compact; the actual video clip from *Spiderman* is about 20 seconds long. My experience of telling this story when teaching is that students often make exclamations and express surprise. Heath & Heath (2007, p. 57) also suggest that we struggle to generate understanding when the information includes a lot of 'useless accuracy'. The 'Spiderman' story has very little detail and has been proven to have a high level of 'stickiness'. People appear to remember the story first, and the principle it illustrates second.

Heath & Heath (*ibid.*) also describe the 'curse of knowledge'. The issue here is that, once we know something in detail or to a sophisticated level, it is difficult to remember what it was like *not* to know. This implies that effective practitioners need to be able to stand aside from their knowledge and experience of how to watch a film in order to understand the perspective of a person with an ASD. Similarly, the teacher needs to remember what it was like to 'not know' in order to communicate at the right level for the students, and for the idea to 'stick'. Using a story such as 'Spiderman' avoids the teacher having to develop this empathy; it is a learning device that works with dramatic effect, whether or not the teacher has the required understanding.

This approach to learning is based on the principle that the source of understanding is the 'lived experience' of individuals (Smith 1998). The story provides a basis for generating an understanding of the whole. 'Stories and poems are slices, metonymically revealing the whole of life' (Bolton 2006, p. 205).

The use of stories

There are illustrative stories or vignettes throughout this book. Each chapter starts with such a story. Typically those of us linked to learning disability services may have a natural tendency to base our practice on what is seen as 'evidence-based practice' and to champion quantitative over qualitative methodology. It can be argued that in the end a story is just a story, and that there may be any number of other stories that counter the point being made.

The clarion call to use 'evidence-based practice' currently runs through nursing. The Nursing and Midwifery Council (NMC 2004, p. 10) states: 'You have a responsibility to deliver care based on current evidence, best practice and, where applicable, validated research when it is available.'

Similarly, the UK Learning Disability Consultant Network (Northway, Hutchinson & Kingdom 2006) states that learning disability nurses should access and use the evidence base in practice.

The 'league table' taught on many learning disability nursing courses would place the following types of evidence at the top of the list.

- Randomised controlled trials
- Strong evidence from at least one randomised controlled trial
- Evidence from well-designed trials without randomisation
- Evidence from non-experimental studies from more than one research group
- Opinions of respected authorities, based on clinical evidence, descriptive studies or reports of experts

Vignettes would be ranked far below these types of evidence on such courses.

The preceding list is based on the traditional principles of medical/scientific methodology. The main concern is that evidence should be reliable, possible to replicate, and possible to

15

generalise from. The lowest level allows for opinion but only from 'respected authorities' and based on 'clinical evidence'.

It would seem to exclude first-hand accounts from those who are 'not respected' and this presumably includes accounts from people with a learning disability. (If they are being 'devalued', it suggests that they are not respected.) There is certainly no mention of the evidence that comes from reflexively utilising one's own experience, as in the 'Spiderman' story presented above.

I believe that in order to answer the questions:

● What do we mean by valuing?

and

● What do we need to do to value people with a learning disability?

it is necessary to look at specific examples from the 'real world' and attempt to understand what is happening. This understanding is what underpins good practice. Randomised, controlled trials are in fact limited in how far they can enable practice to be better understood and performed. Throughout this book, the approach will be based on reflection on illustrative stories, as I believe that this actually constitutes very powerful 'evidence'.

Reflexivity is required on the part of the reader. This changes passive reading into a cognitively active process. Stanley defines reflexivity as '... treating one's self as subject for intellectual enquiry' (Stanley 1993, cited in Thomas 1999, p. 82). We might argue that the outcome of 'intellectual enquiry' is 'data'.

Wetherell et al. (2001b, p. 396) say that, in order to be reflexive, one must 'acknowledge the theories, values and politics which guide the research so these can be taken into account when evaluating the analyst's claims'. This is a way in which we might judge the worth of research. The principle also applies to practice, in the sense that the practitioner should acknowledge the theories, values and politics that underpin their judgement.

Stanley suggested that reflexive research involved 'treating one's self as subject for intellectual enquiry' (Stanley 1993, cited in Thomas 1999, p. 82). Wetherell et al. describe a third sense in which research might be reflexive: '...the way that the researcher acts on the world and the world acts on the researcher, in a loop' (2001a, p. 17). Similarly, the practitioner engages with the world through intervention and thus changes the world.

The learning disability practitioner faces a complex world of practice. What is the 'right' sort of 'evidence' to inform learning disability practice? Burton & Chapman (2004, p. 60) suggest that the scientific response to this complexity is to use a strategy of simplification. This means that, in the 'production of knowledge', the context is controlled, the participants are restricted, the intervention is formalised and standardised. For the practitioner, this unfortunately leads to a common and recognisable syndrome: research papers with appetising titles, promising abstracts, dull content and limited conclusions. Little is said about little.

They describe further problems with the literature:

- If the research does not 'speak to their practice and experience' (*ibid.*, p. 61), the practitioner comes to rely on training and experience. Perhaps we might add 'own reflexivity and reflection'; and of course we might also add 'stories' and 'vignettes'.

- Research is not readily available to practitioners. Academic researchers are under pressure to publish in peer-reviewed academic journals, which require some specialist knowledge to understand. The way the research is presented might thus be a barrier to the practitioner.

- Even when the research is 'pre-digested' by professional journals and textbooks, practitioners may have limited access to the journals and be too short of time (in this era of service targets) to engage in reflective digestion of content.

Burton & Chapman (*ibid.*) suggest that practitioners should draw upon seven significant areas when making a professional decision:

- Experience
- Appraisal of current situation
- Values, attitudes and beliefs
- Theory, which has several layers of explicitness
- Knowledge from multiple sources (personal, craft, scientific, local, interpersonal, feedback from people receiving the service)
- Imperatives, which can be personal, interpersonal, organisational, professional, legal, governmental
- Judgement (an action that draws on the above facets, integrating them, but is perhaps little understood as a skill)

They argue (2004, p. 63) that 'scientific knowledge' is the only factor in the above list that corresponds to what is usually meant by 'evidence-based practice'. They also summarise the central problem with the orthodox evidence-based approach:

> It would be naïve to think that there is a simple recipe for basing practice on one type of input. Yet that is just what is offered by the [evidence-based orthodoxy] ... an almost insultingly mechanical cookbook model is implied: just follow the expert recommendations.

It can be argued that the term 'evidence-based practice' has become reified, a 'taken for granted' tenet in professions involved in supporting people with a learning disability. French (2002, p. 250) claims that the term is imprecise:

> 'Evidence based practice' has become a euphemism for information management, clinical judgement, professional practice development or managed care.

He goes on to state that the term 'evidence' itself is unclear and ambiguous and suggests the following summary and hierarchy (p. 254):

Evidence as truth.

Evidence as knowledge (including tacit, expert opinion and experiential).

Evidence as any relevant information that confirms or refutes a belief.

Evidence as primary research finding.

Evidence as meta-analyses and systematic reviews.

Horses for courses

It might be illuminating for you, the reader, to reflect on your last day of practice. How much of your work do you think was directed by the 'gold standard' of findings from randomised controlled trials? It is possible, for example, that your eight-hour day may have only included ten minutes of practice that was thus directed. The person you were supporting may have had a health need that required knowledge that could only safely have come from such trials.

Another area to consider is communication with people with a learning disability. We may have gained knowledge of the effect of limited linguistic development, and we may have developed other systems of communication, using 'scientific' approaches. But what directs us in everyday practice? The following vignette was from a liaison nurse in a general hospital.

■ The scary camera

A man with autism was having problems with his bowel. He required a colonoscopy, as there were fears that he might have a serious health problem. He was refusing point-blank to have the investigation. The liaison nurse met him to discuss the investigation. It turned out that he had been told that he would have a 'video camera put up his bottom in theatre'. As a person with autism, he heard language literally. The only video camera he knew of was the one his family took on holiday, and the only theatre he knew of he had seen on *Holby City*, with noise, panic and copious amounts of blood. He agreed to just have a look at the camera and theatre. Once he had seen these, he readily agreed to the investigation.

Colonoscopy procedures are based on 'rigorous science'. From the design of the apparatus to the interpretation of the symptoms and on to the interventions used when a problem is diagnosed, there is no substitute for the knowledge gained through randomised, controlled trials. However, the liaison nurse did not need to have much knowledge of the actual procedure. What knowledge did she have and where did it come from? She was able to interpret the man's response based on her knowledge of the world from the viewpoint of a person who is on the autism spectrum.

We might ask where such knowledge originates. Both this practitioner and the one in 'Spiderman' would probably say their knowledge came from long reflective practice. The key cognitive steps probably came from single 'critical examples' from practice. Many of the key vignettes used in this book came from practice and were experienced as 'critical' in this way.

This book is based on stories from practice. These stories have been collected from my own experience, from colleagues, students and people with a learning disability. Other stories have been taken from the media and history. Each is used to illustrate a particular point. I am interpreting the stories in a particular way but it is quite likely that you, the reader, may question some of these interpretations. That is as it should be. I would be very happy to hear from readers who may wish to challenge the interpretations as well as the particular applications of theory. We can learn in a collaborative fashion.

Several of the stories appear in more than one chapter because they can be seen to illustrate several points. This book makes no claim to identify 'The Truth'. Rather, it reflexively tries to make links between theory and practice, in an attempt to understand what is happening. The best we can hope for is that we find 'A Truth'. The underlying aim is to offer tools for deeper understanding for practitioners, and to keep asking 'What was happening here?'

When we understand things at a deeper level, there is a chance that we might act in a more conscious way. Action based on deeper understanding might be more likely to lead to a better experience for the person with a learning disability. Johns' model of reflective practice is based on a similar assumption (Johns, 2000). Thus the main aim of this book is for practitioner action to lead to valuing of the person with a learning disability.

The interpretation and analysis of the stories are both open to discussion. The book does not set out to offer a definitive analysis, nor to provide a list of 'what to do' rules. Its purpose is to raise questions about day-to-day practice and cause the reader to reflect on the following questions:

- What do I mean by valuing?
- Do I actually value people with a learning disability?
- What do I need to do to value the people with whom I work?

Historic Roles

■ Dirty cups

Four people who have resettled from a long-stay institution live in a house, with 24-hour support from a staff team. The staff are well organised. They keep a set of 'staff cups' in a high cupboard. In a lower cupboard there are 'client cups', which are cheaper and older than the 'staff cups'. There is a dishwasher in the house and no one who lives there has a communicable disease.

This is a situation that many readers will recognise from their practice. How has it arisen? The staff have made this arrangement. We might ask whether this arrangement tells us anything about the way they perceive the people who live in the house. We are, after all, only describing the use of crockery. It would be difficult to argue that the staff value the people who live in the house if they are not prepared to share the same cups.

The second vignette is an example from history.

■ Unfit breeders

In Germany in 1932 there was concern about 'hereditary diseases' being passed from one generation to the next. Anyone who had such a 'disease' could legally be made to undergo compulsory sterilisation. The official list of hereditary diseases included 'congenital feeble-mindedness', 'hereditary epilepsy' and 'severe hereditary physical deformity' (Friedlander 1995). Many thousands of people experienced enforced sterilisation as a result of being seen as individuals who might pass on the 'disease' of what we now know as learning disability.

Is there a thread that connects the crockery arrangements in a house to the enforced sterilisation of a whole group of people? The staff in the 'Dirty cups' story are prepared to share cups with each other but not willing to share them with people with a learning disability. When the staff team was challenged about this, the manager argued that the reason was a practical one; there was a risk of infection.

There are two obvious counter-arguments to this. Firstly, shared facilities such as this should have strict hygiene standards in any case. A dishwasher will ensure the cleanliness of a cup, for example. Secondly, if one person has a communicable disease or hygiene issues then their cutlery and crockery should be kept separate from all other people in the house, no matter whether they are staff or other residents. In this particular house, no staff member or person with a learning disability was known to have a communicable disease.

One member of the staff team was able to express his feelings well. He said, 'I don't know why but I just don't fancy using the same cups as the clients.' This staff member would seem not to value the people who live in the house sufficiently to share cups with them but this judgement is a feeling, rather than a fully considered point of view. It appears to be an unconscious judgement.

In the 'Unfit breeders' story, the rationale was that the passing of disease from one generation to another needed to be halted. In both 'Dirty cups' and 'Unfit breeders', people with a learning disability are seen as 'diseased'. The underlying way of seeing the person with a disability is the same, even though the outcomes are at opposite ends of a continuum. At one end of the continuum, the result of this perception is that the people with a learning disability are made to use inferior cups. At the other extreme, they are forcibly sterilised.

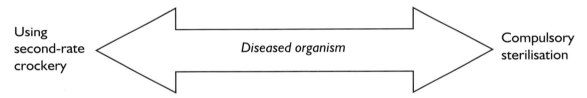

Using second-rate crockery ⟷ *Diseased organism* ⟷ Compulsory sterilisation

The challenge for the reader and practitioner is to be prepared to consider that there is any commonality between something they might do (such as using staff cups) and something they would never expect to do (such as participating in enforced sterilisation). It will be argued here that understanding this commonality enables us, as practitioners, to better understand our relationships with people with a learning disability.

It is possible to see the two issues as related but still believe that the crockery issue is so inconsequential as to be unworthy of serious discussion. However, this book argues that the devaluing experienced by people with a learning disability is sometimes extreme but more often a 'drip, drip, nag, nag', as described by the Equality and Human Rights Commission (2011, p. 5). This 'drip, drip' is important and probably describes the lived experience of many people with a learning disability. It is still devaluing.

There is a body of theory that can help us to understand the ways in which both present-day care workers and the policy makers in Nazi Germany perceive people with a learning disability. It is first necessary to tease out the underlying assumptions in the two examples above. In 'Dirty cups', the staff appear to be saying that other staff are in the group with whom they will share a cup but people with a learning disability are not – they are diseased. In Nazi Germany, policy makers and medical practitioners considered themselves in the group who had the right to reproduce but viewed people with a learning disability as being in another group – those who were unfit to reproduce. Again the reason is 'disease'.

In both cases, people with a learning disability have been perceived as 'other'. Once individuals have been 'othered', they may be subject to different standards of treatment by those who have thus defined them. Wolfensberger argues that the way people are perceived and defined determines the way they are treated (Wolfensberger 1972). He suggests that in the past people who have been seen as deviant (including people with a learning disability) have been seen as occupying deviant roles and that, once this has happened, their treatment is likely to be negative. He calls them 'historic roles' and suggests that there are eight of them:

- Diseased organism
- Subhuman organism
- Menace
- Unspeakable object of dread
- Object of pity
- Holy innocent
- Object of ridicule
- Eternal child

For each one, Wolfensberger (*ibid*.) states that there is an underlying way of seeing people who are perceived as being in that role. He describes this as an underlying ideology. It is possibly such an underlying ideology that makes the staff member unwilling to share cups but then be unsure about why. Wolfensberger argues that these ideologies are unconscious and that the way to revalue people with learning disabilities is to become conscious of them and take on board 'good' ideologies. Whether we, as practitioners, are really able to exert such control over our 'ideologies' is a question that will be considered in subsequent chapters.

These roles are described as 'historic' but they cast a significant shadow over the present. They manifest as unconscious representations of people with a learning disability now. For example, the historic role of *diseased organism* might be seen to apply both to the people with a learning disability in 'Dirty cups' and those who lived in Germany at the time of sterilisation in 'Unfit breeders'.

Each of these historic roles will be discussed in turn and illustrated with stories and examples. In each case, some things will be described that you might well have done and other things that you would never consider doing. As with 'Dirty cups' and the German sterilisation programme, you should consider the common thread and reflect on the implications for your own practice.

Diseased organism

The opening paragraphs of this chapter gave two examples of this role with the 'Dirty cups' and 'Unfit breeders' stories, but we can go further back for historic examples. In the nineteenth century, people with a learning disability (or 'the feeble-minded', in the language of the day) were cast in the role of *diseased organism* and it was believed that they could be 'cured'. They were put in hospitals and cared for by medical professionals and offered a range of 'therapies' such as centrifugal therapy, magnet therapy and even wind therapy. Nowadays we tend to see the prime need of people with a learning disability as educational – hence the use of 'learning' in the label. If thinking had been the same in the nineteenth century, people would have been institutionalised in residential special schools rather than hospitals.

In more recent times, the same underlying *diseased organism* perception has meant that people with a learning disability have been subjected to a vast range of 'therapies'. They may have had art therapy, occupational therapy, horticultural therapy or industrial therapy or – my own favourite – 'rebound therapy'. The word 'therapy' implies that an illness or disease is being 'cured'. The rest of the population was not subjected to this range of therapies and so they might simply paint pictures, rather than 'do art therapy'. Similarly, they simply did crafts (not occupational therapy), had an industrial job (rather than industrial therapy), grew plants (instead of partaking in horticultural therapy) and used a trampoline (rather than having rebound therapy). We now know that learning disability is not an illness and is not curable. Those of us labelled 'learning disability nurse' might reflect on this adoption of health as the primary need of people with a learning disability. The result was that for much of the twentieth century nurses were the dominant professional group caring for people with a learning disability. (This is not a critical point but it does demonstrate how the adoption of a historic role has impacted on a professional group.)

The following story is another contemporary example of a person with a learning disability being seen as a diseased organism.

■ Jacuzzi

A member of staff attended a health club with a man who has a learning disability. His disability is apparent due to his rocking and incongruous laughter. He enjoys sitting in the jacuzzi and rocking. Another health club member complained to the manager of the club that he did not think it right that he should have to share the jacuzzi with a 'subnormal man' (his words).

The other seven historic roles will now be described in turn and historic examples given. Each will also have contemporary examples.

The deviant individual as a subhuman organism

Once a person has been 'othered', they are essentially perceived as different. Such a person might be more valued than the general population but it is more likely that the person with a learning disability will be seen as 'different and less'. If that person is seen as less human, they are also likely to be treated in a less humane way.

Dr Langdon-Down (Down 1867) offers an example of how a person with a learning disability might be seen as 'different but less'. Langdon-Down identified Down syndrome but used the term 'mongolism'. He accepted the idea of racial degeneration and considered that a child born with 'mongolism' had degenerated to a historic and lesser human type, similar to people from Mongolia. He believed that this was due to the degenerate lifestyle of the parents and specifically due to the parents having tuberculosis. This is an example of the 'devaluing' described by Wolfensberger (1972) and so might be seen as *low grade human* rather than *subhuman*. This is indicated by Down's use of the term 'degeneracy' to describe the condition.

An annual report from the Royal Albert Hospital, from the end of the nineteenth century, included a record of a discussion by the hospital committee as to whether it was worth investing in windows in the bedrooms of the most disabled residents. Some argued that it would be a waste of money because 'they' did not feel cold like the rest of us. A more contemporary account is offered by a report previously available from the Down's Syndrome Association. One parent stated:

> **When Daniel had his first heart operation he was in a lot of pain. We were told by staff when we asked for pain relief, 'Oh, he has Down's syndrome; they don't feel any pain.'**

In this case the use of the word 'they' effectively 'others' the person with Down syndrome. 'They' supposedly don't feel pain like 'us'. The consequence is that the child is left in pain. Similarly, in the same DSA report the mother of a 17-year-old commented that 'An eye doctor was unsure of sight loss and said to a nurse in front of me – "never mind, it doesn't matter – she has Down's syndrome."' In this case the child is cast in the role of *subhuman*, as she is not seen as having the same need of sight as any other 17-year-old.

In 2007, the Human Fertilisation and Embryology Bill was debated in parliament (HFE Bill). One proposal in this bill was that the legal limit for termination of pregnancy should be reduced from 24 weeks to 20 weeks. The reasoning was that medical progress now made a 20-week foetus viable. However, it was also being argued that the limit should remain 24 weeks for a foetus that was considered disabled. David Cameron, who was the leader of the opposition at the time, stated (on the Conservative Home website):

My own view is yes, I think that we should change the abortion limit down from 24 towards 20 weeks; I voted that way and I think it would be right to do that. But in the case of parents who have medical evidence that they may have a very disabled child, I would not want to change that.

He went on to argue that the option of later termination should be available to these individuals because of the problems they were likely to face as parents of a child with a disability. This is also interesting because, at that time, David Cameron had a son with cerebral palsy and a learning disability.

His view has significant implications for the value of the life of a foetus with a disability. He is arguing that the 'normal' foetus is gaining extra protection, as life is now viable at an earlier stage of development. To take a life between the age of 20 and 24 weeks would be illegal. The fact that the foetus with a disability is afforded less protection can be seen as an argument that this life is seen as less valued.

In the same article, Jim Dobbin, a Labour MP and Chairman of the All-Party Parliamentary Pro-Life Group, countered this view. He said:

This is an equality issue. [David Cameron's] statement allows abortion for the disabled and this sends out a horrifying message to people with disabilities. This is telling people with disabilities that they have fewer human rights than people without disabilities. Many people with severe disabilities have contributed greatly to humanity.

Dobbin's response appears to value the life of a foetus with a disability more highly, and give it equivalent value to the life of a foetus that is non-disabled. However, he does place a condition of utility on that valuing. He appears to be saying that people with a disability should be valued because they can be useful and make a contribution. This idea of usefulness was also a key issue that underpinned the mass murder of people with a learning disability in Germany and will be further discussed in Chapter 11.

Cameron also appears to be arguing that parents should have the right to choose abortion. It is possibly reasonable to assume that the parent might have an unconscious need to see the unborn child as subhuman in order to make abortion acceptable.

■ The monster

A mother of a child with an autistic spectrum condition was describing her early experiences of her child to a group of professionals who were attending a course:

In those early days he just didn't respond to me. And then he used to scream and scream for no apparent reason. I just thought that I had given birth to a monster and used to wish that he had died at birth.

In England in the 1930s people with a learning disability in England could be seen as biological specimens.

■ Jimmy's brain

Some students were being shown historical artefacts at a long-stay institution. They were interested in (but horrified by) a display cabinet that contained a range of human brains from people with a learning disability, which dated from the 1930s. One of these brains was entitled 'Jimmy, the microcephalic imbecile'. The students were being shown the artefacts by two elderly men who had lived in the hospital at the time when Jimmy was alive. One of the men said, 'Oh, I remember Jimmy, he were a right nice lad.' This occurred in 1988.

Jimmy had resided in the institution in living memory and part of his anatomy had become a curiosity and item for display. It is interesting to note that the display of Egyptian mummies at the British Museum now has notices discussing the ethical and moral issues surrounding the display of any human remains, including those of people who died thousands of years ago. The museum has raised the issue of human dignity and rights. It would appear that such considerations did not apply to Jimmy at this time and so it could therefore be argued that he was seen as *subhuman*.

Wolfensberger (1972) coined the term 'culturally valued analogue'. He suggested that the best way to judge such an issue is to consider it from the perspective of a 'valued' person. For example, when considering whether it is acceptable for an adult with a learning disability to be told when they can have a bath in their own home, it is necessary to ask whether it would be acceptable for an adult without a learning disability to be similarly controlled. The two elderly men in the story above were in the position of seeing the preserved brain of an acquaintance. It is hard to imagine a situation in which those of us without the label of 'learning disabled' might be in a similar position. It is, of course, unlikely that a person with a learning disability would be in that position in the present day either. This is one area where standards appear to have risen.

Two relatively recent news stories offer chilling examples of people with a learning disability being perceived as *subhuman*. Both resulted in death for the person with a learning disability. The first happened in 2006 (BBC 1):

Steven Hoskin, who had learning disabilities, was murdered by people he thought were his friends. He was led around on a dog's lead and then made to hang from a viaduct by his fingertips. He fell to his death when they stamped on his hands.

27

There is something grotesquely symbolic about putting a human on a dog lead, as if the person has been degraded to the level of an animal; in other words they have been recreated as *subhuman*.

The second concerns Brent Martin, who was killed in 2007 after being chased by boys of 16 and 17 and a man of 21 who were all trained boxers. They bet each other £5 that they could knock Brent Martin out with their fists. They increased the ferocity of their attack (*Independent*):

> ...they started kicking Brent, and stamping on him. They removed his lower clothing, at the end, and took photographs of their bloodied selves to mark the occasion.

> Brent died in his mother's arms of a massive head injury. He had been so badly beaten that his uncle did not at first recognise his face. Hughes and the 16-year-old admitted murder, while the 17-year-old was found guilty of murder at Newcastle Crown Court last week, after telling witnesses that 'he was not going down for a muppet'.

However appalling his crime, Hughes did not consider that he deserved to be imprisoned; he did not see his victim as a human but as 'a muppet'. He appeared to consider Brent as insufficiently human for his killing to be considered murder.

The recent report 'Hidden in plain sight: Inquiry into disability-related harassment' (Equality and Human Rights Commission 2011, p. 5) made the following comment in respect of the 10 harrowing cases described:

> In the worst cases, people were tortured. And apparently just for fun. It's as though the perpetrators didn't think of their victims as human beings. It's hard to see the difference between what they did, and baiting dogs.

The following story describes a person with a learning disability who has adopted the attitude that violence is acceptable if it is directed towards someone who is considered of lower status.

■ The low grade

A staff member saw a man with a learning disability pinning a second man against the wall and hitting him. The second man looked terrified. The staff member told the first man to stop and leave the second man alone. He replied, 'It's all right, he is only a fucking low grade.'

An individual who is in a coma is sometimes medically described as 'in a vegetative state'. This sort of language is, by definition, describing the person using *subhuman* terminology.

In the next story, this sort of language was used in a long-stay institution.

■ The 'cabbage'

A referral was made to an occupational department in a long-stay institution. The entry under 'reason for referral' read, 'To stop Mary becoming a cabbage.'

Finally, a student returned from a placement with this story, which she thought demonstrated that she had seen the person with a learning disability as *subhuman*.

■ The nose picker

I was in a room with two people with a learning disability and two members of staff. I did not have a tissue and felt a big urge to pick my nose. I did not want to be seen doing this. The two staff left the room and I took the opportunity to pick my nose. The two people with a learning disability were still in the room but I realised that I did not care what they thought of me.

If the student is concerned about what one person thinks of her but not the other, then that other is being valued less highly. This story is a good example of how historic roles can be illustrated in the details of day-to-day experience in the present.

As with the *diseased organism* historic role, the examples used to illustrate *subhuman* have covered a broad continuum of outcomes for the person with a learning disability. The challenge for you, the reader, is to consider the extent to which your interaction with people with a learning disability demonstrates an underlying ideology of *subhuman*, whatever your conscious intention and however large or small the outcome for the person with a learning disability.

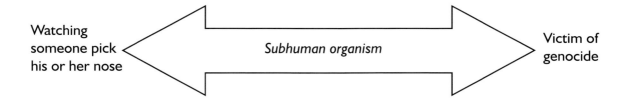

Watching someone pick his or her nose ← *Subhuman organism* → Victim of genocide

The deviant individual as a menace

The historic role of *subhuman* can often lead to that of *menace*. If the person with a learning disability is less than human as well as dangerous in some way, then that person is likely to be contained, restricted or punished. Sometimes the assumption of danger is implicit. It is as if the person is seen as a wild animal.

■ People like that (1)

In the late 1990s there was rapid progress in the efforts made to resettle people from long-stay hospitals. During this period, the mother of a woman with a learning disability died. She left enough in her will for this person to be able to buy her own house. She moved into the house with two rent-paying friends from the hospital. She had been able to buy a house in a desirable neighbourhood. The local residents raised a petition to object to the move and the neighbours contacted the editor of the local paper. The editor rang the service manager and said: 'Are you the manager responsible for that group of sex offenders who have moved into the neighbourhood?'

None of the people who moved into the house had committed a crime of any sort. There was no reason to expect that any of them would be likely to be sexual offenders in the future, any more than any other resident in that neighbourhood. It is possible that the neighbours who contacted the editor had generated the link to sex offenders. It appeared to be the case that the editor had uncritically adopted this representation. This story is expanded and further explored in Chapter 6.

In the old long-stay institutions it was typical for windows to have protective bars. This gave an impression of the people inside being caged and dangerous. For example, the grounds of these institutions were often surrounded by high walls with spikes on top. This could compound the idea that the institution existed to contain dangerous people. People with a learning disability were placed in these institutions ostensibly as an act of asylum in the original sense of the word 'asylum' – 'a safe or inviolable place of refuge' (Collins 1994). However, it is also the case that some people might consider this containment to be about the safety of the public and protection 'from' the people with a learning disability.

The deviant individual as an unspeakable object of dread

Where the person with a learning disability is seen as such a threat that they should be feared, then more extremes of treatment become likely. It is probable that people with epilepsy and mental health problems have been burnt as witches at various periods in history. Wolfensberger (1972) described how children with disabilities were killed, as it was believed that evil spirits possessed them. Frith (2003) discusses how it is likely that children with an autistic spectrum condition (ASC) were seen as changelings. Parents of children with an ASC often report that their children appear to change suddenly. Frith argues that it is possible that in the past parents may have explained this by blaming supernatural creatures for swapping their children with those from another world. These children were often killed out of fear.

Wolfensberger coined the term 'deathmaking' (1984). This described the way in which people with a disability are symbolically and actually 'made dead'. He cites the over-use of tranquillisers, denying of treatment, being given insufficient food and abortion as examples of this.

For lengthy periods in history, people with a learning disability have been denied the opportunity to have heterosexual relationships and have children. In the early years of the twentieth century, the 'science' of eugenics suggested that the over-breeding of 'feeble-minded' people would lead to racial impurity. People with a learning disability could supposedly cause the actual collapse of civilised society. The most extreme result of this belief occurred in Germany in the 1930s, where most people with a learning disability were subject to Nazi genocide. The implications of this are discussed in the penultimate chapter of this book.

The following continuum illustrates the range of outcomes experienced by the person with a learning disability when perceived in the combined roles of *menace* and *object of unspeakable dread.*

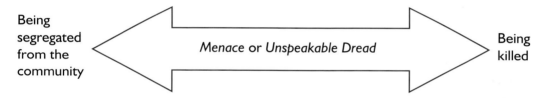

Being segregated from the community — *Menace* or *Unspeakable Dread* — **Being killed**

The deviant individual as an object of pity

With the roles discussed previously, we have seen how negative attitudes and treatment (often taken to extremes) can affect the lives of people with a learning disability. The following set of four historic roles can be seen as more benign or even well intentioned. The question of whether or not the resulting treatment can be seen as 'valuing' is consequently more complex. The first of these apparently 'benign roles' is *object of pity* and this story is a first-hand account from the mother of a child with Down syndrome, describing the child's treatment (Down's Syndrome Association).

▪ Suffering

Professionals don't bother to communicate with him and decline to discuss things with us or gloss over particular concerns. He is due the same courtesies as everyone else, e.g. hello, goodbye, please, thank you. He is not a fool; he just has Down's syndrome. They also refer to him as 'suffering' from Down's syndrome or ask whether there are any health problems other than Down's syndrome. Surely children with Down's syndrome don't suffer; they are born with this disability and health problems are incidental to it. Down's syndrome should not be categorised as a health problem *per se.*

This account offers an example of *subhuman* role, with the professionals not communicating with the child or offering common courtesies. However, the aspect of particular relevance to this section is the idea of 'suffering' from Down syndrome. The mother argues that the syndrome is simply something the child is born with. An analogy might be made with a person with red hair. They are born with the red hair but do not suffer from it. However, they might suffer from the response of others to red hair, which might include being victimised.

The use of the term 'suffering' evokes pity but the following account poses a challenge to the idea of pity.

■ You lot suffer

A lecturer realised that there was one comment he was frequently making when marking case studies written by new students. The students might write 'John suffers from autism' or 'Susan suffers from Down's syndrome'. The lecturer found himself frequently writing the comment 'value judgement – who says he is suffering?' This had been brought home to him when a man with autism, who was speaking to a group of students, had said, 'You lot suffer from neurotypicality. I feel sorry for you.'

This particular person with an autistic spectrum difference considered it a privilege and an advantage to have his condition. He thought that it gave him advantages over 'neurotypicals'. This means that a pity response for this man would be insultingly patronising.

Pity is evident in the fact that the hospitals were built as acts of charity by industrialists in the nineteenth century. The minutes of the first meeting to discuss the building of the Royal Albert Hospital included the following entry (Royal Albert):

THE ROYAL ALBERT ASYLUM.

Nov. 14, 1864.—Meeting of ten Lancaster gentlemen, including Mr. James Brunton, whose offer of £2,000 for the establishment of an Institution was considered and accepted.

The hospital was built as an act of charity. The list of benefactors on page 33 shows 'acres bought' and 'amount donated' by each one in the columns on the right (*ibid.*).

Hospital wards were named after some of the benefactors and these names remained in use until the closure of the hospital in 1996. In 2012, the coalition government was again placing charity at the centre of its 'Big Society' initiative.

Charities often use images that evoke a pity response. For example, the Children in Need logo is a teddy bear with a bandage over one eye. In the 1960s and 1970s, the Spastics Society (now Scope) placed collecting boxes in shops. These boxes were in the design of a girl with a calliper on her leg. She was looking down with a sad expression. The Mencap logo was a simple line drawing of a boy with a tear running down one cheek. He too was looking down. In the 1990s, Mencap changed their logo to that of a man with Down syndrome holding his arms out and appearing more positive and powerful. It was reported that at the time of the change of logo the donations to Mencap dropped. It appears that the donating public more readily gave money to a 'pity image'.

Jly. 26, 1867.—Swainson	Skinner's Flat	2·0	600
Mch. 26, 1868.—Cole	Gardens and Grounds	22·0	3,600
Nov. 24, 1871.—Whalley	Thimbreak	3·2	850
Aug. 26, 1873.—Swainson	Tarn Fields	13·5	2,260
Sep. 16, 1879.—Huntington	Thinbreak	3·1	720
Aug. 14, 1882.—Johnson	Hibbert Plot	1·4	410
Sep. 28, 1882.—Rigby	Cottage Meadow	6·6	1,450
Dec. 31, 1884.—Lamb	Back Thornbreak	7·8	1,400
Feb. 2, 1885.—Sharpe	Brunton House	3·0	(a)
Nov. 19, 1894.—Cort	Patchett's Farm	55·5	4,500
Feb. 2, 1895.—Johnson	Lawson Bridge Strip	0·8	125
Feb. 14, 1895.—Fell	Fell's Fields	7·7	1,140
Nov. 1, 1898.—Walker	Haverbreaks Fields	15·8	4,744
May 18, 1911.—Pickard	Deep Cutting Farm	20·2	2,344
Jly. 30, 1914.—Bailey	Ashford Road Farm	13·2	1,833
Mch. 2, 1917.—Craven	Albert House	0·7	(b)
May 12, 1917.—Douthwaite	Albert House Strip	0·1	60
Nov. 12, 1917.—Huntington	Whinney Carr Farm	61·6	5,000
May 26, 1933.—Gardner	Cemetery Fields	3·6	470
Jun. 29, 1934.—Huntington	Haverbreaks Plots	0·8	400
Jun. 19, 1935.—L. M. & S. Ry. Co.	Canal Fields	2·9	250

Above: List of benefactors of the Royal Albert Asylum

Pity is an interesting historic role. If a person with a learning disability is viewed from this perspective, it is possible that the result will be empathy and giving. But the empathy may well be misplaced and patronising, in the sense of 'poor him, he must be suffering'. Seeing someone as an object of charity is also possibly patronising. To answer the first question (of whether a perspective of *pity* values the person with a learning disability) requires more subtle consideration than with the previous historic roles.

The deviant individual as a holy innocent

■ Bless him

A man with Down syndrome ordered a coffee and cake in a café. When he was asked to pay he said, 'Got no money.' A woman behind him in the queue said to the person at the till, 'I'll pay. Bless him, he doesn't know you have to pay.' And to the man with Down syndrome, she said, 'Never mind love, enjoy your cake.'

A student nurse saw this transaction. She happened to know the man. She knew that he could carry out such a transaction and that he usually carried money with him.

Is the lady in the queue valuing the person with a learning disability by paying for him?

'Not knowing any better' is an important aspect of life for people with a learning disability. In Chapter 4 there will be further discussion of the difference it makes to treatment when staff believe that a person 'cannot help themselves'.

The deviant individual as an object of ridicule

■ The king

A student nurse was new on the ward in a long stay hospital. A man with Down syndrome spotted the student and introduced himself.

'Hello, I'm Terry, the king of the mongols.'

The student was taken aback by this use of archaic language. He replied, 'Who said that? That is a terrible name to be called.'

Terry became tearful, 'I am the king of the mongols. I'm in charge of the ward.'

This happened in the 1980s but Terry still referred to himself in this way until his death around the year 2000.

It is reasonable to assume that staff coined the title 'king of the mongols'. If that is the case, then it is also reasonable to assume that it was not coined to confer respect (that is to value Terry) but as a way of making fun. The abuse is compounded by the fact that he was not party to the joke. He was the subject of the joke.

The following conversation was recorded as part of a critical discourse analysis of staff talking to people with a learning disability (Follows 1995). This took place in a supported living project in the 1990s.

■ Lisa the cat

Bill: We want some sort of pet, do we?

Paul: Yeah.

Bill: What would you call it if you got a cat? What would you call it?

Paul: Tim.

Bill: What if it was a girl cat?

Paul: Dunno.

Bill: What would you call it then?

Paul: Lisa.

Bill: Lisa? (incredulous tone)

Paul: I'm gonna sit outside after…

With this story, we might start by asking who is the person with a learning disability and who is the staff member? The power appears to be one way and the implications of this will be explored more fully in Chapter 9, which discusses discourse analysis. You can probably guess very easily who is who.

In this example, the person with a learning disability has made the error of using a 'human' name, which would not normally be used for a cat. This is quite a subtle judgement and perhaps most people would find it funny if a dog was named Alan or a horse was named Shirley. The reason that this is funny involves category judgements, but for the purposes of this discussion we might assume that Paul is unaware of that judgement. In his mind it is possible that he has correctly picked a girl's name (in this case it was a woman he knew) and he is being laughed at but does not know why. If someone who understood this category rule, and Bill knew that this person understood it, had said the same thing, Bill might have laughed *with* that person. If Bill knows that Paul does not understand the rule, then he is laughing *at* him. It is hard to argue that laughing at someone is valuing him or her. Paul is being seen as an object of ridicule.

Follows identified many examples of humour across the service but he noted that the person with a learning disability frequently did not get the joke. The jokes were often based on irony, understanding of abstract rules (as in the example above) or wordplay. All these types of humour might well prove difficult for someone with a 'typical' learning disability and so to laugh at such responses is to laugh at the consequences of that person's learning disability. Again, it would be hard to argue that this is anything other than treating this person in a devaluing way. An important point here is that, as with all the historic roles, the underlying ideology and treatment of people in these roles is usually unconscious. Bill thought he was just having a laugh with Paul.

The *object of ridicule* role is exemplified historically by the Bethlem Hospital, where people paid to be entertained by 'the insane'. During that period in history, those viewed as 'insane' included many types of people who are now defined as having a learning disability.

The deviant individual as an eternal child

In the early 1980s, the idea of 'valuing' was just being introduced to the long-stay hospitals.

This included extensive training in human rights and Wolfensberger's theories of normalisation and social role valorisation. The following story happened at that time.

■ Equals

A trainer was working with a staff team and introducing them to the idea that people with a learning disability (or 'mental handicap' as it was then called) have the same worth as anyone else. The manager was not convinced that this training was necessary. He told the trainer about his attitude to 'his' adult residents (as people who lived in long-stay hospitals were called): 'I don't know what all the fuss is about! I have always treated my boys and girls as equals.'

The 'boys and girls' in question were all adults, some being over 60 years old.

An ongoing difficulty in the world of professional practice with people with a learning disability is that of mental age. Tilly is now 10 months old. Her mother reported being told, 'She'll never develop more mental ability than a 5-year-old and she'll have a hysterectomy when she is 14' (Down's Syndrome Association).

The fact that adults with a learning disability are often seen as children can affect many aspects of their lives. For example, they may be bought toys for Christmas, have clothes that are typical of those worn by a younger person, and not enjoy the usual adult rights and freedoms. Another example concerns names. Many people, particularly men, will be called by a shortened version of their name. For instance, William may become Bill, and James may become Jim. The person with a learning disability might be called a diminutive of that name such as 'Billy' or 'Jimmy'. One might hear staff saying 'good boy' to an adult who has done well at a task. If they have 'misbehaved', adults with a learning disability might be punished by being denied the opportunity to go out, as if they were children.

One of the diagnostic criteria of learning disability is mental age and this can create some dissonance. The following is a summary of an individual's assessment:

David is 35 years old. He enjoys trips to his local pub and has a particular liking for Guinness. He plays pool and knows several of the regulars. He enjoys pornographic magazines. He has not had a long-term relationship but he has had sexual relationships with men and women.

David has a mental age of three and a half.

Similarly, the following example is taken from a news story (BBC 2):

The story of a pregnant teenager has been making the headlines in India. Lakshmi (not her real name) is 19 years old, but her mental age is said to be only around eight. She became pregnant after allegedly being raped.

The effect of mentioning her mental age changes the impression of the crime from rape to paedophilia. The cognitive implications of these two stories are discussed in Chapter 6.

The effects of being seen in the role of *eternal child* can be seen as benign. If the person is perceived as a child, they might be offered more protection than if they were viewed as an adult. Thus, an act of aggression by a person with a learning disability might be seen as a serious challenge if they are viewed as an adult. They may be perceived in the role of *menace* and the resulting treatment will be punishment. However, if the person is perceived as *eternal child* their aggression might be seen as a tantrum and not be taken as seriously. Whether this can, or should, be seen as devaluing is a more complex, subtle question.

Conclusion

People with a learning disability can be viewed as different from other members of the community. This can be particularly problematic when they are seen as different and 'less'. If they are perceived as 'less', then it is difficult to argue that they are being valued. The way people with a disability are perceived can also influence the way that they are treated. Wolfensberger (1972) suggests a useful model for understanding this perception and resulting treatment. His list of eight historic roles leads to 'treatment', which can range from patronising good intent to ridicule to mass murder. Clearly, none of these can be seen as 'valuing'.

Many of the examples cited in this chapter are taken from everyday practice. As a reflective practitioner, you can consider how the day-to-day details of your practice can indicate your own valuing of people with a learning disability. As Wolfensberger states, one problem is that most of these aspects of valuing are unconscious and possibly therefore more pernicious. It is the reflective practitioner's responsibility to make the unconscious conscious, and in so doing increase the chance that their practice will become conscious and more 'valuing'.

A conclusion that will be drawn repeatedly throughout this book is that few actions on the part of the practitioner are 'value neutral'. Many of the above examples might seem insignificant in the context of the overall problems faced by people with a learning disability. But the effect of these 'minor' details can be compounded by repetition, and this is what causes the overwhelming feeling of being devalued. In this way, the 'drip drip' of devaluing experiences may eventually be experienced as a tsunami.

Metaphor and Attribution

■ Nice boobs

A man with a learning disability was known to say inappropriate things to women he saw on the street. He might say things such as 'nice boobs, darling' and then laugh. In order to help him understand the rules of conventionally acceptable behaviour, his key worker would run through rules such as 'say nothing to women you do not know' before going into a public place. The key worker would explain the rule that if he did know the woman he should just say 'hello' and nothing more. She might then say something like 'how are you?' and they would then rehearse an appropriate answer.

When they were out in public, there would be periodic checks on whether the man had behaved appropriately, and if so a reinforcement would be given.

Many of us who have worked with people with a learning disability will recognise this scenario as an attempt at behaviour modification. The appropriate behaviour is defined and then rehearsed. 'Correct' behaviour is then reinforced. The aim in this case is to help the person with a learning disability to behave according to a 'script' of appropriate things to say. Carol Gray has devised a system of 'Social Stories' (Gray 2010), which enables people with autism to learn complex social rules, where the details of the script are linked to the feelings of the participants in the situation.

In this way, it is possible to see the man's behaviour as a 'performance'. There is an appropriate 'script', which is 'rehearsed' prior to going into public. Once in public, the man 'performs' this behaviour. The staff and public appraise this performance so that, in effect, they become the man's 'audience'. In Chapter 3, we saw how the audience perceived people with a learning disability in historic 'roles'. By using the terms 'script', 'role', 'rehearse', 'performance', 'actor' and 'audience', we are adopting the metaphor of drama to help us understand social processes. The theories discussed in this chapter, as well as Chapter 5, are based on societal reaction theories, including deviancy theory. These utilise the metaphor of drama (Lemay 1999). The terms 'actor' and 'audience' will be used throughout the rest of this book.

The notion of 'script' is central to the metaphor of drama. Schank & Abelson (1977, p. 41) define script as '...a predetermined, stereotyped sequence of actions that defines a well known situation'. Numerous scripts are needed in order to be able to act with appropriate coordination and direction in social situations. Schank & Abelson offer restaurant behaviour as an example, which might take place on a variety of 'stages'. Is it self-service or waitress service? Should there be tipping? How do you order? Actors need to remember scripts and perform them. This performance might need to include some improvisation to allow for the specific stage. There are certain constants (such as actually being served and consuming a meal with appropriate decorum), and any mistakes can lead to social embarrassment. The more socially aware can combine and adapt scripts with more originality. For the person with a learning disability, it may be difficult to learn a large number of scripts and generalise them to new situations. Any errors might lead to social embarrassment and consequent devaluing.

▪ It's mine!

A man with a learning disability went to eat in a restaurant, accompanied by support staff. This man had previously lived in a long-stay institution. The ordering of the meal was carried out appropriately and he waited patiently for his food. Once the meal arrived he ate very quickly, putting food into his mouth in a way that caused other diners to notice. When the waitress came to remove his apparently empty plate he grabbed it back and shouted at her, 'Leave it! My plate!"

This man was an 'actor' performing the role of *restaurant diner*. He knew many of the script requirements of this role, as demonstrated by the appropriate aspects of his performance. Two ways in which his performance deviated from the script were that he ate too quickly and became possessive with his plate. These performance 'errors' were sufficient to lead the audience (the waitress and the other diners) to value him negatively. These 'errors' can, however, be seen as appropriate when the performance is set on another stage. When he lived in a long-stay institution, someone else probably would have eaten his food if he had not eaten quickly and protected his plate. A parallel to this behaviour was observed in a day centre for Jewish people who had survived the concentration camps (Guardian):

Similarly, I notice that a basket carrying big, solid chunks of bread is out all the time, even after lunch has been cleared away. That's a legacy of the time someone took away someone else's bread. 'All hell broke loose,' Lazarus says. The injured party had saved that bread for later, a habit developed seven decades ago and never shaken off. To this day, many of those who endured enforced hunger – whether in a concentration camp or ghetto – need to know there is food available, just in case. So the bread rolls stay out.

In both these examples, the trauma of institutionalised living led the actors to behave in ways that would damage the performance of the role of *eater in public*.

Billig (1987) argues that audience predisposition is critical to the actor. If the audience is positively predisposed to the actor then the performance will work; if not, there will be tensions. This would seem to indicate that the success or otherwise of the performance depends on factors other than the quality and nature of the performance itself. If the audience in the restaurant knew that the actor (either *Jewish person* or *person who had lived in a long-stay hospital*) had experienced hunger and food being taken from them, they might be more likely to 'excuse' the behaviour of being possessive with the food they had.

The roles of 'actor' and 'audience' are based on the social setting of theatre. This metaphor can be further developed when it comes to the predisposition of the audience. For instance, an audience member who had been pressurised to be there would have a different predisposition to someone who was going to see their favourite play being performed by actors they knew had a good reputation. Another member of the audience might like the play but wish other actors were involved. Each would possibly have a different experience of the play, even though it was the same event. Their predispositions would have screened the information being taken on board and would also have loaded it in a certain way. For example, if an actor imposed a big part of their personality onto their part (such as someone who already had a recognisable TV personality), a member of the audience who liked the actor might enjoy the performance. Meanwhile, someone who liked the play, but would have preferred someone else to be playing that part, might find the performance grating. This process is one where both members of the audience have noticed what the actor is doing but their interpretations have been loaded by their predispositions.

Another possibility is that someone might go to see the play with a predisposition that the play would be dull and then be pleasantly surprised by the performance. In this case, experience has had more of an impact on interpretation than predisposition. Furthermore, that experience may have altered predisposition permanently. For example, someone might attend the performance believing that the starring actor is poor but come away having been impressed by the performance.

Billig (*ibid*.) also argues that there should be more allowance for conflict within the drama metaphor. He differentiates between the performance and the preparation. Backstage there may be squabbles and changes of plan but on stage people keep to the script. The 'Nice boobs' story is an example of this. A second difference is the fact that there are two people involved in the planning of the performance, whereas the more usual adult type of preparation is to imagine people's response and plan accordingly. Thus, a support worker might look at

41

each stage of the performance to be enacted and plan it all to maximise the value for the person with a learning disability.

As Billig suggests, there is conflict here. The carer will usually be in a position of power and will direct the person with a learning disability. A further complicating factor is that, whereas in a theatrical performance the director sits backstage or even in the audience with their fingers crossed, the carer as director is often in the situation of taking part in the performance (not in the sense of a Hitchcock cameo role but as a full participant). What effect does this have on the performance of the person with a learning disability and, more importantly, on the audience's perception? In reality, practitioners probably have their fingers crossed in the same way as the director, with as little control over the audience's perception and evaluation.

Goffman (1969) thinks that an audience expects coherence between the setting of the performance, the appearance of the actor and the manner of the actor. Is it possible that getting two of these factors as right as possible but getting the third wrong could actually lower valuation because of lack of coherence? The following vignette illustrates this principle.

■ The dribbling man (1)

A man with a learning disability was eating at a high-quality restaurant with a support worker. He was dressed appropriately and sat quietly eating and chatting to the support worker. The man had some problems controlling his mouth when he ate and he repeatedly dribbled some food onto his jacket.

Playing new roles is a complex matter, and this is something faced by people with a learning disability when they experience changes. These situations might include major changes such as moving from hospital to the community. But they may also include what might appear to be minor changes such as being a shopper in a supermarket or a corner shop. Knowing one's role requires a degree of understanding and intimate knowledge, and there are many situations in which the 'pretender' can be spotted. Goffman (ibid.) describes the problems that can arise for people who rise up to a higher social class. Those already of that class will spot the newcomer. The following vignette illustrates this principle.

■ Incompetent mod

Cohen (1980) carried out a piece of participant observation of mods and rockers in the early 1960s. He presented himself as a mod and took part in damaging property in order to get arrested. He noted that the police seemed to ignore him, and then even when he did get arrested he was quickly released. He came to the conclusion that his middleclass-ness and his Jewish-ness somehow showed through and spoiled the image he was trying to display. He did not know what to do in order to 'pass' as a mod.

Crucially, he did not know what the concrete difference was. Herein lies a potential problem for the person with a learning disability. It is hard enough for anyone to know all aspects of an unfamiliar role but how much harder for the person with cognitive difficulties? The carer might be required to 'do the thinking', but there are extra problems when a third party is managing the presentation in this way. Any learning that takes place is through feedback from the audience. Presumably spotting feedback to someone else is hard enough, but it is when the third party is involved in a performance of their own that the feedback will have most impact.

Finally, here is a summarising quotation from Goffman (1969, p. 63): 'Performance is a delicate fragile thing that can be shattered by very minor mishaps.'

Attribution theory

■ Stubborn

A man with a severe learning disability sometimes screams and tips his wheelchair over. Support staff describe him as 'challenging, defiant, obstinate and non-compliant' when he does this. A behaviour specialist suggests that this man might have a sensory difference, which is common for people with an autistic spectrum condition. The staff's response to this suggestion is that he:

- is just being stubborn
- does it for no reason
- just likes to get his own way
- does it on purpose because he is smiling after it.

He eventually blinded himself permanently by picking at his eyes. After this he was very much calmer.

Using the drama metaphor, the man is the actor and the staff are the audience and see this man's performance of screaming and tipping his chair. They interpret this behaviour according to their predisposition. Their explanation for this behaviour is negative and based on the assumption that he is acting through selfishness and in full knowledge of what he is doing. However, his behaviour was probably due to his visual hypersensitivity. The staff team as a group came to the conclusion that his reasons were 'selfish' and yet it appears that they were wrong. Not only were they wrong, but they had also chosen a negative reason rather than the real justification.

There are many similar accounts from practice, such as the following examples.

■ Attention seeker

A woman with the label 'challenging behaviour' was on a bus trip. She started to vomit. This was happening repeatedly and the vomit was watery brown and smelled of faeces. Staff saw this as just another example of her behaviour. One staff described it as 'attention seeking'. After returning home she was seen by a doctor and diagnosed as having an intestinal blockage.

■ Wind-up

A manager visited a house where she did not know the clients. While she was there, a man with a learning disability fell over and she helped him into the chair. He kept saying 'I'll get up in a minute' but did not seem able to do so and so the manager called for advice from staff who knew him. These staff advised the manager that 'he is playing you up because you are new'. John's care plan was focused on maintaining his mobility following a stroke and there was a constant problem with getting him to leave his chair. He had a reputation of being a 'bit of a wind-up merchant' and enjoying the fuss made when he was ill. He had trouble getting up stairs later but couldn't pinpoint any pain. He said he had stomach-ache and headache. When medical help was eventually sought, it was discovered that he actually had a cracked femur.

■ Lazy

A man with a learning disability had always been a lively man. He became less and less lively and he was seen as becoming lazy. He started to lie in bed for much of the morning and his staff team met to devise plans to get him motivated. A psychologist, who was visiting to make a behavioural assessment, found him dead in bed. A post-mortem discovered that he had died of leukaemia.

■ Pervert

A man who was detained under the Mental Health Act for sexual offences was being treated with a sexual suppressant. The long-term use of this medication had resulted in his breasts developing. He complained to a student that his nipples were very sore. The staff team told the student that he was just getting a sexual thrill from exposing his nipples to her.

Subsequent investigation revealed that his nipples were sore and he was treated effectively.

All these accounts describe situations in which the person with a learning disability was in pain. Staff saw changes in behaviour but put these changes down to negative things about the person. In other words, staff *attributed* a cause to the behaviour, based on their predisposition towards the person. Attribution theory is an attempt to explain this tendency to see events as being caused, rather than randomly occurring (Augoustinos & Walker 1995). When the event in question is the behaviour of the actor, the audience might attribute motivation and intent to the actor's behaviour.

Heider (1958) suggested that there are two main types of attribution: *dispositional* and *situational*. We make a judgement about a behaviour according to whether the causes are perceived as *dispositional* (that is, within the actor) or *situational* (external to the actor). In the vignettes described above, staff explained the behaviour of the person with a learning disability using dispositional reasons: 'They are behaving like this because they are lazy/attention-seeking/a wind-up merchant/stubborn/a pervert.' This type of explanation can be seen as arising out of negative attribution. However, the actual reason in each case was situational; the person had pain arising from a health problem. A situational attribution can be seen as arising from positive attribution. Heider (*ibid*.) said that we tend to perceive negative behaviour in another as dispositionally caused, whereas our own negative behaviour is likely to be described as situationally caused.

The original question this book set out to answer was: 'What do we mean by valuing people with a learning disability?' If a person with a learning disability is given negative and dispositional attribution, then it is difficult to argue that they are being valued. It can be seen that people with a learning disability are frequently given negative attribution.

The audience must decide whether behaviour is intended. Jones & Davies (1965) claimed that socially desirable behaviour is less informative about intent than socially undesirable behaviour. Where the observed behaviour is seen as negative, the attributed disposition is likely to be negative.

As a support service manager, I collected 22 accounts in which pain resulted from illness or injury. Four of these are described above. The people with a learning disability who featured in these stories were 'performing' differently and attracted negative attribution until the health problem was diagnosed. The people who submitted these stories from practice had all felt guilt about missing these problems. In effect, they were all reporting their own negative attribution to people with a learning disability, when they might have expected to have positive attribution. In other words, they were staff who would have expected to value the people they worked with but had unconsciously valued them in a negative way by interpreting their behaviour using negative attribution.

For some staff, the negative attribution continued until after the diagnosis, despite full knowledge of the problems the person faced. The following vignette is an example of changing attribution.

■ The victim

A girl of 17 was admitted to an assessment unit. She was behaving with extremes of violence: biting through to bone on her own knees and wrists, and banging her head on the wall. She also bit support staff, causing an injury that had required hospital treatment. She was disliked by support staff and most tried to avoid working with her.

At the first review meeting for the staff team, it became apparent that this girl's learning disability had been the result of abuse at the hands of her father when she was a baby. Once this became apparent, the staff team were more prepared to work with her. The staff commonly said 'poor thing' about her.

Once the behaviour is negatively evaluated, the person as a whole becomes negatively evaluated, which is an example of global attribution (Trower *et al.* 1988). This suggests that if one aspect of an actor's behaviour is considered 'bad' enough, then they will be seen as globally 'bad'. The implication for the central question in this book is that if a person is seen as globally 'bad', then they are, by definition, being devalued.

Reeder & Brewer (1979) argued that networks of dispositional attribution could affect perception. For example, skilful behaviour will be seen by most people as indicating the possession of skill, whereas an unskilful performance may indicate lack of trying as well as lack of skill. This could have some potential for explaining the tendency of some staff to see people with a learning disability as 'lazy' or 'manipulative'.

The attribution staff make of the people they support will determine the sort of support they offer. Weiner (1985, 1986) described a model that emphasised staff attributions of controllability and stability in relation to the behaviour of people with mental health problems. This model suggests that such attributions determine the emotional responses in support staff. These emotional responses determine, in turn, the extent to which staff will offer helping behaviour to the people they support.

Regarding people with a learning disability, Dagnan & Cairns (2005) found that the best predictor of helping behaviour on the part of support staff was the emotion of sympathy. This emotion was likely to lead to staff believing that the challenging behaviour was not the fault of the person and that the responsibility for resolving the behaviour lay with them, the staff. Dagnan & Weston (2006) concluded that the emotional state of the support staff did not affect the likelihood of them using physical intervention but suggested that there may be some link to the amount of force used.

Similarly, Rose & Rose (2005) found that staff perceptions of their own stress and burnout did not affect attribution. A number of other cognitive variables have been explored in these studies, including evaluations of individuals and their behaviour. Dagnan et al. (1998) explored the evaluation of people with a learning disability by staff, and the resulting response to people with a learning disability. Dagnan & Weston (2006, p. 219) stated, 'Evaluative beliefs are global judgments of worth and would be predicted to strongly affect emotional and behavioural responses to challenging behaviour and the person exhibiting it.'

Weigel et al. (2006) found that staff supporting people with a learning disability were more likely to make negative assumptions about people who displayed challenging behaviour. They considered this challenging behaviour to be due to factors internal to the person – that is, the attribution is seen as dispositional. They described this as 'fundamental attribution error'.

Some researchers have been exploring the attribution ascribed when the audience perceives that the root of the 'problem' is biologically determined, and this has interesting implications for perceptions of learning disability. Attribution towards attention deficit hyperactivity disorder (ADHD) was found to be affected negatively by the belief that the cause was biological (Goldacre 2010). Researchers looking at attribution in relation to mental health problems discovered that the attribution ascribed, where the cause is perceived as biological, is that the person with the mental health problem is dangerous and unpredictable (Read & Harre 2001) and this belief leads to fear and a desire for social distance (Dietrich et al. 2004).

One person with an inherited condition said his family was ashamed of the genetic 'defect' and told others that he had had 'an accident' – to keep secret the 'family condition' (Equality and Human Rights Commission 2011, p. 87). The family in this example had made an assumption about the perception of the audience, in this case a 'generalised other'. They had attempted to manage the impression this other would have of the family. This is termed 'impression management' and is the subject of Chapter 5.

Conclusion

People with a learning disability frequently attract negative attribution. Others often perceive any 'challenging behaviour', lack of skill or misunderstanding as a wilful act by the person with a learning disability. It is commonly seen as part of that person's make-up (or dispositional). Links to the notion of valuing are probably fairly obvious; almost by definition if we value another person it will be the case that we have positive attribution towards them. A devalued person (a person ascribed negative attribution), with the label 'challenging behaviour', will frequently attract comments from support staff such as 'he knows what he is doing' or 'he is deliberately winding us up' or 'he knows how to do it but is just lazy'. If the person is valued (ascribed positive attribution), any challenging behaviour might trigger thoughts such as 'I wonder if he is in pain' or 'he is struggling to understand this' or 'I think things are getting on top of him, I would be angry if I faced these problems'.

If those of us who work with people with a learning disability are to be seen as valuing the people we support, we need to become conscious of the attributions we hold. Through such reflection, we may be able to challenge any negative attribution. A change to positive attribution is likely to lead to a change in behaviour towards people with a learning disability. This might be part of the 'positive ideology' described by Wolfensberger (1972) and discussed in Chapter 3 of this book.

Impression Management

■ The clubber

The clubber was a man with a learning disability who had a reputation for getting into trouble when living in the hospital but was known as someone who had the ability to 'use the system' and make the most of what was on offer at the hospital. He also used to attend the nightclub in the local town. He could pass for an ordinary member of the public and had been known to 'pick up' someone from the club. When asked why he did not do inappropriate things at the nightclub, he replied that he would never be able to get away with that sort of behaviour 'outside'.

This man was able to 'pass' as a member of the local community, specifically the clubbing community. Ginsberg (1996) defined 'passing' as being able to present oneself to the dominant group in a way that conceals the disability. The 'clubber' was clearly able to do this. He also understood how to play the role of *hospital resident* and was able to maximise returns by exploiting what was on offer.

Playing two roles so successfully demonstrates that he knew the social rules and expectations and had a subtlety of judgement. This enabled him to perform each role in a way that led to others having the impression that he was a *clubber* in one context and a *hospital resident* in the other. He was therefore able to manage the impression that others had of him. This included the women in the nightclub, who appeared not to guess that he lived in the institution. He was 'valued' as a participant in the club, a peer to the other clubbers.

Tedeschi (1981, p. 31) defines impression management as '…the behaviour by a person that has the purpose of controlling or manipulating the attributions and impressions formed of that person by others'. In Chapter 4, the story of the 'Incompetent mod' (see p. 42) outlined a failed attempt at impression management by someone who does not have a learning disability.

Previous chapters have attempted to use the drama metaphor to unravel what was happening in the perception of the audience in any transaction. According to this dramaturgical model, the 'clubber' and the 'incompetent mod' were the actors in each vignette. The audiences were the other clubbers and the police respectively. The audience passes judgement on the performance, picking up clues from the performance of the actor, who will in turn do what they can to modify this interpretation. At the same time, the actor will give off unintended signals. The 'incompetent mod' was not able to control those aspects of his performance that gave him away as middle class. The implications of this are quite profound, as highlighted by Tedeschi & Rosenfeld (1981, p. 17):

> **One view is that any behaviour has the potential to convey information about the actor, whether or not the actor intended to convey the information... If one adopts the position that all such behaviour is impression management ... then what is not impression management? Goffman would probably be happy with the answer, 'virtually nothing of importance'.**

Interestingly, the man with a learning disability in 'The clubber' story was apparently better at managing his image than the man who did not have a learning disability in 'Incompetent mod'. It seems that the 'clubber' had more control over the unintended aspects of impression management. Having the ability to plan a performance and anticipate the response from the audience requires a mental faculty defined as metacognition. Rueda & Mehan (1986) define this as the ability to monitor and evaluate actions. Tedeschi (1981) argued that successfully enhancing one's own identity by successful impression management requires that:

● The actor can see how others perceive them

● The actor has insight into the rules of image enhancement

These are key characteristics of metacognition.

Rueda & Mehan (1986, p. 146) studied how students with a learning disability set about managing their impression in a classroom. They argued that:

> **The characteristics of LD students' action lead us to suggest that passing, a concept often associated with con artists, transvestites, and deviants who are trying to manage a tarnished identity, and metacognition, a concept associated with the highly sophisticated reasoning of experts mastering complex bodies of knowledge, are flip sides of the same coin–strategic interaction. Monitoring, and evaluating what is organized in the pursuit of socially sanctioned goals is 'metacognition,' while the use of these same strategies to avoid sanctioned goals while attempting to proceed undetected is 'passing.'**

The 'clubber' had higher metacognition than the 'incompetent mod' although we might more usually find that the person with a learning disability will have a lower metacognition than someone without a learning disability (Torgesen 1980).

The idea that almost every detail of performance conveys information to the audience, whether or not it is intended, underpins one reason why impression management can be such a challenge for people with a learning disability. The following vignette illustrates this point.

■ The newspaper reader

A man with a learning disability was on holiday. He sat in the hotel lounge looking at a newspaper. He was well dressed and groomed and looked 'just right' for a 54-year-old man. His behaviour was appropriate, sitting quietly and drinking a cup of coffee. He was turning the pages of his newspaper periodically but others in the room noticed that he had the paper upside down. Support staff noticed other hotel guests pointing and quietly laughing.

Almost everything was right about this performance but the one 'incorrect' aspect of this image was that the newspaper was upside down. This one fact can be seen to undermine the whole performance. The error can be described as the *salient* feature of the performance; it is the single thing that determines the impression formed by the audience. Schneider (1981) argued that two kinds of impressions could be made:

- *Calculated impression*. This is the immediate aim of impression management.
- *The secondary impression*. The secondary impression of behaviour may be inconsistent with the calculated impression, or even opposed to it.

The secondary impression in this vignette is that the person cannot actually read. An error such as this may elicit the perception in the audience that the man is behaving more like a child. He is 'aping' the performance of reading, much as a young child may pretend to read or write. The essential detail is wrong and so leads the audience to a certain conclusion. Such *faux pas* are the subject of comedy: a woman walking out of a public toilet attempting to look 'cool', unaware that her dress is tucked into her knickers; or a man trying to seduce a woman, not realising that he has spinach in his teeth.

Salience is a key issue with impression management for people with a learning disability. There are many single behaviours or characteristics that might lead to a spoiled impression, however well the other aspects are managed. Some examples are dribbling in a restaurant, shouting out in a theatre or wetting oneself in a public.

Braginsky (1981) suggested that 'being surplus' can profoundly undermine any attempts to manage one's impression. He described how 'being surplus' was a fact of life for many people in an industrialised society. Being surplus may carry a salience that determines evaluation of all the rest of an individual's features. If one is labelled as 'surplus', there may be little one can do to manage the impression others form. He defined being surplus as a state of being unnecessary for a society to function and having no social value. He included the 'retarded' (*sic*) in the category of 'surplus'.

The degree to which someone is expendable is determined by:

● The intensity of the need for the person or the service they perform

● The degree of others' dependence on that person or the service

● The person's independence of those who require them or their service

The following quotation (1981, p. 299) suggests that people with a learning disability are likely to be considered surplus and therefore, in Braginsky's own terms, have no value:

> **Thus if society has no need whatsoever for the services of a person, or if just anyone could perform the services needed, or if the person were totally dependent on others to perform, she [*sic*] would be a surplus person...**

Many people with a learning disability would fit this definition. Braginsky used the following model to illustrate the two dimensions of being 'surplus' or expendable:

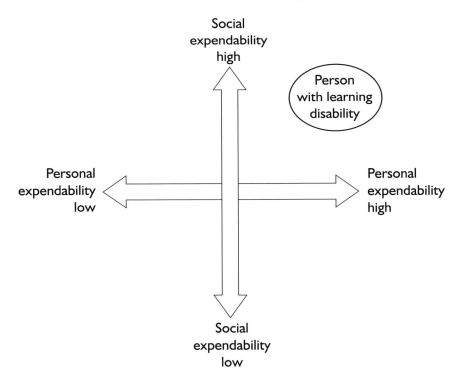

The two dimensions of being 'surplus' or expendable

Someone's position on the horizontal axis determines one's personal perception of status, and one's position on the vertical axis determines one's social value. Thus the top-right quadrant is the position in which one has high expendability, both personally and socially. One of the 11 examples Braginsky uses for illustration is 'mental retardate' (*sic*) in the extreme of this position.

Moving between quadrants represents a real upheaval in life, either negative or positive. Braginsky calls this social transformation. It is, he argues, very difficult to move from one quadrant to another, particularly from high surplus value to low, and even more so when the direction is from high to low in both dimensions. People attempt to reduce their *expendability* through impression management.

One possible implication of this model is that the value of people with a learning disability is really to their staff, whose jobs depend on them. In other words, it might be the case that support staff value the people they support as a means of earning a living. If this is the case, then it is possible that the more dependent (surplus) the person with a learning disability is, the more they are valued. If the person with a learning disability understands this staff perception, they may manage their impression in order to be perceived as needing their staff. Does being needed by the client make staff feel less expendable?

In many services for people with a learning disability, there is a 'key worker system' where an individual member of staff has special responsibility for a person with a learning disability. Many key workers argue their indispensability to the client. This has clear implications for the possibility of the person with a learning disability being empowered and independent.

As well as creating an impression with the audience, the actor may also be managing their impression to themselves, acting as their own audience. Paulhus (1984, 1986) suggested that self-deception takes place in the form of self-attributing unearned positive characteristics.

■ Jarrow Elvis

A television documentary from the 1990s portrayed a man with Down syndrome who performed in a pub as an Elvis tribute act in the town of Jarrow. He believed that he was a convincing impersonator and a good singer and that the audience appreciated his talent. He spent what little money he had on costumes. The landlord said that the night when 'Elvis' performed was his busiest night. He did not pay him, however, as he claimed that this would affect the performer's benefits. The film showed the audience enjoying the performance but they were laughing at 'Elvis' because in fact he could not sing at all. He was unintentionally funny; 'Elvis' had no idea that people were laughing at him.

In this example, we can see that the actor (Elvis) has a literal as well as a metaphorical audience. 'Jarrow Elvis' self-attributed the characteristics of *good singer* and *good impersonator*. This is clearly self-deception. Langdon *et al.* (2010) suggested that men with a learning disability were more likely to present with higher levels of self-deception than men without a learning disability. Did the audience 'value' him? It can be argued that he was very popular and people turned out to see him, which indicates that they 'valued' him as entertainment. On the other hand, there was a lack of respect and it was therefore devaluing. The landlord 'valued' him as a source of business but not enough to pay him. If he had been perceived as a *deliberately* bad singer, the audience might have come to a different conclusion. In effect, they might have been laughing with him. Examples from the world of comedy are Les Dawson playing a piano in the wrong key, Tommy Cooper getting tricks wrong or Ricky Gervais playing a hopeless boss. The audience knows that in each case the mistakes are intended.

The following vignette demonstrates the importance being conscious of an outcome to one's action.

■ Laura Ashley curtains

A manager of a support service to a group of people with a learning disability was talking to a new acquaintance. When they got on to talking about work, the manager described the general neighbourhood where the people with a learning disability lived. The acquaintance was able to name the house, using the language she had heard from others. It was 'the house where the nutters live, the only one in the road with Laura Ashley curtains and posh cars in the drive'. A common assumption, apparently, was that the people with a learning disability could not have chosen the curtains and it was assumed that the staff had chosen them. After hearing this, the manager could not decide whether to remove the curtains and make the house look more run-down, like the other houses in the neighbourhood.

The first point to make is that the presentation of the house led the audience to see it as different. This may be a problem when the occupants are, themselves, seen as 'other'. This point is discussed in Chapter 7 on normalisation. Heider (1958) identified the three attributes that increase the chance of attribution of responsibility:

- The actor could have foreseen the consequences
- The actor intended to produce the consequences
- The actor was not forced or constrained by other factors in situ

If the person with a learning disability is perceived as not being capable of making style judgements and therefore not able to predict the way their house will be perceived, and they are believed to be controlled by staff, then the people with learning disability will not be accorded the positive impression responses that a good 'style' choice might usually elicit. The manager consciously set about presenting the house in this supposedly positive way but the impression management outcome may well have been the opposite to what she intended for the people who lived there.

The discussion so far might lead you to conclude that impression management is difficult at the best of times. Sometimes it is overwhelmingly difficult. Most of us can probably recall the stress of having to perform well in a setting where we were not quite sure of the rules and expectations. This might have been the first day in a new job, at a job interview, meeting the parents of a girlfriend/boyfriend for the first time or the first day at university. The following vignette describes the experience of one man with a learning disability.

■ Blown fuse

A man who lived in a long-stay institution was due to resettle. One thing of concern to the team supporting him was that he sometimes became violent. He was a strong man and could punch and kick accurately in a way that presented significant danger to others. Most of the time he was able to remain calm. The psychologist came to the conclusion that this man was aware of his learning disability and so had to use all his resources to get by in his interactions with non-disabled people. At times this became too much and he 'blew a fuse'. This was particularly the case when others laughed at his mistakes.

Rueda & Mehan (1986, p. 151) described one boy they had worked with:

Adam, in effect, was working on two tasks at once: the management of his identity and the management of the intellectual task put to him. His 'identity work' is particularly relevant and important on those occasions when he did not get the support needed from others. By disengaging from the interaction, including coming close to tears, Adam prompted others to root for him and arranged for simpler questions.

In any social situation, all of us have the dual task of exercising our metacognition and doing whatever task is required at that particular time. Adam and the man in the 'Blown fuse' story both faced an overwhelming task, due to their intellectual (or metacognitive) limitations. Adam also had the complicated task of dealing with impression management in a situation where his intellectual limitations were likely to be highlighted.

55

Sometimes it is possible to exploit a damaged impression, as in the next vignette.

■ Carol singer

Near Christmas, a staff member heard a carol being roared and shouted rather than sung. He then recognised a man with a learning disability who was carol 'singing'. The man with a learning disability then knocked on the door of a house, which opened just a little. A hand was thrust out and money offered. The man recognised the staff member and crossed the road to show him a substantial amount of money he had already collected. The staff member asked him why he was singing like that, to which he replied, 'They are scared of me.' He laughed as he said this.

Barga (1996) argues that although the label 'learning disability' might typically have negative implications and prompt concealment, it can also sometimes be advantageous. She found that some people were relieved to get the label because it offered explanation and also allowed access to resources and support. In 'The carol singer' story, the person was able to use the fear response associated with the label to his own advantage. This is another example of a person with a learning disability using metacognition. He was able to plan his performance by anticipating the response of the public.

The visible signs of a disability are a significant factor in impression management. In any new interaction, these signs are among the first things noticed by the audience. Goffman (1964) described these signs as stigma and produced a seminal work on the subject. As described in Chapter 7, these physical manifestations were significant for Wolfensberger. The following vignette illustrates their power.

■ Surgery decision

A mother of a girl with Down syndrome was deciding whether her daughter should go ahead with surgery to alter the facial differences that are a consequence of the syndrome. She was worried that her daughter's 'bad behaviour' would be less readily excused if it were less obvious that she was disabled. She said that people might wonder why her behaviour was so bad if she looked 'normal'.

The audience is more likely to believe in the existence of a disability, or accept the 'excuse' for the girl in the vignette above, if there is a symbol that suggests a disabled identity (Fitzgerald & Paterson 1995). Similarly, requests for help are less likely to be accommodated if the person appears 'normal' (Mollow 2004).

The mother of a boy who was on the autistic spectrum told a similar story.

■ Good looker

> My son is a very good-looking little boy. He looks so normal. When he throws a tantrum in the street and passers-by show their disgust, I sometimes wish he had Down's syndrome or cerebral palsy and then people would understand.

Gill (1998, cited in Valeras 2010) suggested that when a person's disability is not obvious the audience might assume that their problems are less real than those of a person who shows more obvious signs of disability.

Social situations are often more complex than a simple audience–actor relationship. Participants are seldom simply in one role or the other, and impressions can change from moment to moment. It might be described as a state of flux. The following story demonstrates how roles can change in impression management.

■ The unwanted shopper

> A man with a learning disability was visiting a town for the first time. He entered a newsagent's to buy some cigarettes. He had never been in this shop before. The support staff member stood by the door in order to keep an eye on the situation but enable the man to carry out his own shopping. The shopkeeper walked through from the back of the shop. He saw the man with a learning disability at the counter but did not notice the staff member by the door. The man asked for cigarettes. His speech and appearance indicated that he had a learning disability. The shopkeeper said,
>
> 'Fuck off, I don't want your sort making trouble in here.'
>
> The staff member stepped forward; this was the first time the shopkeeper noticed him. The shopkeeper, appearing uncomfortable, then said to the man with a learning disability, 'Oh very sorry mate, I thought you were somebody else. What did you want?'

In this story, the shopkeeper was the audience to the man with a learning disability and apparently did not value him in the role of *customer*. Furthermore, as an actor in the role of *shopkeeper*, he did not value the person with a learning disability as an audience to himself sufficiently to be concerned about how he would be perceived. (This has some similarities to the 'Nose picker' story in Chapter 3.)

However, the shopkeeper was sufficiently concerned about the support staff as audience to change the management of his performance in the role to appear more 'matey'. In other words, he appeared to value the support staff more highly as an audience than he did the person with a learning disability. The other obvious point here is that the person with a learning disability was unable to manage his presentation in the role of *shopper* sufficiently well to 'pass' and be valued.

Rueda & Mehan (1986) argue that learning disability cannot be defined by the label alone. It is actively constituted in social interaction, in the dramaturgical sense argued throughout this chapter. These performances are interpreted differently in different contexts. The 'Unwanted shopper' story demonstrates the fluid nature of these processes.

'Passing' has been theorised by a range of authors from the 'classic' era when these theories were conceptualised. Examples are Goffman (1959, 1964) and Garfinkel (1967). A particularly relevant study for those of us who work in the field of learning disability is Edgerton's *The Cloak of Competence* (1967). In this book, Edgerton explored the ways in which people with a learning disability, who had resettled from long-stay hospitals, managed their presentation in order to disguise their stigma. Their lives appeared to be a constant struggle to personally deny their 'mental incompetence' [*sic*] and to put effort into 'passing as normal'. The strategies used to achieve the aims of 'denying' and 'passing as normal' started as soon as the person left the hospital. Failure to 'pass', at that time, might mean a return to the hospital.

Edgerton's entire sample preferred to be labelled as almost anything other than having a learning disability. It seems surprising that anyone would prefer to be seen as a 'sex offender' or 'criminal' rather than 'mentally incompetent'. Yet, as suggested above, Edgerton came to the conclusion that to have 'mental incompetence' was the worst stigma to overcome. The film *The Reader* offered an interesting account of the shame of incompetence. An ex-concentration camp guard preferred to take responsibility for an atrocity, and the subsequent punishment, rather than admit that she could not read or write. Edgerton's study and the era portrayed in *The Reader* took place in the aftermath of the eugenics panic in which learning disability was seen as a significant social problem. This is discussed in Chapter 11. Valeras (2010) similarly found that people who had 'hidden' disability disliked the term 'disabled' and chose not to associate themselves with other disabled people.

Many in Edgerton's study claimed that they had never belonged in the hospital in the first place (Edgerton 1967). The reasons they gave for admission to the hospital were 'nerves', mental illness, alcoholism, epilepsy, sex offence, criminal offence, physical illness, need for education and abandonment by parents. This is a powerful pointer to the damage done by being labelled as having a learning disability.

Edgerton identified five main areas in which a person with a learning disability actively managed their presentation in order to disguise their 'mental incompetence':

- **Making a living**: This was, and still is, one of the major gaps in the lives of people with a learning disability. Edgerton reported that many of his research participants described 'being just like everyone else' when they had a job. Many struggled to meet the demands of work such as punctuality, regularity and zeal. Those who had been successful managed to learn these skills; one person appeared cheerful even though he did not like the job.

- **Having a relationship**: The ultimate aim for many was to have a relationship with a person not labelled as having a learning disability, and avoid association with people with a learning disability. 'Second best' was to be married, even if that meant being married to someone with a learning disability. Many talked of marriage making them 'just like anyone else'. Having children was also an important factor and was wanted by most of the men and nearly all of the women in Edgerton's sample. The policy at the time in the USA was to surgically sterilise most people who left the hospitals. Those who had been sterilised actively disguised the fact. Strategies included not telling partners, claiming that the scar was for another operation and falsely claiming that they did not wish to marry when the prospect of children was discussed.

- **Managing material possessions**: Having no material history is a common fact of life for people with a learning disability. Many people in this study invented a past by collecting objects and ascribing a false history to them. For example, one woman collected old photographs from junk shops and made an album, which she claimed was her family history. Another tactic was to display books and magazines in their homes as 'evidence' of their ability to read, even when they were unable to read. Mail was also displayed as evidence of participation in community life. In some cases the mail had been picked out of dustbins belonging to other people. The fact that the letters were to someone else would possibly be a salient factor similar to that in the 'Newspaper reader' story on p. 51. That single error in impression management might lead the audience to the conclusion that the actor had a learning disability. Likewise, several participants kept cars that did not work, claiming that they had no intention of ever driving them.

- **Interpersonal competence**: This is the area where a person's communication and cognitive limitations are likely to be shown up. Strategies employed by the people in the survey included avoiding association with other people with a learning disability and avoiding contact with the outside world whenever possible. When contact with the world at large was required, some people tried very hard not to use hospital jargon, which would give the game away. Some would avoid talking as much as possible.

- **Literacy and numeracy**: When there was a need to read in public, some people pretended they had forgotten their spectacles or had had too much alcohol. This allowed them to elicit help to read without admitting lack of competence. Similar excuses, as well as needing to leave for an urgent appointment, were used when form-filling was required in a public place. Some people carried a piece of paper with their name, address and telephone number in case they were ever asked for this information. Many of the group were unable to tell the time; and even when someone told them the time, the language used might be confusing. To avoid this confusion, some of the group used the hospital style of asking the time such as, 'Is it nine o'clock yet?' Using money caused similar problems, which were often disguised by handing over a large denomination note in a shopping transaction. Other people used public displays to demonstrate their 'ability'. Some used complex language, but used it wrongly, thereby giving the game away. One man copied complex sums onto paper in pencil and then filled these in with ink in public places, claiming that he was on an 'advanced maths' course.

These examples demonstrate the very conscious attempts made by the actor with a learning disability to ensure that the audience gains a more favourable impression; the impression is *managed*.

The label acts as a basic guide for the interaction between the actor and audience. The convention in impression management theory is to describe the audience as 'the target'. It can be argued that in this interaction there is a two-way process of expectation shaping interpretation. Thus a person may consciously manipulate the label placed upon themselves, as well as behave consistently with the label for some purpose.

Staff are the third participant in the interaction but this consideration raises a question: to what end are they managing their impression and that of the person they are supporting? Both in respect of the person with a learning disability managing their own impression and of the staff member managing their own and that of the person they are supporting, the role is potentially so complex that it is unlikely that all the managed parts of the role will be consistent. What effect will this inconsistency have upon the valuing of the person with a learning disability?

▨ Muscle man

An elderly man with a learning disability attended a local community day centre. He was the only member who had a learning disability. He was supported by his key worker, who was a very tall young man who exercised at a gym. The key worker had pronounced muscles and wore revealing T-shirts to show these muscles off. The man with a learning disability asked for a different key worker because he was aware of everyone looking at him. It was established that he wanted someone older to go with him. He had noticed other people looking at his support staff.

Schneider (1981) differentiates between *self-presentation*, as performed by the actor, and *impression management*, which may be managed by a third party. The two are not synonymous: it is possible to present self, which is a conscious act, in a way that may not have a conscious function in terms of impression management. He also makes the point that the self-presentation of the actor may be at odds with the image management carried out by a third party.

In the 'Muscle man' story, the person with a learning disability was conscious of the impact of the staff on his own impression management and the staff member was not aware. More typically, staff may have more consciousness of the impression created by the person with a learning disability. This conscious impression management devised by staff may be at odds with the self-presentation of the person with a learning disability, who may in fact have little understanding of what the staff member is trying to do. What result will this incongruity have on the audience's perception?

Theorists have identified some of the 'rules' of impression management. The following vignette is an example of *avoiding blame*.

■ The biscuit eater

A man with a learning disability moved from a hospital ward, which had a locked kitchen, to a small environment in which he could access the kitchen. In this new environment, he entered the kitchen and ate all the biscuits. When staff asked him about this, he said that he had never had access to biscuits before and did not know how to behave appropriately. The staff member who had asked him about this was unsure what to make of this reply. The staff member somehow felt that the very act of putting this forward as an explanation invalidated it as an excuse. If this man was conscious of the problem, why was he not able to do anything about it?

Tedeschi & Reiss (1981) suggested that one avoids blame by disassociation from the *negative* consequences and actions. They developed a typology of excuses to reduce the impact of a negatively perceived impression, including:

- Denial of volition and assertion of lack of intention
- Denial of volition and assertion of lack of bodily control
- Denial of agency or commission

These points help us to understand the behaviour of the 'biscuit eater', who was effectively saying: 'I can't help it because I've never been anywhere where I could get biscuits.' He was asserting lack of bodily control and agency. Schneider (1981) suggested that mental illness is a form of impression management.

While not necessarily being 'mental illness', we might consider 'challenging behaviour' in a similar way. How much of the challenging behaviour of a person with a learning disability has a function in terms of impression management? Much of the discussion so far has been concerned with the possible limits to the person's ability to deal with all the aspects of image management, but there might also be an under-estimation of the person's ability. If we are to allow for people with a learning disability being more than simply reactive, we should perhaps attempt to understand apparently eccentric behaviour as possibly functional for that person.

Implications of the rules of impression management

Some of the rules of impression management identified by theorists have serious implications for many people with a learning disability. What is being suggested here is that the required skills for impression management may be beyond the capability of some people with a learning disability. If the result, for that person, is a poorly managed impression, then the likely consequence is devaluing for that person.

Tedechi & Reiss (*ibid*.) suggested that one gains credit and social approval by association with the *positive*. This includes:

- Taking responsibility and proving entitlement by saying, for example, 'It was because of me that this good thing happened.'

- Increasing the positive consequences by enhancement by saying, for example, 'My action has changed everything.'

Taking responsibility and increasing the positive consequences require a good deal of skill and judgement. If it is obvious to the audience that the claims being made are being exaggerated, the person will probably be perceived in a less positive light. A significant amount of judgement is required to make an appropriate level of claim.

■ The host

A man with a learning disability had left the family home and moved into supported accommodation. He invited his parents to a meal at his new house. Support staff had suggested this to him. They also suggested the menu, organised the buying of the food and carried out most of the preparation. The meal went well and the parents thanked their son for a lovely meal. His mother winked at the support staff as she said this.

The parents knew the current limits to his abilities and it was clear to them that he had not had much involvement with the meal preparation. Support staff had created this opportunity because they believed that inviting one's parents to a meal after moving away from the family home was a 'rite of passage'. It should lead to that person being seen as more 'normal'. However, it is possible that the actual consequence was to highlight that person's limitations and therefore to damage their impression. This man was not really seen as associated with the positive thing that had happened.

People who are relatively powerless have certain self-presentation strategies available to them, as described by Tedeschi (1981). These allow the actor to establish power over the target person:

- Ingratiation
  - Increase attractiveness of your qualities
  - Verbal self-reference
  - Flattery of the target person
  - Opinion conformity
  - Do a favour for the target
- Intimidation – like me, or the consequences might be scary
- Self-promotion of a particular feature such as intelligence
- Exemplifier such as high moral standards
- Supplication – the last resort of a weak person

Most of these strategies require extensive personal resources. And two of them require an ability to learn how to live in a position of social subservience: 'doing a favour' and 'supplication'. These were at the heart of the following vignette. (For a full account of this incident, see Mee 2012.)

■ The reluctant historian

A woman who had lived in a long-stay institution was part of an oral history group who taught student nurses about the nature of living in such places. She always stated that she was happy to be part of the project. At one stage she was being videoed and was accidentally filmed stating that she was upset about the project when the facilitator, a person without a learning disability, left the room. When the facilitator returned, she changed her demeanour. Without the accidental video, it would not have been apparent that she was upset. She appeared to lack the confidence to opt out of the project. One argument put forward by others was that she wanted to please the facilitator.

The woman remained involved in the project, despite her private unhappiness at doing so. It is probable that she had learned, through 40 years in an institution, to 'do as she was told'. This is a theme that has emerged many times in this oral history project (Royal Albert).

Tedeschi (1981) lists the personal resources required to enact successful impression management strategies:

- Knowledge and expertise
- Objectivity and no apparent vested interest
- Attractiveness – the actor needs to be attractive to the audience
- Myths, legends and slogans
- Credibility – history of truth telling
- Consistency

It would be very difficult for some people with a learning disability to claim these attributes or to be seen as possessing them. However, there are many myths, legends and slogans that apply to people with a disability, and many of these are negative.

Schneider (1981) puts self-presentation strategies into four classes.

- Verbal self-presentation: This has been the main focus of previous impression management studies. All verbalisation carries presentational information. Even simply saying 'hello' illustrates knowledge of rules of interaction. By contrast, saying nothing illustrates rudeness. One can also choose topics of conversation to present oneself. The verbal limitations of some people with a learning disability have obvious implications here. The less obvious point is that *not* saying something will presumably also carry presentational information.
- Expressive behaviours give meaning to the verbal: Examples are smiles, yawns and eye contact. Aspects such as facial deformity and speech impediment may affect these subtleties.
- Artifactual display: Attention is paid to physical appearance cues such as dress, and situational contexts such as living in the right neighbourhoods and being seen at the right places.
- Purposive behaviours: These include ingratiation, conformity, gift giving, aggression and moral condemnation. This may be another area in which some people with a learning disability struggle because of the sophistication of these acts and the judgement required.

Tactical variations, as described by Schneider (*ibid.*), include displaying one's wealth with a modest disclaimer; or, more subtly, criticism can become a compliment if delivered in the right tone of voice. The cognitive skills required to enact these behaviours (including the idea of irony and an understanding of the way another will hear your words and pick up on cues) may arguably be beyond the capabilities of some people with a learning disability. He goes on to argue that the skill to present a proper *mix* of behaviours differentiates a good from a bad impression manager. Furthermore, it is the expressive behaviours (particularly the non-verbal ones) that may modify perceptions of other characteristics.

Schneider (*ibid.*, p. 33) stated:

> The actor must worry about performing a particular self-presentational behaviour convincingly, and she must also be concerned with the salience of various alternative interpretations of her behaviour in terms of situational forces and her past behaviour. Furthermore, she must make some risky assumptions that the target will analyse her behaviour the way she hopes he will. From the perspective of person perception, it is a minor wonder that impression management is ever successful…

Edgerton (1967, p. 218) also reached this pessimistic conclusion regarding people with a learning disability:

> So the desperate search for self-esteem continues. The ex-patients [*sic*] strive to cover themselves with a protective cloak of competence. To their own satisfaction they manage to locate such coverings, but the cloaks they think protect them are in reality such tattered and transparent garments that they reveal their wearers in all their naked incompetence. In a sense, these retarded [*sic*] persons are like the emperor in the fairy tale who thought he was wearing the most elegant garments but, in fact, was wearing nothing at all…

Conclusion

What do we mean by 'valuing'? Impression management theory suggests that the audience forms an opinion about an actor in the light of that actor's performance. The extent to which the actor is 'valued' will be determined in that evaluation. In order for the actor to manage a good impression, a wide range of cognitive skills might be required, many of which may be beyond the capacity of some people with a learning disability.

There may also be facts about the reality of having a learning disability that lead to a secondary impression being created. These might include 'being surplus', disfigurement, strategies devised for survival and the presentation of staff. The actions of support staff in relation to people with a learning disability, and the way they carry out those actions, will have significant impact on the primary and secondary impression management. Yet again, this calls for support staff to work in a more conscious manner and consider the impact of their actions on the people they support and their impression management.

Are people with a learning disability 'valued'? If the theories of impression management are correct, then – at the deepest cognitive levels – they are probably not valued at all.

65

Schemas, Social Representation and Stereotypes

A shorter version of the following story appeared in Chapter 3 as an example of menace. A longer version is used here to illustrate schemas.

■ People like that (2)

In the 1990s there was rapid progress in efforts to resettle people from long-stay hospitals. During this period, the mother of an individual with a learning disability died. She left enough in her will for this person to be able to buy her own house. She moved into the house with two rent-paying friends from the hospital. She had been able to buy a house in a desirable neighbourhood. The local residents raised a petition to object to the move. An extension was added to the house. The neighbours contacted the editor (E) of the local paper and she rang the service manager (M). The resulting discussion is reproduced in full here.

E: Are you the manager who is responsible for that group of sex offenders who have moved into the neighbourhood?

M: I am the service manager but none of the people who live there have broken any law. Who gave you that information?

E: A local resident has been speaking to one of the staff and they say you have kept this fact from the neighbours.

M: I can guarantee that there are no sex offenders in that house.

E: Well, they are making a lot of noise and disturbing the neighbours.

M: What noise is that?

E: There are cement mixers going all day and banging.

M: They are having an extension built. The builders only work 9.30am to 5pm and they will be finished in a couple of weeks. Are you really planning on running this story? What is the headline 'three people move into a house and have an extension built'?

E: Well, what right do they have to move into that house?

> M: *One of the ladies owns the house. (The manager thought this must be the trump card.)*
>
> E: *People like that can't own their own house!*

In the newspaper editor's mind, the idea of a person with a learning disability was incompatible with the idea of a house-owner. The incompatibility was so clear to her that it was stated as if it was fact: 'People like that can't own their own house.' The editor has a preconceived idea of what people with a learning disability are like, and what they can and cannot do.

Schema theory offers a way of explaining what was happening in the editor's mind. Augoustinos & Walker (1995, p. 33) suggest that a schema is '...a kind of mental shorthand that people use to simplify reality'. They define a schema as a mental representation of the world, which is activated at the mere mention of the object the schema represents.

It is relatively easy to become aware of a schema as it is activated. Simply read the following list and consider each object in turn, being aware of the thoughts, images, feelings and judgements that come to mind for each one. This combination of things is your schema for that object:

- Tory MP
- Labour MP
- Vicar
- Holiday
- Manager
- Footballer
- Work
- School

Augoustinos & Walker (*ibid.*) suggest that schemas are mental short cuts so that if an object is experienced (or even mentioned, as we have just seen), a readily available cognitive structure is available to enable the individual to deal with that object. Human beings will use these mental short cuts wherever possible and in this sense we are 'cognitive misers'. This has clear evolutionary potential, as it is best to avoid expending unnecessary mental effort in order to leave spare mental capacity for dealing with any unexpected events.

Rumelhart & Ortony (1977) suggest that schemas have a two-fold function: to enable understanding of the situation and to predict what will happen next. A child's first day at school offers a clear example of this principle. Typically, this first day is approached with trepidation and huge uncertainty. The child is likely to be anxious about what is expected. (Where will I sit? How should I behave? How long will it last? What do I do? Will I like it? What is it for? And will I go home afterwards?)

Eventually the child will develop an 'attending school' schema and will have no need to think about these questions. The child should then have greater cognitive capacity for learning, as less mental effort will be required to make sense of the world of school. When an individual goes on to attend university for the first time it is likely that, even if there is some uncertainty, the 'attending school' schema will offer some ability to negotiate the day. The first lecture will still require the students to sit in rows, looking towards an individual, who will direct the day and 'teach'. The student will still sit largely passively until the lecturer decides the lecture is finished. The student will expect to write notes, and so on.

As well as offering an expected blueprint for what will happen, a schema also contains judgements, evaluations, opinions and decisions. I observed this myself when giving a lecture. Before the start of the lecture, the students were chatting and looked animated and happy. The words 'OK let's start' were enough to make the talking stop. Most people in the room turned to face forward and arrange their papers. Their faces and demeanour also changed – from animated discussion to a look of resigned boredom! The schema value judgement indicated by this change of expression was something like 'this will be boring'. The following vignette offers an example of schema judgement. (It was also used in Chapter 1 to illustrate how a single event can trigger more than one cognitive response.)

■ The cleaner (2)

A lecturer visited a student nurse on placement at a day centre. They found a quiet room in order to discuss the placement in private. A woman dressed in an overall and carrying polish and duster entered the room and started cleaning with her back to them. The lecturer felt frustrated at the disturbance to the meeting but thought that they were in the way. He apologised and said they would move so that the cleaner could get on. The woman turned to the lecturer and he then realised she had a learning disability. His instant feeling was one of, 'It doesn't matter, as she is not a real cleaner'. He was able to over-ride this initial feeling and he and the student excused themselves and left her to do her work. The lecturer later discovered that the woman was employed by Social Services to do the cleaning.

The implication here is that the lecturer would have taken the cleaner more seriously had she not had a learning disability. A schema is activated as soon as the person experiences the object (using the terminology of schema theory). This activation is faster than the speed of conscious thought (Augoustinos & Walker 1995). In this scenario, the initial schema reaction was negative but the lecturer was able to over-ride this with a more 'valuing' judgment.

eThis particular lecturer specialised in teaching about values but in practice he was subject to devaluing schemas for people with a learning disability.

To enable the schema holder to understand the world and to predict future events, the schema must offer a reasonably accurate account of the environment. This requires the schema holder to continually assess whether actual events are compatible with the schema. This happens automatically and largely unconsciously (Neumann 1984). If the reality and the schema are no longer compatible, then the schema may be revised. However, the schema may affect the way the information is interpreted (Augoustinos & Walker *ibid.*). Evidence supporting the schema may be selected and interpreted in ways that are consistent with the schema. It is also likely that factors consistent with the stimulus will be recalled more readily.

The complex and dynamic relationship between the schema and reality is described by Taylor & Crocker (1981, p. 91):

> **The schema contains general knowledge about that domain, including specification of the relationships among its attributes, as well as specific examples or instances of the stimulus domain... The schema provides hypotheses about incoming stimuli, which includes plans for interpreting and gathering schema-related information.**

Fiske & Taylor (1991) suggest that there are four types of schema:

- **Person schema**: These structures account for personality traits and person types.
- **Self-schema**: We have schemas that give structure to our self-concept.
- **Role schema**: These structures account for ascribed and achieved roles. The former would include race, gender or disability. The latter would include mother or politician. These are discussed in detail in Chapter 7.
- **Event schema**: These are mental representations of social events such as attending a class or eating in a restaurant.

The two vignettes earlier in this chapter offer examples of these four types of schema. In 'People like that (2)' (see p. 67), the initial person schema activated in the mind of the newspaper editor is that of person with a learning disability. However, it appears that the role schema of house-owner is also activated but it is excluded from her schema for person with a learning disability. Similarly, the lecturer in the 'Cleaner' vignette (see p. 69) appears to hold a person schema that is incompatible with his role schema for cleaner.

Such a conflict between separate and apparently incompatible schemas is demonstrated when one considers the role schema for *mother* and the person schema for *person with a learning disability*. Mee (2005) identified two schemas, as follows:

1 Mother
- Forming emotional attachment to the child

- Being able to develop a relationship with the child
- Having the intelligence to make judgements
- Having the ability and motivation to hold the child
- Having empathy
- Being altruistic
- Having the ability to remain engaged and focused on the child

2 Person with a learning disability

- Struggling with relationships
- Having low intelligence
- Having a poor concentration span
- Being hedonistic
- Lacking empathy

In attempting to understand the object (to use the language of schema theory) of a mother with a learning disability, the research participants appeared to activate these two schemas. They are inherently contradictory; for example, the *mother* schema includes 'being altruistic', whereas the *person with a learning disability* schema includes 'being hedonistic'. Augoustinos & Walker (1995) suggest that schemas are particularly useful where category boundaries are unclear. If the category boundary is unclear, then it will be difficult to ascribe meaning to that object. Schemas will be activated and juxtaposed to make sense of the object. In the example above, research participants juxtaposed and compared the role schema of *mother* with the person schema of *person with a learning disability*. This was a 'surprise' to some people.

The resulting values conclusion reached by many of the research participants was that a woman with a learning disability could not be a good mother. In other words, a woman with a learning disability was not valued as a mother. This is discussed more fully in Chapter 7.

The extent to which the research participants had experienced mothers with a learning disability also affected the valuation they made. Some of the group were professionals who had worked with mothers with a learning disability. Such schemas are described as 'data driven': they are particular and specific and are based on objects that have been directly experienced in the past. Other participants had no direct experience of mothers with a learning disability and so their schemas were 'theory-driven' or schematic. Such schemas offer a generalised picture and are likely to be activated in a new situation of which the audience has no previous experience or knowledge. It offers a 'best guess' as to the likely outcome in a situation. In this particular research project, it was generally true that those with prior experience, or data-driven schemas, were more likely to negatively value mothers with a learning disability than those who had no experience, and therefore used theory-driven schemas.

Typically, schemas are not purely theory driven or data driven. Fiske & Neuberg (1990) suggested that schemas occur on a theory–data continuum. Any event is likely to have elements of novelty as well as elements of similarity to prior experience. No event is exactly the same, or completely unlike, a previous event. A balance of these extremes will locate the event on the continuum. The more important the event to the person, the more likely it is to be data driven.

As well as personal significance, Forgas (1985) suggested that the more culturally salient and consensual the stimulus, the more likely it is that the schema will be data driven. Conversely, with a stimulus with low cultural salience (which is likely to be a more unique event), the more the schema is likely to be theory driven.

Another aspect of schema theory is that where the audience experiences the 'surprise' of a new object their attempt to create meaning will be conscious rather than unconscious (Meyer *et al.* 1997). Rumelhart & Norman (1978) differentiate between weak and strong variable constraints. Some aspects of an object have strong implications for schema congruence and others have weak implications. In the example above, a feature with a strong variable constraint for *mother* schema might be 'child-like behaviour', while a feature with weak variable constraint might be 'red hair'.

The following vignette offers an example of the principles outlined above. It also appeared in Chapter 1 under the heading 'Revulsion'.

■ Paedophile

A group of managers had been asked to assess how their staff evaluated the clients they were working with. One of the managers worked with a man detained under the Mental Health Act. The man's offences were against children and were sexual in nature. The manager said that her staff showed a positive attitude to this man, seeming to like him as a person. He sometimes punched and kicked staff if told he could not walk past the local school (a requirement of his detention under the Mental Health Act). Despite such attacks, the staff remained positive towards him. This manager was also very fond of him. However, she said that if she thought of this man when she was at home with her young children she felt a sense of revulsion towards him. She never felt this at work.

This situation highlights two very personally important (salient) role schemas for the manager: *nurse* and *mother*. Perhaps the conflict centred on the key schema difference of 'professional objectivity' in *nurse* and 'emotional attachment' in *mother*. Both were data driven for this manager. Secondly, the roles of *nurse*, *mother* and *paedophile* have great cultural salience and so have well-defined schemas. These link to social representation, which is discussed below.

The following vignette shows how schemas can affect our interpretation of events.

■ Different routine

A woman with a learning disability started to change her food preferences (for example, wanting cheese rather than meat paste in her sandwiches), saying that the food she had previously preferred was giving her stomach pains. Staff saw this as positive, as they had been encouraging her to get out of old 'institutional' patterns. It appeared that they had been successful because she was changing her strict habits and trying new things, and exercising choice. It was later discovered that she had had a stomach cancer for this whole period. She was probably only trying different foods because her stomach hurt. After cancer was diagnosed, she admitted that she had not been sleeping for a long time but had pretended to be asleep and so staff had not noticed the change in her sleep pattern.

She died shortly afterwards.

The staff team had been attempting to encourage the woman to socialise with the others living in the house, as she had always kept herself apart. The care plan had focused on reducing her dependence on routine and her isolation from others. She had started to come down to see the others in the house at the same time as she changed her eating habits. Staff saw this as success. Perhaps she just wanted company because she felt ill and afraid, and changed her food because whatever she ate made her feel sick. It is possible that the support staff were focusing on their role as care planners and they had therefore interpreted this woman's behaviour through this schema.

The Michaels Report, 'Healthcare for All' (DOH 2008), outlines the way in which people with a learning disability frequently have their health needs missed and suffer severe neglect. This woman's story is one of neglected needs, but the neglect arose from good intentions. Schema theory can help us to understand what went wrong for her. It had been a matter of some distress to the manager of this team that they had missed this woman's illness. Perhaps we can all be better practitioners if we reflect upon the schemas we hold and their possible impact on the people we work with.

Another way in which schemas affect interpretation is that they tend to be based on the central tendency or average for the category. For example, Rosch (1975) suggested that people saw sparrows as more typical birds than penguins. This indicates that we hold a schema for what is seen as a good example of a category. Different examples of something in that category are seen as 'less typical'. This may seem like a neutral judgement but the assumption of 'typicality' is, in fact, a form of prejudice. One practice implication is that person-centred care plans can often reflect the label attached to the person. For example, compare the focus of the plan for a person with the label 'challenging behaviour' to that of a person labelled 'old'. Rather than a person-centred plan, it may often look more like a 'label (or schema average) centred plan'.

Schemas are clearly linked to the idea of valuing. They are normative structures against which we may ascribe value to an experience. Whether we ascribe value to something negatively or positively may depend upon the schema we hold. An individual who is a good match to a schema with significant negative affect is likely to be disadvantaged. 'Person with a learning disability' may be a schema with significant negative affect. This issue is discussed in relation to attribution in Chapter 4.

Social representations

■ The complainer

The following abstract is taken from a final year student's essay:

Karen is 36 years old and has multiple and complex needs. She has resided in institutions from the age of 18 months. Karen is severely physically disabled and she is non-ambulant due to spastic quadriplegia, bilateral congenital dislocation of the hips and other problems with her joints; she also suffers from poor circulation. Karen has a distended stomach due to bowel problems and for this she receives an enema every three days. Karen has limited comprehension and no speech. She communicates through screaming. Karen also suffers from frequent emotional distress and irrational mood swings.

The student's opinion had been formed by discussion with the rest of the staff team. There was a shared view of what this woman with a learning disability was like, and this is clearly linked to attribution. The staff team attributed mood swings as the cause of her behaviour rather than it being a rational response to presumably painful health problems. This shared view was held unquestioningly. Social representation theory offers a potential explanation for this situation.

Social representations are coherent patterns of thought that help us to make sense of the world. They may be located within the cognitive processes of an individual or in the social domain (Moscovici 1988). In other words, the representation may be located outside the individual but that individual has access to them and shares a common understanding with others in their group. The student in 'The complainer' shared the representation of this woman with the members of the staff team. Representations are thus shared by a collective and are located in common consciousness. They enable an individual to ascribe meanings and attributions to something unfamiliar.

The following vignette describes a situation in which a staff member struggled to make sense of their experiences.

■ It's not fair (1)

A staff member was supporting a person with a learning disability who had accrued benefit to the point where income might be lost unless some large purchases were made. The staff member commented to her manager that she hated the fact that this person had a larger disposable income than she had. The staff member was struggling to pay her bills from an earned income, whereas the person with the learning disability 'had not earned their money'. She also did not like the fact that public money (benefit) was being spent as a means of reducing a bank balance, rather than for genuine need. The staff member felt guilty about these thoughts because she felt that she was being disrespectful to the person she supported.

This member of staff appears to be experiencing conflict between political values, personal values and her relationship with the person with a learning disability. In order to reach a definite conclusion, this staff member needs to compose a coherent idea from this disparate set of beliefs and schemas. This representation then becomes the structure by which the staff member understands the situation. In this case, she has to make a coherent whole out of the following range of understandings:

- Earned income is morally superior to unearned income
- The benefit system is unfair and illogical
- I don't deserve to struggle financially
- I should value my clients
- I should maximise material conditions for the person I support
- I should work in non-judgemental way

To return to the central theme of this book, is it possible to determine whether this member of staff valued the person with whom she was working? Such constructs are further explored in Chapter 8 but we can conclude at this point that such judgement will probably be conditional and variable. De Rosa (1987) believes that we hold multiple representations for a single category. On a day when she has had a reminder of an electricity bill, with no money in the bank with which to pay it, she may resent the person. On a day when she has been given positive feedback at appraisal for giving excellent support to the person with a learning disability, the staff member is likely to value the person positively.

75

Moscovici (1984) argues that social representation enables a person not only to recognise and understand an unfamiliar object but also to ascribe value to it. The object will have a positive or negative value and will be placed in a hierarchy. Regarding the person with a learning disability described in 'It's not fair', the extent to which they are valued probably depends on which object they become in the perception of the staff member. For example, whether they are seen as 'person who draws benefit' or 'person who I support' may lead to different valuing conclusions.

Such multifaceted cognitive responses have been noted in other fields. Katz & Hass (1988) looked at attitudes of white people towards black people and discovered a complex set of representations with a lack of internal coherence. For example, individual white people believed that more should be done to help under-privileged black communities, while at the same time believing that those black communities were not doing enough to help themselves. In other words, they were both 'deserving poor' and 'undeserving poor'. Katz & Hass (*ibid.*) located the origins of these beliefs in the Protestant work ethic and egalitarian–humanitarian values, both of which, they claim, are at the heart of American belief systems. The Protestant work ethic correlated with the anti-black beliefs and the egalitarian–humanitarian correlated with the pro-black beliefs. They even suggest that where progress is made to strengthen a pro-black attitude, there may be no impact on anti-black beliefs. In other words, it appears that anti-black beliefs have a separate 'cognitive life' from pro-black beliefs.

This has important implications for people with a learning disability. Some progress may be made in developing positive attitudes towards learning disability with strategies such as the 'Valuing People' policy (DOH 2001) but these changes might have little impact on existing negative attitudes and beliefs. The following vignette can be understood in these terms.

■ They deserve it

A manager who worked with people resettled from a long-stay institution had staff who expressed the view that the amount of resources needed for people to live in the community could not be justified. He argued that the use of this amount of resources was a way of correcting past injustice to individuals.

The manager's defence of required expenditure included a justification based on righting wrongs; it was not simply a matter of entitlement. Somehow there was still a need to rationalise the cost. Did this manager value people with a learning disability?

Once a representation is anchored, it is possible to classify objects, compare and explain events, and objectify them. Anchoring is the process of fitting an unfamiliar experience or object to a known category. Individuals identify what they consider to be salient features and compare them to their previously formed prototypes. If there is a reasonable similarity, the unfamiliar object acquires the characteristics (including the ascribed value) of that category, and it becomes classified. Where the similarity is poor, the category has to be adjusted to accommodate the object. Alternatively, a new category has to be created (although it is likely to have some relationship to another prototype already held). The next stage in the cognitive life of the representation is that the new category becomes objectified; that is, it becomes reified. It now has a 'common sense' reality (Augoustinos & Walker 1995).

The unfamiliar object so processed may comprise new knowledge. The term 'valuing' has probably become 'common sense' in this way. The term was adopted, even when not fully understood, as a type of shorthand for the changes that were taking place over the period of resettlement from the long-stay hospitals. Thus a new term gained an iconic quality, which culminated in its use in 'Valuing People' (DOH 2001). Moscovici (1984) described processes like this as objectification.

The main difference between schemas and social representation is that schemas are based within the individual and account for cognitive process, whereas social representations exist collectively and account for the interaction between socially produced knowledge and the individual. Meaning is collaboratively created. The following vignette considers a newspaper article that illustrates both schemas and social representation.

You couldn't make it up

Littlejohn (1997) wrote a newspaper article entitled 'Once You Got Arrested and Now You Get a Grant'. The subject of the article was a policy document from Luton Social Services.

The content of the article is outlined below and it might be instructive for you, the reader, to become conscious of your response to it. This may be challenging, as you are likely to have two levels of response. Many of us who have worked with people with a learning disability will have considered the issues raised in Littlejohn's article and will have well-rehearsed counter-arguments. However, underneath this 'intelligent' formulation of ideas, we are likely to have an initial reaction that is more of a 'gut response'. The 'Cleaner' vignette on p. 69 offers an illustration of this principle.

The challenge to the reader is to attempt to be conscious of an immediate response to the arguments put forward by Littlejohn, particularly if this response is one that feels uncomfortable. As you start to read the quotation below, schemas will be activated. By the time you have finished reading the quotation, you may well be aware of a more considered opinion.

Littlejohn's article opens with the following statement:

This week's edition of You Couldn't Make It Up was almost cancelled on the grounds of taste and credibility.

He then offers a warning:

> Readers of a squeamish disposition and those with a high blood pressure should turn away now. So should those inclined towards armed insurrection.

What is it that is potentially so tasteless that it might cause heart failure or armed insurrection? This is the point at which you might attempt to be conscious of an initial response. Littlejohn goes on to describe a Luton Social Services policy, which he says:

> …recommends that Social Services staff should help the mentally handicapped [sic] obtain pornographic magazines and videos. In addition [it] says, 'Some people may need verbal guidance to learn to masturbate successfully. Others may require physical aids and assistance to masturbate'…

He describes how this policy references human rights, which he sets out to ridicule. The needs of people with a learning disability are apparently easy to define clearly:

> The Social Services department should provide food, secure accommodation, transport, nursing and, where appropriate, education and entertainment. But there are limits. And supplying pornography, sex aids and masturbation classes is so far beyond those limits as to be visible only from the dark side of the Mir space station.

And finally he appears to make a capacity assessment:

> Anyway, if people have to be taught how to masturbate how can they be in any fit state to decide whether or not they should be allowed access to pornography?

By introducing the idea that people with a learning disability can be 'allowed' something that is available to most other members of the community (legal pornography), the necessary corollary is that it is permissible to allow restriction of access to these things.

What conclusions about the schemas and representation held by the author of this article might be drawn from these statements? Firstly, there is a need to exercise caution. The article is designed to arouse indignation in readers so the mode of expression is likely to be intended as inflammatory and therefore exaggerated. On the other hand, editorial decisions about the article will have been made with the likely views (representations) of their readers in mind.

Secondly, the readers' views of the article's author are partial and he may, of course, have other schemas of his own which conflict with these views. However, the suggested representation can be seen to have an internal coherence. This schema falls into the category of a person schema. It might also suggest a self-schema for the author of the article.

Person schema – person with a learning disability:

- People with a learning disability should not engage in sexual activity
- The thought of people with a learning disability having sex is nauseating

- People with a learning disability only need basic 'warehousing'
- Some people with a learning disability do not need entertainment
- Some people with a learning disability are ineducable
- Support services should not support people to express their sexuality (this is a self-evident truth)
- People with a learning disability need nursing and therefore have health needs
- People with a learning disability can be denied access to things available to others; they don't know what is best
- People with a learning disability should be controlled

The following is a possible representation expressed in the article.

Representation:

- Human rights are an indulgence and have no application to people with a learning disability
- Social Services is an irresponsible publicly funded body
- The United Nations is a 'bloated' (a term he uses in the article) organisation
- Both organisations waste public money
- Public servants make fatuous claims about people's needs
- The author's views are common sense

On the same page, Littlejohn writes about the law in Muslim countries and the trend of apologising for atrocities (a word he puts in inverted commas) to Maori people. Given the representation above, the reader can probably guess the tone he adopted in these articles.

Does this author value people with a learning disability? He might claim he does. In particular, he might argue that people need 'saving' from the excesses and inadequacies of Social Services. On the other hand, it is possible to argue that denying people the right to express their sexuality is devaluing. This article has resonance with the following vignette.

▮ It shouldn't be allowed

A manager of a support service to people with a learning disability wished to introduce a policy that would give guidance to staff when supporting people with a learning disability to express their sexuality. He sent round a questionnaire to staff, hoping to establish what sort of help they needed to fulfil this role. He was surprised to receive a large number of responses indicating that staff did not think it appropriate that people with a learning disability should be enabled to express their sexuality.

79

In this particular case, the support staff who worked within the learning disability services had a similar view to that of Littlejohn regarding people with a learning disability having a sex life. None of them appeared to accept this possibility. The reader might consider how many people with a learning disability they know who have an active sex life. My own experience is that very few people do and so we might conclude that people with a learning disability are not generally valued sufficiently to have a sex life.

Stereotypes and prejudice

Stereotypes are a type of schema and usually involve evaluation of the subject (Augoustinos & Walker 1995). As a schema and, to a certain extent, representations are unconscious responses to an object, it can be argued that they are a prejudicial response by definition; they do not involve conscious judgement. Stereotypes can be defined as a mental representation of a social group (Hamilton & Sherman 1994). They are also a cognitive structure with a mental and social life. Stereotypes are schemas that organise and integrate information and colour the retrieval of information. Social stereotypes are 'objectified knowledge structures in collective and social life' (Augoustinos & Walker *ibid*., p 209).

If we consider the 'Cleaner' story again (see p. 69), the initial devaluing response was prejudicial. It corresponded to a stereotype that a person with a learning disability couldn't be a 'proper' cleaner. In this vignette, the lecturer had this stereotyping initial response and then had a more considered, 'judicial' response. A key issue here is that, however developed his understanding of disability issues, he still had a prejudicial response. 'Prejudice' and 'stereotyping' have pejorative loading; they are seen as bad things, characteristic of an unthinking person. Professional training will usually label stereotypes as 'bad'. It is being argued here that prejudice and stereotyping are inevitable responses to an object for anyone who holds a schema and representation – in other words, for nearly all of humankind. They are not optional and cannot be suppressed. However, as the 'Cleaner' story suggests, they can be consciously over-ridden.

Furthermore, social stereotypes are shared and more or less universally identifiable by all members of the culture. This is not a moral judgement on stereotypes but a factual position: stereotypes exist and are often universally understood in a culture. Augoustinos & Walker (*ibid*.) also suggest that stereotypes and fact have some relationship. This has been an uncomfortable line of enquiry for cognitive psychologists because stereotypes themselves are often seen as negative, due to their association with negative evaluation of minority groups and social outsiders. However, not only are stereotypes a social fact, they may have some association with 'truth'. In their discussion, Augoustinos & Walker skirt round this aspect of stereotypes and seem to conclude that its ramifications are too uncomfortable to engage with. Is it the case that a stereotype that had no basis in fact could not survive as a cognitive tool for long?

The tone of the following quotation from 'Valuing People' (DOH 2001, p. 81) can be considered in this light:

> **The number of people with learning disabilities who are forming relationships and having children has steadily increased over the last 20 years. Parents with learning disabilities are amongst the most socially and economically disadvantaged groups. They are more likely than other parents to make heavy demands on child welfare services and have their children looked after by the local authority. People with learning disabilities can be good parents and provide their children with a good start in life, but may require considerable help to do so.**

Thus, if it is the case that people with a learning disability are, statistically, more likely to make inadequate parents, then a negative stereotype such as 'people with a learning disability do not make good parents' has some basis in reality. The 'Calpol' vignette on p. 82 might be considered in relation to this point.

Also Booth & Booth (1994) suggested that the main challenges facing parents with a learning disability are social and economic disadvantage. This point is mentioned in the quotation above but it is followed by the sentence: 'They are more likely than other parents to make heavy demands on child welfare services and have their children looked after by the local authority.' The sentence begins with 'They'. This means that a category is being suggested. It appears that 'They' is referring to the category of 'parents with a learning disability', rather than 'parents who face economic and social disadvantage'. If this is the case, then 'Valuing People' (DOH 2001) is locating the problem of poor parenting with the disability, not the economic and social condition. Any problems experienced by the parent with a learning disability will be attributed to their disability rather than their experiences such as poverty and lack of family support. Booth & Booth (*ibid.*) found this to be the case.

It is not a simple matter to ascertain the 'truth' in the stereotype 'people with a learning disability make poor parents'. Indeed, we might ask whether 'Valuing People' (DOH 2001) does actually value parents with a learning disability.

The contents and judgements in a stereotype vary according to the changing social relationships of the two groups. Augoustinos & Walker (1995) refer to three pieces of research into American stereotypes of Japanese people. Research in the pre- and post-war periods and during the 1960s showed the post-war stereotype to be most negative, with positive content pre-war and in the 1960s. However, the positive content altered to reflect the changing power of Japan to include, for example, 'progressive' in the 1960s. This appears to be a huge switch in attitude in a short period: from 'hated enemy' to 'progressive' within 20 years.

In terms of this book, the Japanese appear to have switched from 'devalued' to 'valued'. We might reflect likewise on changes in social relationships between people with a learning disability and 'others', and consider any possible changes in stereotypes. No particular conclusions are being suggested here but you, the reader, may wish to reflect on any changes in your own mental constructs in recent times, such as:

- Professionals have a different social relationship with people with a learning disability from the general public.

- People with a learning disability have changed their relationship with the public, staff and their families, following their resettlement from long-stay institutions.

- The hegemony of certain attitudes in the Thatcher and post-Thatcher era (such as demonising those living on social security, being 'anti' Social Services, and believing that reward should only be given for effort) may affect the way people with a learning disability are stereotyped. So, for example, there may be a shift from 'helpless' to 'scrounger', reflecting changing social attitudes generally.

- Policy initiatives such as 'Valuing People Now' (DOH 2009) have suggested the 'correct' way to view people with a learning disability. Person-centred planning, for example, suggests changes in relationships.

- Recent events, such as the Stephen Lawrence racism convictions, the Football Association response to allegations of racism, the acknowledgement of hate crimes against people who are gay and disabled and reports such as that of the Equality and Human Rights Commission (2011) have all indicated a change in relationship with many minority groups. It is likely that these will, to some extent, change relationships with people who have a learning disability.

Duncan (1976) and Sagar & Schofield (1980) studied inter-group attribution. They found that a push from a man who is black is perceived differently to a push from a man who is white. A push from a black man is seen as an act of aggression; from a white man it is seen as 'playing around'. In other words two acts, which are ostensibly similar, are seen as different according to who is committing the act. The following two vignettes illustrate this point.

■ Calpol

A young mother with a learning disability gave Calpol to her daughter in their back garden. A neighbour was watching from an upstairs window. She observed the mother give 14 spoons of Calpol to the child and so she rang for an ambulance. The child was tested for paracetamol (the main ingredient in Calpol). Virtually no paracetamol was detected. Further enquiries by the community nurse revealed that the child had been spitting out the Calpol and the mother had been scooping the medicine off the child's chin and back into her mouth. During the hospital visit, the child was removed by Social Services. At the time of the research, several months after the incident, the child still had not returned home. The community nurse is pessimistic about the chances of the child ever returning.

■ Spider

A paramedic had a daughter who was terrified of spiders. The daughter found a large spider in her bedroom. She screamed and shouted for the spider to 'get away from me'. She carried on screaming and both parents tried to calm her. This ended up with the parents raising their voices to shout above her screams. This went on for a long time.

This family lives in a semi-detached house. The neighbour from the adjoining house left the house at the same time as the paramedic the following morning. There was an embarrassed silence and then the neighbour received an unsolicited explanation from the parent. The paramedic felt unsure as to how well this story had been accepted. She wondered what would have happened had she actually been abusing her daughter. Would the neighbour have done anything? She believed that if she had a learning disability, the neighbour might well have reported the incident and she would have been asked to account for the screaming to someone with the authority to remove the child.

These stories are about apparently similar acts by a parent. Both were nurturing acts – offering pain relief and attempting to calm a distressed child. The differing responses suggest two stereotypes in operation: 'mothers with a learning disability are incompetent' and 'a mother who is a paramedic should be believed'. These two stereotypes led to radically different outcomes. In some cases, the 'who' is more important than the act itself.

Low expectations for children with a learning disability were researched by Gibbons & Kassin (1987). They looked at stereotypic responding in impression formation when their research participants judged artwork that they believed had been done by children with a learning disability, as compared to artwork done by children without a learning disability. They found that the work that the participants believed to be painted by learning disabled children attracted a negative evaluation, based on a cursory examination. They suggested that the participants had a schema of negative expectation for children with a learning disability.

Devine (1989) argues that there are two mental processes in our access to stereotypes. The automatic process is immediate. All individuals in a society will activate their mental representations of a stereotype given certain triggers, irrespective of their degree of prejudice. There is a delay before conscious thought intervenes. However, people have different levels of prejudice, and a person with a low level of prejudice will be able to consciously activate a more positive mental representation. One other important aspect of Devine's model is that we all develop our mental representations in our formative years and they become so well rehearsed in day-to-day life that they become automatic. These are linked to social representations.

One negative schema held about a group may well lead to other negative schemas being deduced. Shifrer et al. (2011) suggested that being a member of a devalued ethnic minority resulted in a greater chance of the child being diagnosed as having a learning disability.

Conclusion

Schemas, social representations and stereotypes can be seen to have great significance for the ongoing question in this book. Many readers of this book will wish to affirm, 'I value people with a learning disability.' I have heard such statements many times. It is as if 'valuing people' is a simple case of making a commitment to do so. However, it seems likely that it is not cognitively possible to make a claim to be non-judgemental practitioners; the body of theory covered in this chapter suggests that the cognitive reality is more complex than that. We all hold mental representations, which include judgements. These are activated every time we experience an object. Perhaps the only honest statement we can all make is: 'I have devaluing representations for people with a learning disability.' It can be argued that the only way to actually value people with a learning disability is to become conscious of the negative cognitive representations we own and to attempt to over-ride them with conscious thought.

It also appears to be the case that we all hold numerous mental representations for an object that are activated at different times. This range of representations may include both valuing and devaluing elements. To this extent, we may all be shown to both value and devalue people with a learning disability. The commitment we must make therefore is not simply to value people with a learning disability but to be honest and attempt to reduce the impact of any devaluing representations that may drive our behaviour. Perhaps this is the only way we can strive to value people with a learning disability. This, of course, is at the heart of reflective practice.

Normalisation

■ Thomas the Tank Engine

A man with a learning disability had a routine of going into the local town on a Saturday morning to buy a coffee in a particular café. He then went to the children's library to find a *Thomas the Tank Engine* book. He would sit at one of the tables and 'read' the story out loud. He made the words up and used comic voices for the characters in the story.

One Saturday morning, a support staff member from the service who supported this man took her child into the library. She saw the man reading the *Thomas the Tank Engine* book. She was shocked by the image that presented itself. The man was in his sixties and dressed quite scruffily. He had coffee spilt down his shirt. He was unshaven and his hair unruly. He was speaking very loudly and could be heard from a distance. He was a tall man and looked too big to be sitting in a child's chair at a low table. Some of the children were staring at him. When he noticed this, the man said 'hello little boy' and smiled and waved.

The staff member overheard a mother complain to the library assistant that this man scared her child. She questioned whether the man was safe to be in a children's library and she asked for him to be asked to leave. The assistant said that she could not do this but she did ask the man to speak more quietly.

The image this man presented (actor) to the other library users (audience) was clearly problematic. If the audience had been asked how they perceived this man they would probably have suggested 'weird', 'childish', 'danger to children' and even abusive terms such as 'idiot'. They might also have said something patronising such as 'harmless but odd'. But it is hard to envisage them saying anything positive. In other words, it is unlikely that the audience would value this man.

One area of theory that offers the potential to unpick this scenario is Wolfensberger's idea of normalisation. Wolfensberger (1983) claimed that the collective unconscious in a society determined the way in which devalued people were labelled and treated. Once a person with a learning disability is cast in a role, or labelled, the reaction of others to that label will keep the person in that role. The labelled person will fulfil the expectations of that label. The man in the vignette above is displaying devalued behaviours and characteristics and, so the argument goes, this could harm his life chances.

Wolfensberger (1972, p. 28) defined normalisation as:

Utilisation of means which are as culturally normative as possible, in order to establish and/or maintain personal behaviors and characteristics which are as culturally normative as possible…

The man in this vignette looked scruffy, odd and out of place. His behaviour was similarly odd and might even be perceived as dangerous in an era of moral panics about paedophiles. Normalisation requires that people develop 'behaviours and characteristics which are as culturally normative as possible'. The man in this vignette might be seen as acting abnormally and displaying culturally abnormal behaviours and characteristics.

Normalisation includes the idea of historic roles, which were discussed in Chapter 3. It is possible that the audience perceive the man in 'Thomas the Tank Engine' as *eternal child*, *menace*, *object of ridicule* or *object of pity*. These are all roles in which people with a learning disability are typically cast, which lead to them being devalued. Wolfensberger (*ibid*., p. 25) argued that it is essential to reverse or prevent this process of devaluing: 'Reversal is generally pursued by means of education, training and treatment, which may also apply to prevention.'

In other words, the support service should seek to change the things that lead to that person becoming devalued. Wolfensberger suggested that these could be addressed by attempting change in:

● The person

● The direct systems affecting that person

● The wider social and policy systems

Wolfensberger's focus on devaluing and valuing makes his theories central to the question that runs through this book: what do we mean by valuing? Regarding the man in 'Thomas The Tank Engine', it would be possible to attempt to make each of the following changes in order to reduce devaluing (and thereby increase valuing).

The person:

● Improve his hair and clothing

● Change his library behaviour – for example, so that he sits quietly, sits in the adult section and ignores the children

The immediate systems:

● Insist that support staff attend with him

- Negotiate a change of plan with the man – e.g. he could take the book home rather than read it in the library
- Stop him from carrying out this activity by making a multidisciplinary decision
- Advise the library staff

Wider social and political systems:

- Provide public education
- Design a quiet area with adult chairs in the children's library

Each of these changes has the potential to remove or reverse any devaluing that the man might have experienced. Many readers will be familiar with such decision-making. As in the 'Pie man' story in Chapter 1 (see p. 9), practitioners are presented with a conflict between the man's rights and some obligation to assess and protect. In the last instance, there is the choice between respecting the man's right to do as he chooses and on the other hand to protect his image. Which of these might be seen as the best way to value him?

As with the 'Pie man' vignette, practitioners are likely to lean naturally towards the side of either rights or control, and supporters of both sides would be able to justify their argument and might claim to be valuing this man. It should be added that in the real-life scenario it did boil down to the choice between rights and image protection for the man in 'Thomas the Tank Engine' because he perceived any change in his routine as denial of his choice.

Wolfensberger (1995) was clear as to what decision should be made when faced with this dilemma. He argued that in the last instance the practitioner should decide on the best way to protect a person's image and that this might involve denial of choice for that person. He believed that the person with a learning disability might not have the level of understanding required to fully appreciate the impact of certain choices on the way they might be perceived. In recent years, it has become common to conflate normalisation with choice. But Wolfensberger (1980, p. 93) stated that the right not to be segregated and devalued is a bigger issue than the right to choice:

> **...for the largest number of devalued persons, the right not to be different in certain dimensions of living is actually a much more urgent issue than the right to be different.**

Herein lies one of the criticisms of Wolfensberger's normalisation theory, proposed by those who err on the side of the right to choice for people with a learning disability. For example, Briton (1979) argued that Wolfensberger ignored the perspective of the person with disability. He claimed that Wolfensberger was not concerned with the person's sense of self and internal quality but with behaviours and their applicability. He saw normalisation as a blind endorsement of conformity. In my own experience, I have seen the following things being done and being justified using normalisation:

- A man enjoyed carrying cuddly toys around with him. He thought of them as his babies. In the name of normalisation, and specifically 'age appropriateness', these toys were taken away from him. This caused him great distress and he resorted to hiding any cuddly toys he could find under hedges, away from support staff.
- A man bought a pair of Paddington slippers from the local town. A manager saw him wearing the slippers in his own house and confiscated them. They were thrown away. Again, the justification was 'age appropriateness'.
- Also in the name of 'age appropriateness', a woman was stopped from watching children's TV in her own lounge.
- A man who appeared to find security in wearing his familiar clothes returned home to find that staff had thrown his old clothes away and replaced them with new ones. He had not chosen these new clothes.

Each of these decisions, being justified as 'normalisation in action', would have been rationalised as attempts to increase that person's value in the eyes of any audience. On the other hand, they might also be seen as riding roughshod over choice and therefore devaluing.

Unlike Wolfensberger's formulation, earlier forms of normalisation were based on human rights and took no account of the audience's perception. For example Bank-Mikkelson (1980, p. 56) described normalisation as:

Making normal mentally retarded [sic] people's housing, education, working and leisure conditions. It means bringing them the legal and human rights of all other citizens…

This definition is based upon standard social indications of quality of life. The Scandinavian approach to normalisation was developed in Sweden in the 1960s and defined by Nirje (1969, p. 33) as:

Making available to all mentally retarded people [sic] patterns of life and conditions of everyday living which are as close as possible to the regular circumstances and ways of life of society…

Further to this, Perrin & Nirje (1985) outline the broad base of the theory as humanistic and egalitarian, with emphasis being placed upon the self-determination of the person with a learning disability. It was this Scandinavian perspective on normalisation that was adopted in the United Nations Declaration of the General and Specific Rights of the Mentally Retarded (United Nations 1971).

Wolfensberger (1980) acknowledged Nirje and Bank-Mikkelson as originators, but claimed that his version 'sociologised' the theory and focused on the presentation and interpretation of the person. The Scandinavian versions outlined the entitlements of people with a learning disability; whereas Wolfensberger's version is a theory, which offers an explanation of how valuing works. Brown & Smith (1992, p. xvii) ask the question, of normalisation: 'Is it a theory, a movement or a principle?' Wolfensberger claimed that his version was definitely a 'theory'. Being rights based, the Scandinavian versions describe the 'principle' of what is the correct thing to do. Race (1999) claims that there is virtually no critique of Wolfensberger's work as a theory; most of the published work either refers to the 'movement' or the 'principle'. This is still true today, with Richardson (2011), for example, including several versions of normalisation in a chapter entitled 'Values Based Support'.

O'Brien (1987) took the essential elements of Wolfensberger's theories and produced an 'action list' for service providers: the Essential Service Accomplishments. These essential accomplishments for people with a learning disability are:

1 Being **present** in the same places as ordinary citizens

2 **Participating** in the life of the community and making relationships

3 Making **choices** in all aspects of their life

4 Developing **competence** in all areas of life

5 Gaining **respect** from ordinary citizens

O'Brien's concern for human rights led to *choice* being included on the list. For Wolfensberger, the audience perception of people with a learning disability is the central concern. For O'Brien, *respect* is the only accomplishment that considers the perspective of the public. The man in the 'Thomas the Tank Engine' story (see p. 85) was exercising *choice* but did not appear to earn *respect* from the other library users.

The Ordinary Life (King's Fund 1980) movement is largely a reworking of the Scandinavian model, with a return to its emphasis on rights. People with a learning disability should live their lives in ordinary communities, in ordinary houses, with ordinary jobs and with whatever support is required. As stated in Chapter 6, this model has, incorrectly, become 'short-hand' in support service discourse for social role valorisation (SRV).

The following vignette is an account of a person with a learning disability who was aware of the perception and resulting valuing ascribed by her audience.

■ She's not mental

A woman who had resettled from a long-stay institution described her life in a block of flats. She was very keen for her neighbours to see her hanging out her washing. She described their response to her: 'Look at her washing, it proves she's not mental.'

Wolfensberger (1987) suggested that it was essential to view normalisation as a development model with a requirement to develop competence. This woman was aware that demonstrating competence with her washing was a key aspect of her image. This becomes critical when the person is 'placed' in a valued role which carries with it expectations of competence.

The woman in 'She's not mental' can be seen as part of the community in that neighbourhood. Wolfensberger (1972) suggested that one of the factors that had led to people with a learning disability being devalued was that they had been segregated (from the wider community) and congregated (with other people with a disability). It was therefore important for people to be dispersed and integrated into the local community. He argued that if people with a learning disability were congregated, then the devaluing would be higher than the sum of their individual devaluing characteristics. This idea was supported by a comment from a disabled person in the recent report 'Hidden in plain sight: Inquiry into disability-related harassment' (Equality and Human Rights Commission 2011, p. 103): 'Another respondent in this group commented: "Unfortunately, if they group you together you then become a prime target."'

Integration is the key to the successful implementation of normalisation. According to Wolfensberger (1972, p. 48) the aim is:

> ...integration ... when he [sic] [the person with a learning disability] lives in a culturally normative community setting ... can move and communicate in ways typical for his age, and is able to utilise, in typical ways, typical community resources... Ultimately, integration is only meaningful if it involves social integration; i.e. if it involves social interaction and *acceptance*...

The following vignette describes a peculiar scenario in which the people with a learning disability were neither integrated nor segregated.

■ The crocodile

A service manager was enjoying a day by the seaside when he saw a group of about ten adults, most of whom had Down syndrome, walking with two support staff. One member of staff was at the front and one took up the rear. The leading support staff member was attached, wrist to wrist, with the first person with a learning disability by the sort of 'reins' that some parents use to keep children safe in busy places. The people with a learning disability were then attached wrist to wrist, and the second member of staff was attached at the rear.

This was a congregated group that was present in a community setting but not really integrated. Very little in this scenario could be perceived as 'valuing'. This set-up portrayed the image of *incompetent*, *eternal child* and *object of ridicule*. Because it is typically animals that are 'walked on a lead', this treatment could even promote a perception of the people with a learning difficulty as *subhuman*.

In attempting to decide what 'valued' means for a person with a learning disability, we should not fall into the trap of simply measuring the person's circumstances against those of other people with a learning disability. The real issue is whether those circumstances would be valued by a valued person of the same age. This type of comparison is a 'culturally valued analogue' (Wolfensberger 1972) and it is important in terms of the question running through this book. When we ask 'What do we mean by valuing a person with a learning disability?', we also need to ask 'Is the person with a learning disability being offered the same opportunities, aspirations and circumstances as those valued by a non-disabled person of the same age?'

Social Role Valorisation (SRV)

■ The educator

A man with a learning disability who had lived in a long-stay institution told his stories to groups of student nurses and others. These had a profound effect on the students (see Mee 2010 for an account). This man was awarded an Honorary Fellowship by the university for his contribution to teaching and learning. He died and at his funeral his relatives were told about this work in some detail.

One relative said they knew he had been involved in education but had assumed this meant that he attended an art class or something similar. They said it would have been nice if they had been able to express their respect to the man during his lifetime.

A student who had attended these sessions said, 'The individual becomes the educator.' Furthermore the role was carried out in a skilful way: 'They really told their stories in a frank and honest way, and it absolutely gave no opportunity for you not to be completely engaged'.

The family wished to express their respect for this man because he was fulfilling a role that they would not have expected of someone with a learning disability. Their response suggests that they valued him more highly because of these unexpected roles: *Honorary Fellow* and *lecturer*. This respect, or valuing, was ascribed to him because of 'what he did', not because of the details of his appearance, specific behaviour or any of the other things that normalisation suggests would lead to re-valuing. Similarly, the student perceived this man with a learning disability to be in the role of *educator* and very skilled in the task.

This example is consistent with the changes in theory that Wolfensberger suggested in 1983 (p. 234). His reasons for this development of his theory were twofold. Firstly, the term 'normal' (part of normalisation) carries a great many connotations. Wolfensberger was therefore concerned that people were paying scant regard to the complexities of the theory because they were jumping to conclusions based upon their preconceived notions. Secondly, and more importantly, he argued that

> ...the most explicit and highest goal of normalisation must be the creation, support and defence of valued social roles for people who are at risk of devaluation. All other elements and objectives of the theory are really subservient to this end because if a person's role were a socially valued one then other desirable things would be accorded to that person almost automatically...

The man in the 'Educator' story had two social roles that could be described as 'valued'. Performing these roles appears to have resulted in him being valued more highly.

Wolfensberger extended this argument to suggest that if the person becomes valued then any attribute (even one that was formerly thought of as negative) would come to be viewed positively. He illustrates this point with examples from other cultures. For example, someone who has hallucinations would be thought of as mentally ill in one culture but held in awe in others – such as some indigenous American tribes and some Arab peoples.

Wolfensberger stated that disability was valued in the Far East (he was no more specific than that) because people's hands were rendered useless if they were of a high social status. This disability demonstrated that they were sufficiently high in status to have servants to deal with their every need. Wolfensberger imagined a world in which having no limbs at all was valued, and suggested that people would even have limbs amputated to copy those who were already valued. He suggested that offering these people artificial limbs would be seen as insulting or even deviancy-making. Wolfensberger called the new theory social role valorisation (SRV).

The following vignette suggests another aspect of SRV.

▪ Get the sack

The problem of support staff not being respectful to people with a learning disability was being discussed at a service meeting. Two members of People First, both of whom had a learning disability, were there. Also in attendance was a woman without a learning disability, who was employed as a scribe and a facilitator for the People First members. The discussion was exploring the lack of sanctions in relation to support staff who were disrespectful. The woman employed as a scribe said, 'If I was disrespectful I would rightly get the sack. My employers have a learning disability.'

What appears to make a significant difference for the members of People First is that they have a significant and powerful role – that of *employer*. If one person has power over another, they may well have the power to 'command' respect (especially if showing lack of respect might lead to loss of employment).

A later definition of SRV was (Thomas & Wolfensberger 1999, p. 126):

> **SRV proposes that people who hold valued social roles in society are more apt than people in devalued roles to be accorded the 'good things of life' by their society...**

The People First members in the vignette above can be seen to have the 'good things in life' in the sense that they can ensure that people are respectful to them because they have the power that comes with the valued social role of *employer*.

Thomas & Wolfensberger comment further (*ibid*., p. 135):

> **What 'the good things of life' are considered to be will vary somewhat from culture to culture, and over time. Still, if one looks across cultures and time, one will find a great deal of convergence on what these 'good things of life' are: respect, acceptance (or at least tolerance), positive relationship [*sic*], integration into the valued activities of society, access to material goods and welfare, housing that is decent according to the standards of that place and time, functions (work related and other ones) that are considered important and contributive...**

The following two vignettes, one historic and one contemporary, suggest a link between the 'good things in life' and valued roles.

■ The tenant

Resettlement from the long-stay institutions started in the 1980s. The service aims of the time were clear. The most desirable model was that the person became a tenant in their new accommodation, with all the rights that entailed.

A group of three people lived in one house. They were a brother and sister and their best friend. They had lived together since childhood. The house was owned by a housing association. The house was large enough for four people and the suggestion was made that another person should move into the house. The three tenants of the house decided that they did not want to have a fourth person and chose to pay a little more rent each to cover the difference. They all had control of their own money and so they could make this decision.

In this example these people with a learning disability had the role of *tenant*. This brought with it legal protection and rights and allowed them to make significant choices, including who they lived with. Having control over their money was important, as they chose to forego some spending in order to stay as a group of friends. The valued roles of *tenant* and *financially independent* allowed this group of people the opportunity to have the 'good things' Wolfensberger predicted, namely to live with people of their choice. This model of support services and accommodation is perhaps rarer now. However, I have noted that the change from tenant status has included a change to viewing an unoccupied bed in a house as a 'vacancy' – rather like a 'bed' in a hospital. It must be filled.

The following vignette is contemporary.

▪ The chattel

In 2009 a care organisation decided to sell a property that housed three people with a learning disability. This organisation was bought out by another care organisation. The new owners decided that they would use larger houses, and sold all the smaller properties. The group of three was moved into a house that could accommodate five people. These people had not met before the move. Each person had a small weekly allowance and the care organisation kept control of the rest of their income.

In this example the people with a learning disability do not occupy the valued roles of *tenant* and *financially independent*. In comparison to the people in 'The tenant' story, they have no choice or autonomy regarding whom they live with. They have been moved for reasons of corporate profit. It is possible that they are valued by the organisation, but mainly as a source of income.

We scarcely need to ask which model of support values the person with a learning disability most highly – the one described in 'The tenant' or the one described in 'The chattel'? The answer is very clear.

The following vignette suggests that role interpretation can also be retrospective.

▪ The tattooed man (1)

A student nurse met a man for the first time in a unit specialising in people who display challenging behaviour. This man had soiled and smeared himself and the nurse was helping him to have a shower to clean up. The nurse was not enjoying the task and was struggling to see the man in a positive light. He noticed that the man had 'good quality' tattoos and thought this was unusual for someone with a learning difficulty. He had seen people with a learning difficulty with tattoos that were self-inflicted, but never professionally done work.

This prompted the student to look into the man's history. He discovered that the man had been a plasterer and taxi driver who was married with children. He had tried to commit suicide by hanging. He was discovered, unconscious, by his ten-year-old child who raised the alarm. The man survived but had acquired brain injury from anoxia. Acquired brain injury was an unexpected personal history on this unit, as its purpose was to support people with a learning difficulty. His behaviour was considered challenging and so he became a resident of this special unit.

The nurse considered his response to this story as a critical incident. The student realised that the man had never previously been in an institution, having had a past very similar to his own. This similarity produced a feeling of empathy: the person with a learning difficulty was no longer 'other'. The nurse acknowledged that this made the client appear different from other clients and he admitted that he 'valued' this client more for having not always been impaired. The implication that concerned the nurse was that this necessarily meant he valued people who have always been impaired less than those who have not. He had formerly believed that he unconditionally valued people with a learning difficulty. He now wondered whether this increased empathy and valuing might lead to this client being a 'favourite'.

The building where this service is provided is a grand old house with disused stables. The service manager was planning to have the stables renovated and turned into a games room for the people who lived there. Part of the requirement for this renovation was to plaster the bare brick. The man with the brain injury had been a plasterer. The nurse suggested that this man might be given the chance to do the work himself. The man's behaviour included exaggerated swaying from side to side and looking backwards at the end of each swing. He would also make a moaning sound. He did the plastering and completed the task well; however, he continued with his swaying behaviour while plastering.

The other staff discussed this man and agreed they all saw him in a different light now he had completed the plastering job to a high standard.

This man had occupied a range of 'valued' roles in the past. These had included *father, husband, worker, wage earner* and *householder*. Furthermore, in the role of wage earner he had been a *small-business owner* (taxi driver) and a *skilled worker* (plasterer). These facts had positively changed the nurse's perception of the man, particularly given that the initial perception had been that he was a *smearer of faeces*. This story is explored in some detail in Chapter 10.

Although the theory of SRV can help us understand valuing in relation to roles, I have reflected upon my own responses to people with a learning disability and have concluded that narrative and 'back story' are also significant factors. The following vignette demonstrates their importance.

■ Moral defective

A nurse was working with an elderly woman who lived in a long-stay hospital. The elderly woman had been cleaning an area of the ward when another woman who lived there walked where she had just been cleaning. The 'cleaner' became very angry and abusive towards the woman who had walked on the clean floor. The nurse stepped in to calm the situation and also received a barrage of abuse from the 'cleaner'. He saw the 'cleaner' as 'bad tempered' and 'unpleasant'.

He later discovered that the 'cleaner' had been admitted to the long-stay hospital in the 1920s. She had become pregnant 'out of wedlock' and had been classified as 'a moral defective' and institutionalised.

Much later the nurse discovered that this woman had been in service at the time and it was reasonable to assume that someone in the employer's family had sexually exploited her as a teenager.

This narrative produced a sense of outrage and injustice in the nurse. The elderly woman was now seen in the role of *victim*, which is not a valued social role but did lead to more positive valuing. Suddenly this woman's anger while cleaning seemed more understandable. This line of discussion can cross over into the area of attribution, as discussed in Chapter 4.

A similar example is that of a person I once met who lived at a long-stay hospital and had been brain-damaged by whooping cough vaccine. This situation led me to see that person's disability as 'avoidable tragedy' rather than 'genetic inevitability'. It seems clear that the role of narrative in perception would make an interesting area for research.

Role

Thomas & Wolfensberger (1999) argued that there are such things as valued and devalued social roles and suggested the following examples to illustrate this principle (Thomas & Wolfensberger 1999, p. 128):

- **Valued roles:** wife/husband, parent, friend, confidante, president, scholar, champion athlete and union leader
- **Devalued roles:** subhuman, social menace, garbage picker (litter picker), sponge and black sheep

Anyone occupying the valued roles would benefit in terms of ascribed value.

However, the following vignette offers a challenge to this assumption.

■ Surprising mother (1)

A community learning disability nurse described how one of her clients became pregnant. Her initial reaction was to be horrified. She saw this woman as someone who was manipulative, hedonistic, deceitful, with poor self-help skills, and potentially aggressive due to a low tolerance of frustration. Furthermore, she had been diagnosed as having Munchausen syndrome, in which the sufferer causes self-harm in order to get hospital treatment. The community nurse and her colleagues were sure this mother–child relationship was doomed to failure; in fact they thought that she would be a disaster as a mother.

In this vignette the woman was devalued in the sense that she was perceived as 'manipulative' and 'deceitful' among other things. When professionals discovered that she was pregnant, they anticipated that this would be a disaster. The woman was not re-valued when it became apparent that she was about to take on the ostensibly valued role of *mother*. If anything, she was now likely to be more closely scrutinised and perceived as more of a problem.

If SRV is to be considered as a useful theory then it should offer some ability to predict an outcome, namely an improvement in the way the woman was perceived. This did not appear to happen and this suggests that the theory is not adequate. Thomas & Wolfensberger (1999, p. 126) stated: 'Because the concept of social roles is so central to SRV, it is important to first clarify what social roles are.'

They went on (*ibid*.) to define a role as:

> ...a combination of behaviors, privileges, duties and responsibilities that is socially defined, is widely understood and recognised in society, and is characteristic or expected of a person occupying a particular position within a social system.

We can gain an understanding of what happened to the ascribed status for the woman in the 'Surprising mother' story by further considering role theory. The person carrying out the role and the perceiver (or audience) share expectations. Thomas & Wolfensberger (*ibid*.) described how expectations are a critical element of role: '...in our society it is expected that parents should rear and take care of any children they bring into the world and not mistreat them.'

All roles therefore carry expectations as part of their 'role schema' (see Chapter 6) and also have a perceived value. Thomas & Wolfensberger (*ibid*.) claimed that within a society there will be a 'continuum of perceived value'. They illustrated this principle by arguing that the roles of *subhuman, social menace* and *garbage picker (litter picker)* are at the devalued end of the continuum. At the valued end, they placed roles such as *president*, *scholar* and *champion athlete*.

This raises an important question: valued by whom? Placing *garbage picker* at the devalued end of the continuum says something about Thomas & Wolfensberger's value sets. In other words, they may not ascribe positive value to *garbage picker* as a job for themselves. However, many people might ascribe positive value to garbage pickers, as their work creates a cleaner environment (even if it is perhaps not the sort of work that many of those people would want for themselves).

Secondly, there are problems in using the term 'role' to define both the *garbage picker* and *subhuman*. The latter is, of course, one of Wolfensberger's historic roles as described in Chapter 6. *Garbage picker* is clearly an identifiable role with a set of 'expected behaviours, responsibilities and duties' as defined by Thomas & Wolfensberger. However, the same could not be said of a *subhuman*. There is no corresponding responsibility or duty and it is doubtful that there would be much agreement over the precise behaviour expected in the role. Neither is there a corresponding role position with clear entry conditions.

Lemay (1999) believes that the latest SRV formulation integrates role theory and is therefore an improvement on past versions. He also argues (p. 236) that SRV offers role theory a '…practical and comprehensive usefulness'. Although he makes this claim, closer examination reveals fundamental omissions in Wolfensberger's theory. In order to unpick this, it is necessary to consider what established role theorists suggest.

Biddle (1986, p. 67) sees roles as 'characteristic behaviour patterns'. He assumes that 'persons are members of *social positions* and hold *expectations* for their own behaviours and those of other persons' (*ibid.*, p. 67). Biddle & Thomas (1979, p. 29) define a role as 'the set of prescriptions defining what the behaviour of a position member should be' and, more specifically, 'those behaviours associated with a position'.

Biddle & Thomas (1979) suggest that 'role position' and 'role behaviour' are two separate entities:

- Role behaviour is action. Action is goal related and conscious and may be described as performance, which carries expectation on the part of the audience.
- Role position is a category of person, which would be recognisable to most people in a culture. Thus the category of 'mother' is clear. It has clear entry conditions, name and essential behaviours.

Regarding the role of *mother*, the 'role position' is clear – the act of giving birth or adopting would place the woman in that role. On the other hand, the 'role performance' is variable and detailed, with certain standards applying to these expectations. For example, an expectation of 'performance' might include playing with the child or not smacking the child.

Thomas & Wolfensberger (1999) do not differentiate between 'role position' and 'role performance'. In the list above, they include *sponge* and *black sheep* as devalued roles, neither of which might be seen as a 'role position' in the sense described here. On the other hand, they describe *parent* and *worker* as valued roles, which both have clear entry requirements for 'role position'.

Thomas & Wolfensberger (*ibid*., p. 131) state: 'Partial filling of a role may be enough to cast a person into that role' and:

> **A person who goes through the marriage ceremony and shares a dwelling with his or her spouse will be cast in the role of husband or wife, even if that person fails miserably at those things expected of a spouse, such as faithfulness, child rearing, financial and other support and so on.**

Here is an illustration of how position and role have been combined. Partial or complete filling of the role appears to make little difference in the story of the 'Surprising mother (1)' (see p. 97). The woman with a learning disability is about to occupy the 'role position' of *mother* but the expectation is that her 'role performance' as *mother* will be poor. It is this anticipated role performance that dictates the value ascribed to her by the professionals. They expect that she will be a bad mum and therefore devalue her.

Finally, to define a role as 'valued' or 'devalued', as Wolfensberger does, assumes that role consensus exists but Biddle & Thomas (1979, p. 30) question whether this is the case. Thomas & Wolfensberger's list on p. 96 illustrates this point. For example they include 'union leader' as a valued role. Whether this is a valued role or not would depend on the political orientation of the audience.

Valuing in everyday settings

This section describes a series of scenarios that the reader may recognise as typical for those of us who have supported people with a learning disability. Each raises questions about whether Wolfensberger's theories of normalisation and SRV help to explain valuing consequences for the person with a learning disability.

Those of us who worked through the era in which Wolfensberger's theories were commonly seen as underpinning service provision can probably remember explicit decisions being made to 'implement' normalisation and SRV. This implies that these ideas are principles that can be implemented. However, if they are viewed as theories, with the potential to explain why things happen as they do, then it is not appropriate to talk of 'implementing' them any more than it would be appropriate for a parachutist to talk of 'implementing gravity'. This has significant implications for practice. If ascribing value is an inevitable cognitive process then everything practitioners do with people with a learning disability will have implications for the way that the person with a learning disability is 'valued'. This will be the case whether the practitioner is aware of Wolfensberger or not. It will also be the case, whether the practitioner's behaviour is conscious or unconscious. It is therefore the practitioner's responsibility to be reflectively conscious of the impact their actions will have on the way the person with a learning disability is valued.

The following vignette describes someone with a learning disability who was in the 'valued' role of *customer*. He also performed the role in a 'valued' facility (a good restaurant) and it involved carrying out a 'valued' activity (*eating out*) so there was congruence about the whole activity.

■ The dribbling man (2)

A man with a learning disability was eating at a good-quality restaurant with a support worker. He was dressed appropriately and sat quietly eating and chatting to the support worker. The man had some problems controlling his mouth when he ate and he repeatedly dribbled some food onto his jacket. The other customers looked away when he did this.

This vignette was also used in Chapter 4 to illustrate attribution. Regarding normalisation, the fact that the other customers averted their eyes suggests that they did not value him. The positive role, setting and activity were apparently not sufficient. The act of dribbling appeared to be salient and undermined the possibility of positive valuing. It could be argued that this devaluing would have been less likely if the person had been eating in a fast-food restaurant or a bus station café. These venues might be seen as less 'culturally valued', yet their use might lead to less negative ascribed value for the person in the 'Dribbling man' story. This is not what would be predicted by normalisation and SRV.

The following vignette describes someone in the 'valued' role of *worker*.

■ The shelf stacker

A woman with a learning disability got a job at a supermarket. The employment support services provided her with one-to-one support. She was required to pack shelves but had to follow her employment support worker's lead. She seemed unable to direct her own work. Other employees were overheard complaining about her. One said, 'She gets the same money as us but is not able to do the job!'

It appeared that being in the 'role position' of *worker* was not sufficient; the 'role performance' was the key thing by which she was being valued. The actual outcome of performing a 'valued' role incompetently led to her being devalued. Wolfensberger (1983) did suggest that developing competence was a key issue for SRV. He also stated that a way of developing competence in the devalued person is to model appropriate behaviour. This is what the employment support worker was doing in this vignette. However, because he allowed the audience to see him modelling the appropriate behaviour, the woman's lack of competence was highlighted.

■ Undeserving tenant

A man with a learning disability and complex needs resettled from a long-stay institution into a new bungalow. His mother visited him and said to a member of the support staff, 'It is all very well but it seems so unfair. My other son has worked hard all his life but could never afford to live anywhere as good as this.'

The valued role of *tenant* and the valued setting of a 'desirable house' were not enough to elicit positive ascribed value from this man's mother. This standard of housing might be seen as one of life's 'desirable things', included in the definition of SRV (Wolfensberger 1983) mentioned above. However, the means by which the person obtains these 'desirable things' seems to be significant. Media coverage of 'fat cats' in public services, bankers' bonuses, premiership footballers' wages and people living on benefits suggest that detailed and value-laden social representations of financial means, living standards and justice exist in our culture. For this mother, it is less just for a person who lives off benefits (even though disabled) to have a nice bungalow than it would be for someone who earns their living to have the same bungalow. This has important implications for ascribed value for people with a learning disability, as very few people with a learning disability have the opportunity to earn their living.

■ The harp man

A man with a learning disability is able to play the harmonica to a reasonable standard. He can play recognisable tunes. When he walks around the town, many people know him by name and many of them will ask him to play a tune. He is always happy to do this, which has resulted in him playing in the middle of a supermarket and at a funeral, for example.

Wolfensberger (1983) coined the term 'conservatism corollary'. He argued that there was a compounding effect with devaluing characteristics. In other words, the effect of a devaluing characteristic on a person who is already devalued is likely to be greater than that for an individual who is valued. For example, an otherwise valued person might get away with behaving in a childish way occasionally, whereas a person with a disability who behaves in the same way might suffer serious damage to their image and reputation. According to the conservatism corollary principle, the service to the person with a learning disability has to 'overcompensate' for the damaged image by taking the most conservative option among those available. As an example, Wolfensberger said that if a social event allows for formal or informal dress the devalued person should choose formal dress, which is the most valued option. The 'Harp man' story describes an individual who behaves in a flamboyant way in settings (a supermarket and a funeral) where valued people would typically behave in a conservative way.

It is difficult to determine whether the people who ask this man to play in public value him or not. Is he being seen as an *object of ridicule*, as described in Chapter 3? His harmonica playing is reasonable but a person without a learning disability would possibly be perceived as insufficiently skilled to play in public if they played to that standard. It would be possible to see the harp man's performance as 'clowning' or even the type of behaviour that might be expected from the historic figure of a 'village idiot'.

On the other hand, the man appears to elicit genuine affection. Some people say that if they meet this man in town he 'brightens up the day'. He makes people laugh and they are possibly laughing *with* him. One student nurse who visited the local town reported that the man was acknowledged by dozens of people who knew him by name and treated him with some warmth. It appears that he was valued as an acquaintance and an entertainer. Is this 'valuing' actually patronising? One thing is clear: if the support services were to act according to normalisation, and specifically conservatism corollary, they would attempt to stop this behaviour. This would deny him his main means of demonstrating competence and connecting with local people. This is another illustration of Briton's argument (Briton 1979) that normalisation is a blind endorsement of conformity.

■ His own kind

A man with a learning disability was good at socialising at his local pub. He was able to drum well enough to 'guest' with the house band. Although he enjoyed this, he showed a preference for attending the Mencap club on karaoke night. He performed the 'master of ceremonies' role at this club and the others there looked up to him. The two events clashed.

Support services were unsure what to do about this. The man's preferred choice was clear but the normalisation and SRV arguments outlined previously contradicted his decision:

● The conservatism corollary principle meant that he should take the most valuing option, which was playing the drums at the pub.

- Wolfensberger (1983) said that a person with a learning disability should, in all aspects of their life, be integrated into the same places and in the same activities as 'non-devalued' people. This places the person in a valued role, in a valued place, and is likely to enable modelling of competent behaviour.

- The support staff would be more aware of the impact of each option on his image and should direct his choice.

- Mencap is segregated and therefore devaluing.

- *Drummer in a house band* is a more socially valued role than *Mencap MC*.

In reality, his desire to go to the Mencap club was respected. To some of the support staff this had an unfortunate resonance with the argument against resettlement from the long-stay hospital that some staff had used: 'They are happier with their own kind.' This man may have felt most valued at the Mencap club because he was the most competent person present and perhaps felt that he had some power and authority in that setting. A 'valued' audience might have perceived him in a patronising way in the role of MC, which would indicate a low level of valuing. However, it is true that a 'valued' audience was not present and so no such valuing took place.

Conclusion

People with a learning disability are a devalued group with a damaged image. Harm to image leads to reduced life chances and so attempts should be made to modify that image in a way that leads to the devalued person becoming valued. This may be done by attending to the characteristics and behaviours of the devalued person, adjusting the support services to that person, and making changes to the wider social and legislative systems in our society. It is also desirable to enable a devalued person to obtain valued social roles.

If support services follow Wolfensberger's theories too rigidly, the rights of the devalued person are at risk of being over-ridden. This presents support services with a possible dilemma – how to balance the rights of the person on one hand, with damage to their image in the eyes of the audience on the other. It is impossible not to affect the image of the person with a learning disability. Virtually everything the support services do may have an implication, both for the person's image and for the choices they make. This will be the case whether or not the support staff members are aware of these theories. The audience will ascribe value to people with a learning disability, and the behaviour of support staff will have an impact on the resulting valuing. It is therefore important that staff become conscious of the impact of their input.

In conclusion, it seems that Wolfensberger's theories are not entirely adequate when it comes to roles, which means that they are less useful when explaining how valuing takes place.

Social Construction of Disability

■ Key note

A man with a learning disability lived alone in a house and needed support with some aspects of day-to-day living. He worked and it was difficult for him to get everything ready and leave for work on time. The two stumbling blocks seemed to be ensuring that he always had clothes ready for the morning and remembering to put his house key in his pocket. He had locked himself out on a number of occasions.

For a number of years, a staff member arrived at his house each morning to help with these two details. This proved to be problematic. The man was often worried about getting everything right and this was compounded by the fact that different staff members did things in different ways and this confused him.

In the end, a very simple solution was worked out. He stuck a picture of a key by the front door. Likewise, by his bed he had a pictorial instruction to remind him what clothes he needed, as well as all the other required small tasks in the order they needed doing. He was now able to get himself ready with no staff member present. This significantly reduced his anxiety.

Although this man is described as having a learning disability, when the picture of the key was placed beside the door he could overcome his problem with remembering complex tasks. As he is now able to leave the house without help when using this picture, he can be seen as not being disabled at all in respect of this task. The key sign actually enables him.

Many people would probably find another illustration of this principle easier to understand, as provided by the following vignette.

■ Stairs

A man who uses a wheelchair is unable to get into the local bank because it is an old building, with steps up to the front entrance. However, he is able to get into the supermarket because it has automatic doors and is on one level.

He cannot get into the bank without help from staff who have to lift his wheelchair up the steps, whereas he can go to the supermarket unaided in the same way as any ambulant person.

Both these stories require us to consider what is meant by 'disabled'. The man in the 'Key note' story does have a limit to his cognitive functioning but if the picture is in place he is not disabled in respect of managing to get to work unaided. Without the picture he is disabled. Similarly the man in 'Stairs' may have a spinal injury but he is not disabled in respect of entering a building if there is a ramp in place. Without the ramp he is disabled. We might say that the picture and the ramp enable the person. If this is the case, the disability is not a characteristic of the person but of the environment in which they find themselves.

This viewpoint has been central to the debate in disability studies. Historically, disability was defined by the medical or 'personal tragedy' model (Oliver 1993). The medical model was at the core of the World Health Organisation (WHO) classification of impairment, disability and handicap as recently as 1980 (Wood), and had three elements:

- **Impairment:** lacking all or part of a limb, or having a defective limb, organ or mechanism of the body
- **Disability:** the loss or reduction of functional ability
- **Handicap:** the disadvantage or restriction of activity caused by disability

This model leads us to interpret the man in 'Key note' as having:

- **Impairment:** a brain that functions at a level that is less than average
- **Disability:** the inability to remember and carry out the tasks required to get to work
- **Handicap:** the inability to get himself ready for work and leave the house safely

This way of perceiving disability can lead services to approach support in a way that is, in itself, disabling. In this case, the practitioners initially saw what the person could not do and put in staff to make up that deficit. This is a clear example of the application of the medical model of disability. This man was perceived to have a deficit in his function and so services 'treated' that deficit by putting in staff to compensate for it. Before the pictorial signs were put up, the man was treated in a similar way to a patient who has been confined to bed with an illness. This type of care appears to be based on the medical model. Thomas (1999) describes the causal link in the medical or personal tragedy model as:

impairment ⟶ disability ⟶ handicap.

This definition sees the impairment as being at the root of the 'handicap'.

In 1972, before the WHO model had been proposed, the Union of the Physically Impaired Against Segregation (UPIAS) published the first definition of these terms produced by people with a disability:

- Impairment: lacking all or part of a limb, or having a defective limb, organ or mechanism of the body
- Disability: the disadvantage or restriction of activity caused by a contemporary social organisation, which takes no or little account of people who have physical impairments, and thus excludes them from the mainstream of social activities (cited in Thomas 1999, p. 14).

In the case of the man in 'Key note', this model suggests;

- Impairment: a brain that functions at a level that is less than average (the same as with the medical model). This means that he struggles to remember and cannot write.
- Disability: an inability to get ready for work and leave the house safely because of a social convention that personal routines are memorised, and diaries and reminders are written, and staff support which is designed to do the job for him.

Thomas (1999) describes the causality in this definition as:

social barriers ⟶ disability.

Personal impairment is now excluded from any causality in disability. Also the idea of *handicap* is excluded from this definition. This is known as the social model of disability.

Oliver was a key theorist in the development of the social model of disability. He wrote (1996, p. 22):

> **In our view, it is society that disables physically impaired people. Disability is something imposed on top of our impairments by the way we are unnecessarily isolated and excluded from full participation in society. Disabled people are therefore an oppressed group in society. To understand this it is necessary to grasp the distinction between the physical impairment and the social situation, called 'disability', of people with such an impairment…**

In other words, the social model of disability suggests that disability is in the social setting and is a result of *barriers* that the impaired person has to face. These barriers can take three forms:

1 Individual and institutional attitudes
2 Policy and legislation
3 The environment

The key point is that these barriers are not fixed. If they are changed, it might mean that the person no longer experiences disability.

The following story illustrates these three types of barriers in practice.

■ The shopper

The assessment of a man with a learning disability had identified that he

- did not like crowds

- could not read
- had a concentration span of ten minutes
- got confused in a busy environment
- had difficulty choosing from more than three things
- could not follow complex instructions
- would not be able to remember something planned on a previous occasion.

His routine was to choose a week's menu on Sunday and then go to the supermarket on a Tuesday, taking the shopping list produced on the Sunday. The staff reported that he did not show much interest while at the supermarket and sometimes he became very impatient and started trying to push the trolley towards the exit. On occasions, this man would become so anxious that he would start to moan and bite his hand, at which point a member of staff would take him back to the car.

You, the reader, have probably carried out a similar activity with a person with a learning disability. I find it strange that this scenario appears to be so common: a bored-looking person with a learning disability pushing a trolley and, when the staff member tells them, taking an item from the shelf. The person seems to take little part in the shopping or paying. If we consider the typical environment in a supermarket and compare it to the assessment in 'The Shopper' story, we can see there is a complete mismatch.

Supermarkets are challenging environments because:

- They are usually crowded
- They bombard the senses with music, announcements over the public address system, eye-catching displays and bright fluorescent lighting
- Shopping takes an hour of concentration
- Shopping lists are usually written
- There is a huge choice for every single product (and all the choices made by the person with a learning disability were made three days before)
- The shop layout is complex
- It is unlikely that the person will know the staff at the checkout

In other words, the shopping experience is entirely at odds with what the assessment has already told us about this person. Taking one example, the activity takes an hour; yet we know the man has a concentration span of ten minutes. It would appear that this exercise is beyond his capability. It is likely to cause him anxiety and undermine his confidence. It is yet another activity in which he becomes dependent on the support staff. He will probably never be able to carry out most of the things required in this activity so why does it take place? It appears to be another example of the 'drip-drip' of undermining experiences that has been mentioned throughout this book.

This scenario offers a classic example of an *environmental* barrier. The environment in the supermarket disables the man. The staff team are colluding in that disabling by carrying out this activity. As the staff members are colluding in the activity, it can be argued that staff *attitude* is also a barrier to the person with a learning disability. The support service *policy* probably states that the person with a learning disability should carry out everyday activities and should be present in their local community and may well justify supermarket shopping in these terms. Yet the policy and the staff support are actually disabling the person. This is clearly not valuing the person.

It is interesting to consider why so many people with a learning disability are subjected to the same kind of experience as the man in the 'Shopper' story, when it is typically so unsuitable. Possible arguments are those mentioned above, some of which may appear in the service policy.

It may also be argued that supermarket shopping can save the person money on their weekly shopping bill. The following story suggests other motivations.

■ The corner shop

An elderly man with a learning disability had resettled from a long-stay institution. He enjoyed going to his local corner shop every morning. The people in the shop knew him and were able to help. They knew his name, they knew he needed some help with paying the right amount and they were used to his usual choices. The man liked to get a newspaper, some rolling tobacco, a fizzy drink and something for his lunch that day. He could carry out this activity unsupervised.

He was usually a quiet man and was happy to be left alone. The one exception was when he went to the supermarket. He had hit the staff who were with him. The staff team called in a behavioural specialist to advise them on how to manage his hitting. The specialist suggested that, as the man did not become aggressive anywhere else, the 'problem' could be simply solved by no longer using the supermarket. 'Big' shopping could be done online, as there was a supermarket that delivered to this area. The man could continue his daily trip to the local corner shop.

The specialist was surprised that his advice was needed for this solution. He was also surprised that the team resisted this change of plan. When he probed further one of the team said, with some anger, 'We all have to go shopping so why shouldn't he?'

Such an attitude is a further example of an *attitudinal* barrier. There are, of course, some people with a learning disability who enjoy shopping at a supermarket, but when people like the ones in 'The corner shop' and 'The shopper' are *made* to go, can it really be argued that the staff team are valuing that person? Actively disabling people in this way does not appear to equate with valuing them.

A further example of a barrier is described by Bell et al. (2001). People with a learning disability who are not detained under the Mental Health Act are legally entitled to vote. However, it is a fact that very few people with a learning disability actually do vote. Bell et al. suggest that the barriers to voting are the requirement to be literate, the problem of getting to the polling station and, possibly most significantly, the attitude of support staff. Redley (2008) found that there were environmental barriers present in the way that support services enabled people to exercise their vote.

Finkelstein (accessed 4 April 2012) describes an interesting imaginary scenario that allows those of us without an impairment to understand the true nature of this oppression. He describes a world in which the majority of people in a society use a wheelchair; and only a small minority can walk. The government in this society, like any government, wants to save money wherever it can. One way to save cost would be to build rooms that are only high enough for wheelchair users. This would save a huge amount on building materials but would mean that ambulant people would have to bend over or crawl when they were indoors.

The film *Being John Malkovich* depicts a world of low ceilings such as this, which creates a very claustrophobic atmosphere. In such a world, non-wheelchair users would develop back and joint problems. Numerous professionals would be needed to treat these back and joint problems with various therapies. There would be an industry created to build support aids for these people. Here is a vivid example of a disability being created by social oppression, and the oppressed person having their difference pathologised and treated. Oliver's imaginary world simply inverts the 'normal' world.

Similarly, we might try to imagine a world in which the majority of people have a learning disability. In this world there would, perhaps, be far less written material available. Communication might be through pictures. Authors of books such as this one might be seen as over-intellectual and might be treated for their excessive concern with things of questionable practical value. Academic pursuit might be pathologised. (Indeed, some might argue that this attitude already exists in Britain!) In this imaginary world, no government would dare to cut disability benefit because people with an impairment would constitute the majority of the electorate. (Of course in the real world, where disabled people are in the minority, the government is indeed cutting disability benefit.)

I have challenged groups of student nurses to imagine this world and describe the detail. This has proved to be a difficult task. These students frequently find it quite easy to imagine a world in which the majority of people use a wheelchair, or the majority have Asperger's syndrome. It is a different matter when they try to visualise a world in which the majority have a learning disability. You might like to try this exercise. This ongoing difficulty might be surprising, given that as long ago as 1999 Barnes *et al.* explicitly broadened the idea of impairment to include sensory, intellectual and developmental impairments.

Goodley (2001, p. 211) highlights a clear implication for this exclusion of people with a learning disability from the social model:

> **Thrown into the category of naturalised, irrational 'other'. Closed in, isolated and confined by a 'mental impairment' devoid of meaning and history, pre-social, inert and physical. People with 'learning difficulties' are personal tragedies of their unchangeable 'organic impairments'. That these assumptions are so strongly held is particularly worrying in light of the concerted attempts by disability theorists and activists to expose the social character of humanity in relation to disablement. Are people with 'learning difficulties' really that non-human?**

He is suggesting that to exclude people with a learning disability from the social model is to deny their humanity. This has a certain resonance with the discussion of historic roles in Chapter 3.

He goes on to suggest that the political concerns for all people who are disabled are the same (Goodley, *ibid.*, p. 211, [original emphasis]):

> **Perhaps we are not really convinced that the social model of disability is a viable epistemology for understandings of disability? For me, following the advice of the 'first wave' of disability theorists ... disability is a societal and political concern and, hence, so is 'learning difficulties'. Moreover, a turn to impairment as a social and political phenomenon necessitates an inclusion of 'learning difficulties'...**

The following quotation is from a person with a learning disability and indicates the double barriers she experiences (Simone Aspis, of London People First, cited in Goodley 2001, p. 210):

> **People with 'learning disabilities' face discrimination in the disability movement. People without 'learning difficulties' use the medical model when dealing with us. We are always asked to talk about advocacy and our impairments as though our barriers aren't disabling in the same way as disabled people without 'learning difficulties'. We want to concentrate on our access needs in the mainstream disability movement.**

Some theorists suggest that the experience of disabled people does not divide neatly into impairment and disability. French (1993) thinks that there is 'something in between'. She describes how her visual impairment gets in the way of ordinary social interaction by, for example, leading her to feel that when she is lecturing she cannot pick up visual clues when students wish to participate. Thus, for her, the quality of the interaction with students is impaired. Similarly neighbours, who know of her impairment, stop bothering to acknowledge her when they have to initiate every interaction, as French does not know the identity of people she cannot see. This problem in transaction does not seem to fit neatly into either the social or medical models of disability.

Secondly Thomas (1999) describes how some restriction of activity for an impaired person may come about because of their impairment and not be socially created and therefore not a disability. She describes this as 'impairment effect'. For example, if a person has no legs they cannot walk unaided. The inability to walk is an impairment effect. However, if the person is deemed incapable of work because of their impairment then they are being disabled.

The following summary of an assessment of one woman offers an account of extreme impairment.

■ Assessment

Jane has cerebral palsy and is unable to move independently. She needs total support with her living skills. She is unable to communicate using speech. She does not gesture. She screams when she is distressed and her carers are sometimes able to determine what is distressing her. This is sometimes the fact that she is wet, hot or hungry.

It is difficult to imagine any barrier that could be removed to undo the disablement in this situation. It might be argued that Jane's impairment is so extreme that the impairment effect is more significant than socially constructed disability in her day-to-day experience. Thomas and other theorists (Morris 1991 and French 1993, for example) raise the problem that in defining all disability as socially constructed, the reality of impairment for the individual is denied. In other words, the disability is significantly (but partially and not totally) located outside the person in the form of disabling barriers. The person may also perceive the impairment itself as barrier. The following vignette is an example of mental impairment being experienced in this way.

■ The stroke

A man who had been an academic had a stroke. He had been very articulate and loved to engage in political discussion. The stroke badly affected his speech and even those who knew him well struggled to understand him.

His family took a copy of the Guardian into hospital so that he would know about the latest news. The family read from the paper. He attempted to comment on one item but the others could not understand what he said. He became upset and the words that did come across clearly were, 'This is cruel torture'.

Another aspect of impairment is the fact that it is not a fixed physical condition. This, of course, is how the medical model also defines impairment. One critique of the social model is the constructionist perspective. This position, as explained by Thomas (2004, p. 23), states that:

> ...there is nothing inherent or 'essential' in an individual's body, character or behaviour that would predispose them to being a disabled person. Rather, those who wield power through the authority conferred upon them by the status and legitimacy of their knowledge – doctors, state administrators and legislators – can impose the category 'disabled' upon individuals in their purview. A person who is socially constructed as 'disabled' may often come, in turn, to construct reflexively her or his self-identity in the image of 'disabled person'.

This should lead all of us who are involved in the assessment of people with a learning disability to reflect deeply. We have power resulting from knowledge, professional status, local policy and legislation to carry out our role. According to the social model, the act of assessment can be seen as actively *constructing* that person's disability and not just passively identifying and describing it. As a consequence of this, the person goes on to construct their own identity. We may claim that the act of carrying out the assessment is well intentioned and any negative consequences are unconscious. But, in terms of outcomes, it is difficult to argue that this process values the person with a learning disability.

The next two vignettes illustrate these points. The first is offered with a personal guarantee from me that it is true. With the passage of time the story appears more incredible, but I was one of the characters! The challenge to the reader is to guess which one.

■ The immigrant

In the 1960s a man who was serving in the British army brought a teenage boy from Kenya to England. The boy was found apparently wandering in the bush. He was thought, in the language of the time, to have a 'mental handicap'. He was eventually placed in a long-stay institution and assessed. This assessment 'confirmed' that he had a 'mental handicap', noting that he displayed the following behaviours:

- Throwing hot drinks at staff
- Refusing to sleep on a bed and insisting on lying on the floor

- Refusing to use eating utensils
- Stripping off his clothing
- Making grunting noises

In the late 1980s, when resettlement to the community was underway, this man was considered and assessed. A social worker, who had previously worked in Kenya, thought that the man looked physically similar to the Kikuyu people she had met there. She knew of a group of people from the same tribe who were attending the local university. She arranged a meeting.

A nurse who was also involved thought that this was unnecessary; the man clearly had a mental handicap (to use the language of that time). Such a meeting seemed a little 'precious' to him. The meeting did take place and the Kenyans made the following observations. It is unlikely that this man had ever had many hot drinks prior to coming to England. His cultural norm would have been to sleep on a mat on the floor, to use his fingers for eating and to wear minimal clothing much of the time. Also he was still able to use his own language, the 'grunting noises' mentioned in his assessment. In other words the behaviours cited as 'evidence' of his learning disability in the assessment were his normal cultural practice.

The postscript to this story is that his family were traced in Kenya and they had assumed he had been killed in the bush 20 years ago. They had suffered shame because they were deemed not to have cared for their son. They had considered him 'slow' and it was because of this that he had been allowed to wander more freely than the other children in the village.

The second vignette is a further example of how the mental impairment of a person with a learning disability has been naturalised to such an extent that the professionals' perception of the person's behaviour is constrained.

■ Headache

A woman presented with challenging behaviour. She bit herself and others when distressed and could cause serious damage. She lived on a specialist assessment unit that had a good reputation and had achieved some success with people referred to it. A team of specialists had devised a range of programmes for her, most of which were based on behaviourist principles.

One day the woman was particularly distressed and the staff were struggling to manage her as she was banging her head against the wall. The unit cleaner was present. She suggested that the woman be given a paracetamol as it seemed obvious she had a headache. This was tried and the head banging ceased. The assessment team had missed this solution, as their focus was behavioural.

Two months later this lesson had been forgotten and the head banging was again being treated with behavioural programmes. The barrier appeared to be staff perception.

The theorists who first engaged with the social model, with disability as oppression, are now described as 'first wave' theorists (Goodley 2001). There have since been attempts to re-theorise the medical model–social model divide and explore how far the social model still considers impairment as personal tragedy instead of something that is also socially created. For example, the International Classification of Function, Disability and Health (ICF, accessed 4 April 2012) has produced a definition of disability that was adopted by the World Health Organisation (WHO) for international use in 2001. This definition integrates the medical and social models and this is termed a 'biopsychosocial approach'. The ICF claims to synthesise the various perspectives of health from biological, individual and social perspectives (WHO 2001).

Kershaw (quoted in Goodley 2000) comments:

> 'Learning disabilities' – I don't like that, disability makes you believe that we are in wheelchairs and we can't do anything for ourselves, when we can. We've got jobs now, we've got paid jobs.

This can be seen as an example of an attitudinal barrier to people who are physically disabled existing in the perception of a person with a learning disability. Kershaw appears to have a perception of people with a physical impairment as being unable to do anything for themselves or to work. The implications of such assumptions have been explored in previous chapters.

■ Reluctant bather

A man with a learning disability hated having a bath or shower. He had lived in a long-stay institution and his fear had probably come from his experiences at that time. When his current staff even mentioned the word 'shower' he would scream and strike out. He was doubly incontinent and as he used a wheelchair his skin was likely to break down. He was made to have a shower, as a multidisciplinary team had decided it was in his best interest.

A qualified member of the team was charged with the responsibility of writing up this man's person-centred plan. In the 'personal hygiene' section she wrote, 'I can carry out many self-help skills but I need encouragement to have a bath.'

Those of us who work in services for people with a learning disability have become used to assessments and person-centred plans that use the first person in this way. It can be argued that the person who has actually written this statement has twisted the truth. For a start, the person whose words these allegedly are, cannot write. Secondly he would not understand words such as 'self-help' or 'encouragement'. Thirdly, even if he were able, he would be unlikely to want any 'encouragement' to have a bath or shower, as he appears to be scared of any mention of such an activity. The support organisation has chosen to put words into this man's mouth. It is very likely that these particular words are not what he would choose to say if he were able.

If this man could write his own entry in the 'personal hygiene section' of his person-centred plan he might write:

> **I am scared of having a shower or bath as I was once hit and ducked under the water by a staff member who was cross with me.**

Or possibly:

> **I hate people giving me any personal care because I can't control what they do to me.**

Or even:

> **I have undiagnosed autism and the smell of many bathing products makes me feel very ill.**

These three statements are made up of course, but they are no less truthful than the one that was actually written in the person-centred plan. In fact it is very possible that the first comment is fairly near the truth of the real situation described in the 'Reluctant bather' story.

To return to the theme of the power of the unconscious in determining the way a person with a learning disability is treated, we could consider the possibility that the man in 'Reluctant bather' might experience care with different emphasis, depending on which statement is included in his plan. As stated above, there is a choice between:

> **I can carry out many self-help skills but I need encouragement to have a bath.**

And:

> **I am scared of having a shower or bath as I was once hit and ducked under the water by a staff member who was cross with me.**

How might these comments change the way this man is perceived and treated?

This theme is discussed more fully in Chapter 4 ('Metaphor and Attribution'). The barriers experienced by this man are at the level of policy and attitude.

Choice of terminology

One form of oppression in the social model is the terminology used by the powerful group. The organisation People First, a self-advocacy group, has made a very clear statement about the terminology they prefer on their website (accessed 22 November 2010). They prefer the term 'learning difficulty' to 'learning disability', as they see support needs as changeable over time. Proper support will lead to more independence. They suggest that the use of the term 'learning disability' suggests that the difference is curable – a clear reference to the medical model of disability. Yet the White Paper 'Valuing People Now' (DOH 2009, p. 2) states: 'The strategy is driven by the views of people with learning disabilities.'

This policy statement may appear to be ironic. The government claims that its strategy is driven by the views of people with a 'learning disability', when the stated preference of that category of people is to use the term 'learning difficulty'. Practitioners define these terms and it is these definitions that have been adopted. It is clear where the power lies.

People First faces barriers to its wish being fulfilled. One barrier is at the level of policy. The previous White Paper 'Valuing People' (DOH 2001, p.15) stated: '"Learning disability" does not include all of those who have a "learning difficulty", which is more broadly defined in education legislation.'

'Valuing People' (ibid., p. 14) defined learning disability as including the presence of:

A significantly reduced ability to understand new or complex information, to learn new skills (impaired intelligence) with;

A reduced ability to cope independently (impaired functioning);

Which started before adulthood, with lasting effect on development.

'Valuing People' adopted the term 'learning disability'. It was also confused regarding the social model of disability. The above definition is problematic because it combines 'impairment' and 'disability' in the same category; 'disability' is defined in terms of 'impairment'. So learning disability is defined both as 'impaired intelligence' (impairment) and 'reduced ability to cope' (which is concerned with functioning). Learning disability is defined as lack of ability to function.

Similarly Gates, the author of a major text, writes (1997, p. 7) that learning disability is a term used to:

...describe a group of people with significant developmental delay that results in arrested or incomplete achievement of the 'normal' milestones of human development. These relate to intellectual, emotional, spiritual and social aspects of development. Significant delays in the achievement of one or more of these milestones may lead to a person being described, defined or categorised as having learning disabilities...

The statement 'this person has a learning disability' clearly makes no sense in terms of the social model of disability. If the disability is a result of barriers external to the person then the person cannot be seen to 'have a disability', they 'are disabled' by the environment. To use the word 'have' in this way suggests that the disability is intrinsic to the person, which is of course more consistent with the medical model of disability. However, that person can be said to '*have* an impairment'.

These issues are starting to be considered in the world of professional journals. For example, *The Journal of Learning Disability* has been renamed *The Journal of Intellectual Disability*. But it can be argued that to be consistent with the social model the intellect of the person does not relate to the disability but to the impairment. Therefore a more 'social model-consistent' title might be *Journal of Intellectual Impairment*.

Can services, policy writers and practitioners and journals be said to value people with a learning disability if they use different terms to describe that group of people from the ones they would choose to describe themselves? And furthermore, can I (the author of this book) claim to value this group of people if I too choose to use the term 'learning disability', which I have done up to this point in this book? The only 'values-consistent' decision would be to adopt the term 'learning difficulty'. From this point onward, I will therefore drop the term 'learning disability' and start using the term 'learning difficulty'.

One final aspect of power is what Duffy (2003) describes as the 'professional gift model' of service provision. According to this model, people pay taxes to the government, which then gives professionals the responsibility of assessing people in need and allocating these resources accordingly. In carrying out this allocation, the professional will decide how that service is to be provided. The professional's relationship with the 'client' (and that term indicates the nature of the relationship) is determined by the power. There is the overt power of directly telling the client what to do, and also the implicit power that will pervade the relationship (Lukes 2005). The person with a learning difficulty just accepts that another person has this much power over them.

Is it possible for the professional to be able to say that they value the person with a learning difficulty while at the same time exercising such power over them?

The conflict between Oliver and Wolfensberger

The final section of this chapter raises some theoretical questions that emerge from a comparison between the theories outlined in Chapter 7 and this chapter. While considering the conflict between the interactionist perspective of Wolf Wolfensberger and the materialist perspective of Mike Oliver (as well as other social model theorists), you (the reader) should also consider your own position. Some readers may choose to skip this discussion without compromising their understanding of subsequent chapters. However, for those readers who enjoy engaging with comparative theoretical discussion, it might prove interesting. There are no supporting vignettes or stories. This is only a brief synopsis of the arguments and for those interested in gaining a fuller understanding it would be beneficial to go back to the primary sources.

Oliver has played a key part in the emergence of the social theory of disability in Britain (Thomas 1999). He has directly criticised Wolfensberger's approach (Oliver 1999), largely because it is based on symbolic interactionist and functionalist sociology. Oliver is a Marxist and his account is materialist, placing 'disability' as a category produced by capitalist relations of production. His criticism of Wolfensberger's account of the emergence of long-stay institutions is similar to that of Scull (1977). For Wolfensberger, the institutions were the result of 'bad' ideology, whereas for materialists like Scull and Oliver they emerged because industrial production required a workforce capable of working to a minimum level of competence. Oliver goes so far as to say (Oliver 1999, p. 164):

> Attempting to incorporate Normalization in a materialist account, however, does not mean that I believe it is of much use. Based as it is upon functionalist and interactionist sociology, whose defects are well known, it offers no satisfactory explanation of why disabled people are oppressed in capitalist societies and no strategy for liberating us from chains of oppression

Personally, I consider Oliver's disregarding of symbolic interactionist thought too glib. Feminist and post-modernist thought would also challenge both symbolic interactionist and Marxist accounts of disability.

Oliver's second criticism is that Wolfensberger provides no explanation of oppression and offers no strategy to gain liberation from oppression. Oliver further comments (*ibid.*, p. 163):

> And I will ... argue that already this theory [the materialist theory of disability] has had a far greater influence on the struggles that disabled people are themselves currently engaged in to remove the chains of that oppression than Normalization, which is, at best, a bystander in these struggles, and, at worst, part of the process of oppression itself...

This is arguably true. Those of us who worked in support services in the 1980s experienced SRV and normalisation being used to justify oppressive practices such as denying a person a sex life and removing a person's property when it was deemed 'age inappropriate'. However, it is questionable whether it has ever been argued that normalisation and SRV are about oppression and, therefore, emancipation from it.

Wolfensberger's aim is to attempt to 'fit' people with a learning difficulty into their society, not emancipate them from it. Meanwhile, Oliver (1999, p. 166) describes how changes in ideas still result in services oppressing the people they claim to serve:

> In the world of late capitalism, the same people, albeit with different job titles and perhaps in plusher buildings, are doing the same things to disabled people although they may now be calling them 'doing a needs led assessment' or 'producing a care plan'...

119

To this list could be added 'Giving someone a valued role' or 'Advising on the best way to enhance their image'. It is a list of things professionals 'do' to people, with or without their consent. And I think it is fair to say that, in practice, normalisation and SRV have become tools for professionals. Perhaps it could be argued that person-centred approaches have also become tools for the professional.

Oliver (1996) claims that normalisation and SRV have not been taken up by a single disabled people's organisation. This is strong evidence against the usefulness of the theory to people with learning difficulties. However, Oliver's claim is not entirely true. At least some groups from People First, an organisation of people with a learning difficulty, have some sympathy with normalisation and SRV. People without a learning difficulty who are employed as spokespeople by People First are themselves advocates of the theory. This, of course, raises important questions about power.

Despite Oliver's antagonism towards Wolfensberger, it is interesting to note their similarities. For example, Oliver (1996, p. 25) refers to the UPIAS Statement of Fundamental Principles:

> **It is obvious that this struggle requires a major rethinking of old attitudes and ideas about the *Social Roles* of disabled people. It will be necessary to draw the mass of disabled people (of whatever age or type of physical impairment) into the great movement to raise our consciousness of our social identity. A general mass movement of disabled people, and our increasing integration into normal work and other social situations, will radically improve our social status as a group.**

The above statement can be summarised as: 'If disabled people adopt normal social roles, their social status will improve.' On the face of it, this sounds remarkably similar to the intermediate definition of SRV (Wolfensberger 1983, p. 234 [original emphasis]):

> **...the most explicit and highest goal of normalisation must be the creation, support and defence of valued social roles for people who are at risk of devaluation. All other elements and objectives of the theory are really subservient to this end because if a person's role were a socially valued one then other desirable things would be accorded to that person almost automatically...**

The link between role and perception of the audience is clearly common to both theories. But they differ greatly in context. The UPIAS work is concerned with *disabled people acting for disabled people*, whereas Wolfensberger's work is focused on *professionals acting for disabled people*. At a more fundamental level, it is clear that the advocates of a social model see materialist causes of disability, while Wolfensberger sees ideological causes. However, both perspectives see the cause of disability as being external to the impaired individual.

Listening and Talking

■ I told them

A long-stay institution ran a camp each summer for the people who lived there. It was expected that people would attend even though some did not enjoy the experience. One man expressed his dislike of going to camp at the time. He (J) described his experience to the Author (A):

A: Did you like camp?

J: No I didn't, no.

A: Did you have to go?

J: I had to go, yes.

A: What would have happened if you had said 'I don't want to go'?

J: They wouldn't listen.

A: Wouldn't they? You had to go?

J: Yes.

A: Did you tell them you didn't like it?

J: I told them and told them and told them (cough). I told them and told them.

A: What did they say?

J: They wouldn't listen.

(This video may be seen at Unlocking the past, 12' 36" to 13' 15", accessed 30 November 2011)

This man was clearly expressing his view but he was not heard. There is a sense of desperation and hopelessness in the way he says 'I told them' five times. This is an example from the past but we might ask whether things are any different today. If no one listened to people then, were they valued? And if we do not truly listen now, can we be said to value people today? The government White Paper 'Valuing People' (DOH 2001, p. 24) stated:

> Like other people, people with learning disabilities want a real say in where they live, what work they should do and who looks after them. But for too

many people with learning disabilities, these are currently unattainable goals. We believe that everyone should be able to make choices. This includes people with severe and profound disabilities who, with the right help and support, can make important choices and express preferences about their day-to-day lives.

It went on to say (*ibid*., p. 45) that a related challenge for services is 'fully involving them in decisions affecting their lives'. It then suggested (*ibid*., p. 49) that one way of doing this is to create person-centred approaches to care. This means that: '...planning should start with the individual (not with their services), and take account of their wishes and aspirations.'

Given that the intention of 'Valuing People' was to create a clear blueprint for services, the wording of this intention was perhaps surprisingly half-hearted. To 'take account' of a person's wishes is very different from 'being directed by' or 'basing planning on' that person's wishes. 'Taking account' can be interpreted differently from 'listening to'. 'Taking account' suggests that the service maintains control over the plan and decision-making and the extent to which we might be expected to listen to the preferences expressed by a person with a learning difficulty. This attitude (even if unintentionally expressed) can be seen as an attitudinal and power barrier, as defined in the social model of disability and described in Chapter 8.

To return to the original question in this book, is it possible for a service to claim that it values people with a learning difficulty if the words used in a person-centred plan are not those of the person concerned, if the time allowed is less than that required for long discussion and full transcription, and if the agenda is controlled by the service? The following vignette is an example of a person with a learning difficulty having control.

■ Laser control

A service manager devised a process for managing a person-centred plan meeting in which the agenda and content were put onto a power-point presentation. The person with a learning difficulty who was the focus for the meeting held the laser control switch and could therefore switch to the next item at will. He also decided what to place on the slides so that others at the meeting would have to seek meaning from him.

At one point the manager was explaining how a particular issue might be addressed when the person at the centre of the plan moved the agenda on by clicking the control. The manager was aware of feeling personally powerless and also feeling indignant that he had been 'cut short'. When he reflected on this incident later, the manager became aware of the power he usually exerted. He also experienced a sense of empathy with the person with a learning difficulty.

He wondered how often this person had been able to exercise such power over discussions about his life.

Other aspects of the process are often organised in a way that that is not really person-centred at all, and similar points are raised in Chapter 8 (which discusses the social construction of disability). Records of the meeting are frequently written for people who cannot read. There are sometimes pictorial representations of the records but the person at the centre of the plan often has little understanding of these pictorial records. The wording may be similar to the 'official' records and the picture can be seen as a token addition to the content, which merely gives a sense of satisfaction to the service planners who can then claim that they have met the 'user-friendly' target.

The conceptualising of the decision-making process is bounded by the worldview and the perception of the professionals. For a start, there is often a meeting that requires a number of people to gather together and use a structure of minutes, discussion, goals, timescales, reading from past minutes, and talking about the future. This all takes place in an office or large meeting room. All these elements may well inhibit the person with a learning difficulty and prevent them from taking a meaningful part in proceedings. The reality is that the person at the centre of the plan often ends up having someone else speak up on their behalf.

The following example illustrates how difficult it can be to cope with having the ability to control a person-centred plan, even for a man with a marginal learning difficulty.

■ The mechanic

Andy is a 17-year-old who lives with his family. He has a learning difficulty, autism and cerebral palsy. He offered to take part in resilience research and over an hour he talked about his life. He was on a mechanics course and described his experience with others in the group:

Just calling me names like spastic and retard and all that for no reason. Just because they think it's fun to do it. I said to them, 'I find that word very offensive so don't use that word again.' That's when I started threatening to hit them.

He had completed the course but was deemed unsuitable to go on to the workshop experience. S asked him how he felt about this:

S: What did you do when you first found out?

Andy: I just thought 'That's quite strange, I've had this dream and now there's barriers up saying I just can't do it.'

S: Yeah. So did you have to stop going to the garage? ... Do you understand why it has happened?

Andy: Well I can understand that there are a few problems like my concentration and all that but what I can't understand is why can't I go into the garage to actually work? That's what I want to do.

S transcribed the interview verbatim. One hour's talk took five hours to transcribe. Andy allowed the family to read his account; they were shocked. However well they thought they knew him, some of the detail had never been fully described. His mum said:

Andy's story was a reality check for me … he was isolated at home, talking to himself and immersed in a fantasy world, fearful of going out. It was there, written in black and white. It was a true reflection of Andy's life at that time.

Andy now had his story on paper and he chose to present it at meetings. It helped him to speak, giving a full account. His mum commented:

I feel that Andy's life story enabled Andy to make a real impact upon his social worker, who worked with Andy to complete his RAS. I was present during the assessment and I believe that the social worker used the information contained within Andy's story to guide him in answering the questions.

She thought the transcript played a very important part:

Andy's story provided him with a sense of pride. This was his story. Although he had been involved in the statement process in respect of special educational needs, this was not a process led by Andy. Because of the open nature of the interview, I would suggest that he was in some way able to lead the process, although he was answering your questions, you were capturing verbatim his actual responses, and thereby capturing the significance of these responses – you may have noticed that he didn't always directly answer your question, but you allowed him to continue and this approach enabled you to capture other aspects of his life which opened up – for example, how else would you have known what Andy's ideal 'race world' would have been like?

What had started as a transcript of a research interview became a powerful tool, which enabled a man with learning difficulty to gain personal power and ultimately shape his own life.

It might be instructive for you, the reader, to consider the last person-centred plan with which you were involved:

1 How much of the personal account was in the person's own words and how much of it was mediated by others? If the first person was used, could you describe this as genuinely their own words? Can you justify the use of the first person if that person never said those things?

2 Consider the time used to create the person's own story in the example above (one hour-long interview and five hours spent transcribing). How long was dedicated to obtaining the person's story in the last person-centred plan you were involved with? If your plan involves less time than the six hours noted here, can the service be seen as listening and acting?

3 Was the person whose plan you are considering given 'free rein' to talk about whatever they wished or did they answer a series of questions from a pro-forma? Can we be said to 'listen' in a valid way if the questions asked were not those deemed important by the person speaking?

(This example was first published in Dennison & Mee 2011.)

Person-centred planning is rooted in the 'Valuing People' (DOH 2001) agenda, which specifies the essential four principles of service design: rights, independent living, control and inclusion. These principles appear to have become the shorthand version of the 'values base' adopted by service providers. Burton & Kagan (2006) see the agenda and structure of 'Valuing People' as being determined by the neo-liberal ideologies that have been dominant in recent times.

In the next story, a person with a learning difficulty challenges this inclusive, neo-liberal approach.

■ Your world

A man who service providers might describe as 'on the autism spectrum' describes himself as 'autistic'. He states that he is categorically different from 'neurotypicals' (a word coined to describe the non-autistic majority). He once said to a group of professionals who were attending an autism course: 'Why do you insist on trying to integrate me into your world? There is nothing in your world for me. Leave me alone.'

'Inclusion' is at the heart of much learning disability policy and practice at present. Wolfensberger argued that the primary service aims should be 'integration' into community life and 'dispersal' throughout that community (Wolfensberger 1972). O'Brien included 'community participation' and 'presence and integration' in his five service accomplishments (O'Brien 1987). Likewise, 'Valuing People' (DOH 2001) and 'Valuing People Now' (DOH 2009) made 'inclusion' one of the four fundamental principles for learning disability services.

Yet we might ask the question 'Who has requested the goal of inclusion?' Wolfensberger and O'Brien were responding to the fact that so many people with a learning difficulty had been subjected to forced exclusion from society at that time, and their concerns are therefore understandable. But has forced exclusion since been replaced by forced inclusion?

The inclusion policy includes a strong emphasis on the central importance of work, preferably paid work. Yet Burton & Kagan (2006) see this focus as another example of the neo-liberal agenda.

■ Dog handler

A man with a learning difficulty had been known to challenging behaviour services for most of his life. He had been seen as a 'good worker' and had been involved in various local community-based employment projects, including a garden centre and a picture-framing business. He demonstrated significant skills in both of these projects. Yet he chose to leave both and had appeared 'challenging' in both settings.

At a later date, he became a volunteer with an animal charity that looks after unwanted and problem pets. He demonstrated skill in dealing with hard-to-manage dogs. He is proud of his skill and volunteers most days of the week for no remuneration. He also teaches student nurses about his work but refuses payment for this. When asked why, he says, 'If you get paid it just means you have another boss ordering you about.' When questioned further about this, it appears that he is really referring to the fact that if you are paid it means, yet again, that a person without a learning difficulty is in a position to order you about. He clearly loves his work but believes that payment would spoil things.

So who asked for paid work to be so central to the concept of inclusion? For most people with a learning difficulty, work means low-paid jobs of low status. This sort of employment may, of course, be what some people with a learning difficulty want, but it may equally be the case that the policy-making process has involved very limited listening to their voices. It might be well worth researching and analysing the participation of people with a learning difficulty in this area of policy making.

In person-centred planning and policy making, it is not easy to include the voice of the person with a learning difficulty in anything more than a tokenistic way. The voices of people with a learning difficulty have been largely absent from many areas of society (Allen 2009, Atkinson 2005, Jukes 2009, Ryan & Thomas 1981).

The history of learning difficulty has also been written in a way that has largely excluded the people with a learning difficulty (Atkinson & Walmsley 2000). Written accounts are largely from the perspective of the policy makers and professionals. If the voice of the person who has actually experienced this history is to be valued, then the individuals must be seen as 'expert witnesses' (Birren & Deutchman 1991). Some examples of histories that have included the voices of people with a learning difficulty are Hunt (1967), Edgerton (1967), Braginsky & Braginsky (1971), Fido & Potts (1989), Booth & Booth (1994) and Atkinson & Williams (1990).

Talking to people with a learning difficulty

An everyday conversation with someone with a learning difficulty might begin: 'You get yourself ready and then we can go to town to buy your DVD.' On the face of it, this might seem straightforward enough. It might also seem that the day has some potential – if this is what the person wants to do. If the person has asked to buy the DVD, then this situation looks like a good example of a service staff member listening to what the person wants to do and then ensuring that it happens.

However, when one has a learning difficulty, by definition, understanding of language is impaired. A speech and language therapist I know is of the opinion that support staff members almost always over-estimate the linguistic ability of the people with whom they work. She told the following story.

■ Feed the birds

A woman with a learning difficulty enjoyed feeding the birds in the garden and watching them through the lounge widow. She would go into the kitchen, take the bird seed from under the sink, go into the garden and place the seed on the bird table when staff suggested it. Staff reported to the speech and language therapist that she understood the request to do this task.

The speech and language therapist asked the staff to make the request while keeping their hands behind their backs and maintaining eye contact with the woman. When the request was made in this way the woman did not act; she appeared to have no understanding of what to do. The speech and language therapist had noticed that staff looked out of the widow at the bird table and then towards the kitchen. This was reinforced with hand gestures. It appeared that the woman had gleaned her understanding from these gestures and eye movements and the words had conveyed no meaning at all.

One aspect of having a learning difficulty is that one's language development may be 'stuck' at a low level. The usefulness of the labelling device of 'mental age' has long been in question but a person with a learning difficulty may understand language at a level that is more usually typical of a child. For this reason, an understanding of the typical patterns of language development may be useful. The Institute of Parenting (accessed 29 December 2011) has produced a table that outlines this development. Here are some examples of typical development at different stages.

At 18 months, the child:

- has a vocabulary of approximately 5–20 words
- cocabulary is made up chiefly of nouns
- is able to follow simple commands.

At 24 months, the child:

- can name a number of objects common to his surroundings
- is able to use at least two prepositions, usually chosen from the following: in, on, under
- can use two pronouns correctly: I, me, you (although me and I are often confused)
- is beginning to use 'my' and 'mine'.

At 36 months, the child:

- uses pronouns I, you, me correctly
- uses some plurals and past tenses
- knows at least three prepositions, usually in, on, under
- handles three-word sentences easily
- understands most simple questions dealing with environment and activities
- is able to answer such questions as 'What must you do when you are sleepy, hungry, cool, or thirsty?'
- should not be expected to answer all questions, even though he understands what is expected.

At 48 months, the child:

- names common objects in picture books or magazines
- knows one or more colours
- can repeat four digits when they are given slowly
- can usually repeat words of four syllables
- demonstrates understanding of over and under
- understands such concepts as longer or larger
- readily follows simple commands even though the stimulus objects are not in sight.

Some of these examples may have relevance to people with a learning difficulty. If the person with a learning difficulty is 'stuck' at a linguistic stage that is more typical for 36 months, for example, then they will have problems understanding the apparently simple sentence, 'You get yourself ready and then we can go to town to buy your DVD.' This sentence might simply be too long. Verbal communication requires complex cognitive skills, which include attending, listening, processing, storing and recalling. In order to understand a long sentence, one requires an auditory memory. This means that one must be able to retain a number of words while they are cognitively processed (Cusimano 2010). Many people with a learning difficulty have an auditory memory of only four or five words. By the time the sixth word has been spoken, the first part of the sentence has been lost (audiblox).

Note that the above list has a child of three understanding a three-word sentence. I recall hearing a simple but aggressive-sounding demand being made to a person in a long-stay institution. The words 'Smith, bath, now!' were shouted at a person with severe learning difficulty. He jumped up and carried out the instruction. In three words the staff member had made it clear who was being spoken to, what was expected and when. The tone used indicated the urgency of the request.

Many support staff today would use more respectful and polite communication. We might hear, for example, 'John, do you want to have a shower now and come down in your dressing gown to watch the football on telly?' This sounds like a pleasant way to spend an evening and this way of speaking might be seen as 'valuing' the person with a learning difficulty. However, if valuing is defined as using language that the person can understand, the three-word command might actually be *more* 'valuing'. All the pleasantries and apparent giving of information in the sentence 'John, do you want to have a shower now and come down in your dressing gown to watch the football on telly?' might lead to confusion. In that sense, it is therefore a devaluing communication. The tone of voice, body language and facial expression, rather than the number of words used, might be the key to making a simple command 'valuing'.

A second problem with 'You get yourself ready and then we can go to town to buy your DVD' is that it is not sufficiently concrete. What does 'get yourself ready' mean? Does that task involve a shower? Getting dressed? Putting on shoes and coat? Is it the same as 'get ready' for bed? Does it mean the same as another member of staff saying the same words? Many people with a learning difficulty may remain largely concrete thinkers. This means that they struggle to see the similarities between different situations, viewing each one as a separate entity (Turkington & Harris 2006).

Another abstract question often put to people with a learning difficulty is 'What do you want to do today?' This might appear to be 'valuing', in the sense that it appears to be offering choice. However, if the person is unable to visualise the alternatives then it is devaluing because no account is being taken of the confusion this might cause. A way round this problem is to have pictures of activities or places that the person is known to like, from which to choose.

A third problem with this request is that the sentence starts with the pronoun 'you'. As we have seen, full understanding of pronouns typically develops by the age of three or four. But this may simply be beyond the understanding of many people with a learning difficulty. A problem with the use of pronouns is that the same person can be indicated by more than

129

one pronoun, depending on who is addressing whom. So, for example, the person with a learning difficulty will be 'me' from their own perspective but 'you' from the perspective of the support staff. Confusingly, these terms are reversed when the perspectives are switched, so the support staff member now becomes 'me' from their own perspective but 'you' from the perspective of the person with a learning difficulty. In other words the person with a learning difficulty is both 'you' and 'me', as indeed is the support staff.

In order to understand that one is 'you' from the perspective of another requires one to imagine the perception of that other person. This ability has been labelled 'theory of mind'. Its absence is usually mentioned as a diagnostic feature of autism (Baron-Cohen 1995) but it has more recently been proposed as a characteristic of some people with a learning difficulty (Ashcroft et al. 1999). If a person does not have theory of mind, the use of pronouns can be confusing. The label that remains constant, whatever the perspective, is the person's name. This is another reason why 'Smith, bath, now' might be clearer for some people with a learning difficulty than a question such as 'Would you like a bath now?' The implications of this may seem counter-intuitive; the use of pronouns when talking to some people with a learning difficulty can be seen as devaluing but the use of the person's name might be valuing.

Another common but complex linguistic feature is the use of negatives. With a sentence such as 'Throw that chair', simply placing the words 'do not' at the beginning can reverse the meaning and turn the sentence into a request to not do something: 'Do not throw that chair.' The implications are obvious if this request is made to an individual who does not understand the use of negatives. If 'do not' carries no meaning, then 'Do not throw that chair' will be heard as 'Throw that chair.' A further problem is that this sentence causes the listener to visualise throwing the chair, even if the negative is understood. Likewise, if someone says to you 'Do not think of David Beckham', you will almost certainly immediately think of David Beckham. For clarity in communication, one should use positives. For example, it is preferable to say 'Put the chair down' rather than 'Do not throw the chair'.

People with a learning difficulty may also struggle to understand a sequence of events. 'You get yourself ready and then we can go to town to buy your DVD' involves two stages. The buying of the DVD is the last thing mentioned and might be the only aspect of the task that the person latches on to. If that person is then asked to 'get ready first' they may not make any link between the tasks. It might appear that the opportunity to buy the DVD has now been lost and the person may become upset. Many of us who have supported people with a learning difficulty have experienced this problem, and perhaps the person has been labelled as having challenging behaviour.

There is a further problem with sequencing. As we have seen, understanding of the past tense occurs at 36 months. The future tense is understood at a later date but has been used in the request 'and then we can go to town…'

Conversation

People who are disabled can face a constant stream of oppression. Chapter 1 included the following quotation from the Equality and Human Rights Commission report (2011, p. 5):

> The really serious cases catch the headlines. But what about the constant drip, drip, nag, nag of the so-called 'low-level' harassment that many disabled people face on a daily basis. It ruins their lives. They don't have the confidence to go out. It undermines their ability to be part of society. It makes them behave differently.

One aspect of this 'drip drip' is the way in which everyday conversation is experienced by people with a learning difficulty. In order to make sense of the following section, it is important to understand that language conveys meaning at many levels. The way something is expressed will convey the meaning in the words as well as in a sub-textual message. The latter may be unintended but it conveys meaning nonetheless. We implicitly understand the rules about these sub-textual meanings without ever being taught them. We all use them in speech, whether or not we are conscious of the rules. Language conveys information about power that will be understood by the speaker and the listener. One example is the way in which a question is asked.

For a question to be understood as such, there are two requirements. Firstly there should be a rising intonation at the end of the sentence (shown by an upward arrow in the extract below, on p. 132). Falling intonation (shown by a downward arrow in the extract below, on p. 132) indicates to the listener that mere agreement is being sought. Secondly it should not be a tag question, in which a statement is turned into a supposed query (for example, the statement 'nice day', followed by the apparent question 'isn't it?'). As with falling intonation, the listener will hear this as a statement, 'nice day', that does not require confirmation. In both cases the listener will not perceive this tag question or a question with falling intonation as a genuine request for an opinion; it feels like 'being told'. Asking a genuine question is obviously important if we are attempting to establish choice for a person with a learning difficulty for their person-centred plan. We might all ask ourselves whether our attempts to ask a question have sometimes, in reality, been nothing more than the seeking of confirmation. If we do not genuinely seek the preference of the person with a learning difficulty, then we probably cannot be described as valuing that person.

It is also important to understand that natural conversation (the sort of conversation one might have with friends) is fluid and unpredictable. Where there is equality of power between people engaged in conversation, each participant will take turns and have different roles in the conversation, changing between 'listener' and 'storyteller' or 'informer' and 'seeker of information' for example. These roles have relative power and prestige. Typically, we might seek to achieve a balance between them. For example, in a group of friends one person might have more than their fair share of the powerful roles, and this might lead the others in the group to avoid them. Over the course of a day, most of us change situations and experience different roles in conversation and achieve an overall balance in power. For instance, we might sit in a lecture and receive information, chat with friends, put our children to bed and talk to a partner. A person with a learning difficulty might typically experience only the least powerful conversational roles most of the time. Constantly being told, informed, corrected and having to listen is a good example of the 'nag nag' described in the quotation above. It is instructive to consider what life might be like if one was permanently in the least powerful role. Spending all your waking hours in a lecture, an appraisal or with significantly more knowledgeable people sounds like a good definition of hell!

One piece of small-scale research sought to establish the nature of this conversation (Follows 1995). Everyday conversation between people with a learning difficulty and staff was recorded and then analysed, using critical discourse analysis. This work was used as a training exercise, in which staff teams were taught the principles and studied transcripts of the conversations recorded during the research. Despite being taught the principles and understanding what was being observed, when these teams were in turn recorded, they fell into exactly the same conversational traps. This suggests that the mental constructs that guide our conversation are deep-seated and unconscious. This research was small in scale but many of us who have worked in support services will probably instantly recognise the conversations. Some of the main principles are discussed below, with some illustrative transcripts, to give a flavour of the research.

The following conversation took place between the researcher, a person with a learning difficulty and a care staff member. They are D, S and M.

S1: Have you been working this week 'D'?

D1: I have been working in the furniture shop just Tuesday mornings. Just got back about one o'clock was it? ⬆

S1: So you were working this morning were you? ⬆

D2: I worked this morning, yeah.

S3: What sandpapering?

D3: Sandpapering wood and stuff, I'd like to go there another day, actually I quite enjoy going.

S4: Do you? ⬆

M1: Maybe in the pipeline, yeah.

D4: Yeah, I'd like to go another day.

M2: It's just like a furniture repair shop. It's got a good business really. Not bad is it? ⬇

D5: Are you on next Tuesday 'M'? ⬆

Although it has not been defined, you can probably work out who is who in this short three-way conversation. It is possible to get a sense of the relative power of the participants even with little understanding of the rules of critical discourse analysis. 'S' is the researcher, 'D' is the person with the learning difficulty and 'M' is the member of staff. The principles illustrated by this example are:

- The person with a learning difficulty starts in the role of 'telling' about their work. This powerful role is taken over by the staff member at M1.

- At M2 the staff said 'Not bad is it?' ⬇. This is both a tag question and has a falling intonation and therefore is not a question; it is a statement that seeks confirmation. All the other questions in this discussion are true questions.

- The 'question' at M2 had the effect of closing what had been a free-flowing conversation in which the person with a learning difficulty had been in the role of 'informer' and 'furniture repairer'. He responded with the universal 'are you on tomorrow' type question which most of us will recognise!

- At M2 the staff member gives an unsolicited opinion about 'D's' place of work. 'D' indicates that he values the work and M responds by saying it is 'like' a furniture shop when in fact it *is* a furniture shop that operates as a proper business. 'M' uses 'really' in his second sentence, which is a hedged response, not fully confirming the fact. Finally he describes it as 'not bad', which does not convey the same meaning as 'good' or 'excellent'. These comments, in combination, have put down 'D's' work experience.

- M1 suggests that power to arrange the extra days rests elsewhere, not with 'D'.

- M1 is an uninvited contribution. 'S' and 'D' are having a two-way discussion until that point.

It is possible to view such analysis as 'nit-picking' and inconsequential. But if one experiences this sort of disempowering 'drip drip' all day, every day and for a lifetime, then the effect is one of overwhelming oppression. In terms of the question that runs through this book, it is certainly devaluing.

Here are some suggested contributions 'M' could have made that would have indicated valuing:

- Saying nothing at all. 'D' is doing fine.

- If M is to say anything then M1 could be something like 'Would you like to do extra days D?' This might lead to a conversation about what they would all need to do to ensure this happens. This would obviate the need for M2.

- If something like M2 is required, then it could be more affirmative – something like 'The work there is excellent, a lot of staff use it' (which was actually the case).

Follows' research noted a significant amount of passivising, in which staff would unintentionally *dis*-empower people, as in the following example:

L1: Are we getting a cat 'A'?

A1: I'll get you a cat if you want one.

Again, in this example it is possible to guess who the staff member is. At A1 the staff member is actually responding to the request from the person with a learning difficulty. However, the manner in which it is expressed indicates that the staff member has made the decision and will carry out the task on behalf of the person with a learning difficulty, as if they were a child. A more enabling (and therefore valuing) way of expressing A1 would be:

A1: Would you like one? 🠕 *Would you like to organise getting one?* 🠕

A similar interaction was:

L1: I want to go to town.

A1: I'll take you then.

A more empowering statement would have been:

A1: Should we go then? 🠕

Another indication of power is the extent to which one person corrects another, either in their use of language or in the information they are trying to convey. This is particularly disempowering if a correction is made where the meaning is already clear. Follows found many examples of correction, including:

A1: Where did you go, paper shop?

P1: No.

A2: Which shop did you go to for your chocolate?

P2: Paper shop.

A3: That's what I just said, daft bat.

This is another example that might be seen as a 'bit of banter', but it is important to remember the idea of the 'drip, drip' of devaluing that runs through this book. P has a learning difficulty. She frequently struggles to understand, and this interaction has highlighted her deficient understanding. It would, presumably, be devaluing to use such names to a blind person who made a mistake in describing the visual appearance of an object or a partially deaf person who made the same error as P. Such banter is only acceptable when both people in the interaction have similar power and competence.

Follows created the following list of recommendations, which I have used in training:

● Conversation is a creative collaborative act. It is something we need to help each other with. (Follows found few examples of staff supporting people to engage with conversation.)

- Think about the number of people in a conversation. The person with a learning difficulty may need more help to participate, the greater the number of participants. (Follows found that typically where there were more than two participants in the conversation the person with a learning difficulty was likely to be excluded.)
- Use real questions. Truly listen to the responses.
- Encourage the person to tell you stories. Share stories.
- Don't use passivising forms of speech.
- Don't put the person into a defensive position where they have to account for their actions.
- Support the person's listening and speaking with visual aids and gestures. Do not make them rely on language alone.
- Be cautious. For example, do not be too eager to contradict or correct the person. Work harder to establish what the person actually means.
- Be tentative. Allow room to negotiate meaning and truth and do not push for absolute rights and wrongs. Don't worry about who is right or wrong and agree to differ.
- Don't offer unsolicited advice. It is usually rejected. Work collaboratively.
- Don't be too keen to provide a service for the person.
- Encourage the person to contribute to the agenda.
- Don't interrupt the person and don't assume the person is missing the point.
- Don't over-use the person's name as a form of manipulation. Make a conscious decision on how to address the person in conversation.
- Use the least directive form of language.
- Encourage the person to self-correct errors in their speech. To directly correct is perpetuating the parent–child relationship.
- Don't be too keen to advocate, encourage self-advocacy.
- Create opportunities and actively encourage the person to interact verbally.
- If the person is distressed, empathise rather than rushing straight in with advice.
- Reflect on your conversation with people with a learning difficulty. Record these conversations and really hear your interaction. Do this as a team.
- Ensure the environment is free enough from distractions to enable the person to interact.

All these actions can be seen as ways of valuing the person with a learning difficulty. Yet Follows found them to be deficient or even absent in his research. It is significant that the support staff who took part in this research were volunteers who were keen to do their work well. Their practice was probably therefore better than average. Nevertheless, conscious appropriate use of language was not very evident when they were speaking to people with a learning difficulty.

Brief mention should be made of the article, 'Black swans: conversation analysis of interviews with people with learning disabilities' (Rapley 1995), which is one of the few pieces published in the area of critical discourse analysis and learning difficulty. It makes particular reference to the discourse running through assessment schedules. Rapley notes that the fixed nature of these schedules limits the power of the person with a learning difficulty.

Conclusion

In policy, practice design, person-centred plans and history, the voices of people with a learning difficulty have frequently been absent or diluted. But if people with a learning difficulty are to be truly valued, their voices should be dominant in this discourse. Similarly, it can be argued that to truly empower and value people with a learning difficulty those of us who work in the field need to use language that is understood by those we work with. Furthermore, we need to understand the rules and conventions of conversation and use them in our own transactions to maximise the power of people with a learning difficulty.

Yet this understanding would appear to be rare. Can any transaction not based on these principles be said to value the person with a learning difficulty? Can any service that does not prioritise these principles be said to value the people it supports? Can any professional education that does not train people in these skills claim to value people with a learning difficulty?

Valuing In Practice

This chapter analyses four vignettes using theories described in previous chapters. Although these stories are quite specific and detailed, their essential features will probably resonate with many readers as they are typical of practice. Throughout this chapter, it will be assumed that you have understood all the preceding theory chapters. No further explanation of the theory will be given. This chapter offers examples of the processes involved in valuing in action. The following vignette was previously used in Chapter 7 to illustrate the problems of role performance deficiency in a salient role. In this chapter the story is teased apart further in order to demonstrate valuing in practice.

■ Surprising mother (2)

A community learning disability nurse described how one of her clients became pregnant. Her initial reaction was to be horrified. She saw this woman as someone who was manipulative, hedonistic, deceitful, with poor self-help skills, and potentially aggressive due to a low tolerance of frustration. Furthermore, she had been diagnosed as having Munchausen syndrome, in which the sufferer causes self-harm in order to get hospital treatment. The community nurse and her colleagues were sure this mother–child relationship was doomed to failure; in fact they thought that she would be a disaster as a mother.

The community team put a support package in place and resolved to try their best. The mother surprised them all and responded well to the responsibility of parenthood. She did not do as well as one might expect of an 'average' member of the community. In fact, were she not to have a learning difficulty she might have been seen as a poor mother, but she did far better than anyone had anticipated. The support team viewed the mother in a more positive light than before, including having more sympathy for her problems. They respected her new competencies. The nurse was proud of her, and proud of her own professional achievement in supporting her. She thought that this mother had been given a rough time by the courts and social services and she said, in her own words, that this success felt like 'two fingers up' to those who had previously judged her client negatively.

Some problems did emerge and the community nurse became the mother's advocate when custody of the child was debated in a magistrate's court. The nurse felt that the police and social services had conspired behind her back to get the child removed. The courts did eventually remove the child.

This nurse also described a relative of hers, who has a successful career that has made him well off but takes him all over the country. This relative has children who have been professionally cared for as infants and attended boarding school as children. The nurse thinks that if you have children you should look after them yourself. She says that 'despite this' the children have grown up to be nice, balanced people. She regrets not having children herself.

To return to the central question in this book, 'Was the woman valued?' In this real situation, the answer appears to be multifaceted and varying. At the start of the story she attracted negative attribution and so was not valued. When she became pregnant she became even less valued. However, she did better than expected as a mother and the team were proud of what she and they had achieved and so she was valued. If she had not had a learning difficulty, her performance of the role of mother would have been perceived as inadequate and so she would have been devalued. The courts, social services and police appeared to devalue her, or at least they did in this nurse's narrative. The story concludes with the nurse using a culturally valued analogue of a relative and notes that this woman is no different really, which implies valuing.

There are, therefore, several aspects we can explore when considering this question of whether the mother with a learning difficulty is valued:

- The cognitive response of the nurse
- The cognitive response of the rest of the team
- The actions of the nurse and the team
- The actions and motivations of the legal and social services
- The changing valuing in different contexts

In order to answer the question, different parts of the narrative will be considered in the light of several aspects of the theory described so far in this book and some models of valuing will be suggested. References for these theories will not be repeated in this chapter. The discussion will use themes taken from research into valuing (Mee 2005). Where a theme is demonstrated, it is indented and in bold. The complete list of themes appears at the end of this chapter (see p. 156).

Activation of more than one schema

When an audience (initially the community team in the 'Surprising mother' story) evaluates the actor (the mother with a learning difficulty), more than one schema is activated. The audience holds schemas for many different phenomena. Where more than one schema is activated for one event, the audience ascribes value to the object as a result of interactions between these schemas. Figure 10.1 (below) illustrates this. The schema elements included in the diagram are only intended to be illustrative. The actual schemas would have more elements and be more complex in structure. The nurse in the 'Surprising mother' story describes an element of her own schema for good parent when she uses the culturally valued analogue of her relative.

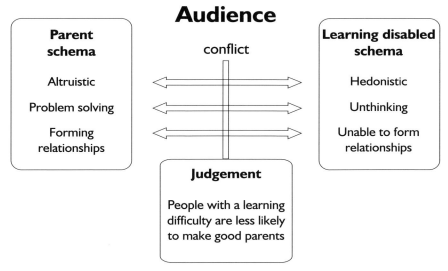

Figure 10.1 Activation of more than one schema

Theme 25

The schema for 'good parent' is juxtaposed with the schema for 'person with a learning difficulty'.

The schema for *parent* is in conflict with the schema for *person with a learning difficulty*. The resulting expectation and ascription of value is likely to be negative. Where the audience anchors the conclusion 'people with a learning difficulty cannot make good parents' as 'truth', then the actual behaviour of a parent with a learning difficulty is likely to be interpreted in the light of the attribution resulting from that 'truth'.

It is possible that an audience might not consider the object *mother with a learning difficulty* as salient, in which case it would not evoke a strong evaluative response. It may have no particular relevance to, or interest for, the schema holder. The schema may be vague and theory-driven, with little knowledge content. If the audience members have not experienced that object, they would only have had a theoretical schema upon which to draw. This schema may be so vague that there is no 'readily available' evaluative script, and they might not have a reason to create one. The 'cognitive miser' principle may be enough to inhibit the formation of an evaluative element. It is possible to hold a schema in which there is a weak, or even absent, evaluative element. However, for the nurse in the vignette, *mother with a learning difficulty* is clearly a very salient and data-driven schema. Furthermore, it is a well-developed schema based on many years' practical, professional experience. In other words, the nurse is 'bringing something to' the evaluation.

Theme 12

Unknown objects may be referenced to a belief system.

Furthermore,

Theme 32

The role taken by the audience in relation to the actor will influence the value ascribed.

Whether that ascription of value is negative or positive is likely to depend upon the outcome of the effect on the actor.

In the model below, these three factors are combined into one category and termed 'the audience's own agenda'. This agenda has a defining impact on the audience's resulting evaluation.

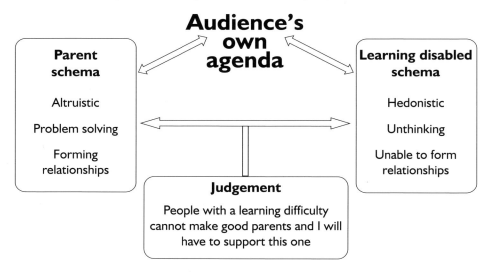

Figure 10.2 What one brings to ascribing value

The nurse in the 'Surprising mother' vignette ascribed positive value to the role position of *mother* in the sense that she would like to become a mother herself.

Theme 38

The audience is more likely to ascribe positive value to an actor who occupies a role to which they aspire.

The nurse's self-schema included the expectation that she would become a mother one day. An inner conflict was expressed when she admitted to being disappointed at not yet having achieved that status. In this case she was being audience to her own actor, ascribing negative value to the fact that she had not yet achieved that role.

Regarding role performance, her *mother* schema includes clear expectation of certain conditions. She believes that the parent, and particularly the mother, should stay at home with the child. She also states a clear priority of conditions: spending time with the child is more important than the material conditions in which the child is raised.

In her professional role, the nurse was in a position to ascribe value to the clients she supported. She was required to assess the clients' behaviour as parents in order to establish their competence. It is interesting to consider whether the positive value she ascribes to the role position of *parent* has had any bearing on her decision to focus on parents with a learning difficulty professionally and to what extent this affects her professional judgement.

The nurse ascribed value to the *client* role in general, and this client in particular. She valued the role position of *client* in the sense that she took her professional role seriously and wished to remain 'client-centred'. This particular client had taken up a disproportionate amount of time, according to the nurse. This begs the question of whether spending time equates to ascribing positive value. The nurse had a *person* schema for this client that included 'manipulative', 'not responsive to support 'and 'untruthful', which all have negative connotations.

Wolfensberger (1984) describes *client* as a devalued role. He also describes *friend* as a valued role. Which of these roles did the client play in relation to the nurse? It is easy to imagine this client having low value as a friend. I have reflected on this question and I have concluded that in my professional life a client has regularly become a friend and becomes part of my life, but seldom seems to be a *significant* friend. A *friend* schema possibly includes reciprocity and it is possible to view a person with a learning difficulty as more needy than a friend would usually be. In the case of the nurse in this vignette, the mother with a learning difficulty has been ascribed positive value as a client ('devalued role') but not ascribed positive value as a friend ('valued role'). In other words the person is ascribed more positive value in an ostensibly 'devalued' role.

Theme 32

The role taken by the audience in relation to the actor will influence the value ascribed.

In the 'Surprising mother' story, the roles are *friend* and *nurse*.

1 The nurse ascribed positive value to this client above all others. She thought frequently about the client, even when she was not at work.

2 The nurse might be seen as exploiting the client in order to work out her own particular agenda. In this case, the client was being ascribed positive value as a means to the nurse's end, to challenge authority. This is one of the factors the nurse brought to the context.

3 It is possible that the client was utilised as a means by which the nurse could manage her impression with colleagues. According to the service ethos, there was a belief that the nurse should advocate for the client, even at personal cost. Using the impression management terminology, she is showing justification for her action, demonstrating exemplifiers such as 'moral courage', 'loyalty' and 'professionalism'. This might have the potential to raise other people's perception of her. There was also an 'anti-social service' view that was widely expressed in health services at that time.

It could be argued that in fact all these three senses of ascribing positive value were in play. It is possible to hold more than one motivation, and for any of these to take centre stage at any time depending on external factors. Thus, the second sense of ascribing value was prompted by the action of the courts and social services. The implications of this are significant. It would be possible for an audience to attribute either of these motivations to the nurse's behaviour.

When the client became pregnant, the nurse reported that her initial reaction to the news of the pregnancy was to be horrified. As discussed above, the nurse's data-based *person* schema and theory-based *parent* schema were juxtaposed, leading to the conclusion that the client would be unlikely to be a 'good parent'. What the nurse brought to this ascription of value was the role of *professional with responsibility for this client*. It seemed highly likely, particularly given her long professional experience of assessing parents with a learning difficulty, that the client would fail, leading to an unpleasant professional experience. The nurse might well have had to support a distressed mother following the removal of the child.

At this point, the schema was somewhere between data-based and theory-based on the continuum. The new object was *this particular person* with a learning difficulty as a mother. General knowledge of this client was data-based but knowledge of her as a mother was theory-based because she had never been a mother before. All that could be said was that in a situation that is categorically similar, such as needing to empathise, she had not been perceived as performing well.

Theme 11

The audience will reference new objects to a known schema, and this is likely to be data-driven.

When the nurse reported the situation to her colleagues, there was a very negative tone to their discussion. The social representation created in this professional context was not a discussion she would have wanted an 'outsider' to hear. They spoke disparagingly about the client and used language that would not be considered professionally appropriate. This group of professionals colluded to create a negative evaluation of this new object.

Theme 2

New objects may be ascribed value in a collaborative way.

Theme 6

The audience may respond to 'permission' from a significant other to both form and express an ascription of value that is perceived as contentious.

Theme 7

Active collusion may take place where collaboratively produced negative ascriptions of value cause discomfort for the participants.

Theme 39

Incongruity between the roles being played by the actor is likely to activate the audience to ascribe value.

The team members were demonstrating an awareness of audience in this discussion, as they alone heard the discussion. This is a key requirement of impression management.

Expectations of parental success in the *person* schema for this client were low. The team provided support with little hope of success. She surpassed their expectations, although her performance as a parent was not as good as might typically be seen as appropriate. The nurse reported that the professional team members were proud of her and themselves. The mother got praise and kept the baby for a while. She was ascribed positive value, in the sense that people valued her for not having done as badly as everyone had predicted.

Theme 36

Where expectations are low, the audience is less inclined to ascribe negative value if the actor performs badly.

Now the schema for this person as a mother had become data-based, expectations were rising. However, her performance was nowhere near what the audience would have expected from a non-learning-disabled mother. Perhaps that level of support would have been unavailable to other client groups and the child would have been removed. The nurse's agenda may have affected her ascription of value: she had achieved a result that reflected well on her professionally, with positive implications for her impression management. In other words, the target (client) is ascribed positive value in her role as aid to the nurse's impression management.

Any object is likely to activate multiple schemas in an individual. At any event there may be several schemas available for activation at the same time. These schemas will not have equal weighting, and their relative weighting may change in different circumstances. The factors that help determine weighting include:

- The constitution of the audience or the other actors in the situation
- One's role in that situation
- One's dominant beliefs

The courtroom was the new context for ascribing value to the client.

Theme 1

The social context will influence the value ascribed.

In the courtroom the nurse ascribed negative value to the role of the court and social services. In her data-driven schema she saw herself as frequently having to advocate for the client against these agencies. She believed that there was collusion against her client. Her *professional role* schema included a clear view that her responsibility was to act as an advocate for the client. She would have presented her evidence in a way that supported her client most strongly.

Theme 4

The context in which the ascription is made will determine the terms of reference and the discourse used to ascribe value.

The nurse supported the mother despite the mother's shortcomings as a parent. The ascription of value evident in the court report was the opposite to that expressed in the nurse's initial discussion with colleagues.

Theme 5

Different contexts may produce different ascriptions of value for the same behaviour by the same actor to the same audience.

The nurse also had her 'political' schema influencing her behaviour, causing her to take the side of the 'underdog'.

In the context of the courtroom, for this nurse the *professional role* schema and the *courtroom* event schema have more salience than the *client* person schema and the *mother* schema. It can be argued that the nurse's action in that context was consistent with ascribing positive value to that person as a mother. Her stated opinion in the court would also have been consistent with ascribing positive value. This is represented in Figure 10.3.

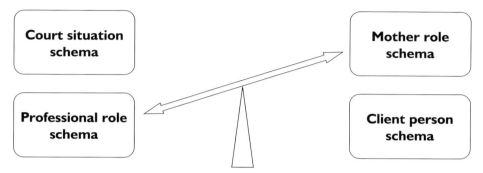

Figure 10.3 *The balance of schemas in the courtroom*

When the nurse first heard about the pregnancy, the following balance of schemas may have been activated.

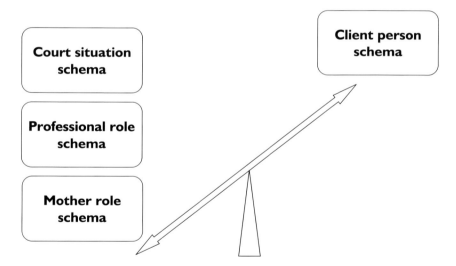

Figure 10.4 *The balance of schemas when talking to a colleague*

Ascribing negative value to the potential for the client to become a mother is the same as in the courtroom scenario. However, the context is now different. The nurse was in the company of trusted colleagues who knew the client as well as she did. Thus the *person* schema for the colleague prompted the nurse to behave in a trusting and honest way with

145

no requirement for 'professional' behaviour, with its related impression management (such as acting as advocate or using non-judgemental language and behaviour). The weighting of *professional role* schema was lower in this context. The nurse's ascription of value to the client becoming a mother could now be seen as negative.

An underpinning belief to the professional behaviour might be something like: 'My client has the same right to have children as any other person. My role is to support that person. There is legislation to protect the child.'

Theme 12

Unknown objects may be referenced to a belief system.

In this case, rights became an absolute value, which absolved the nurse from stating her personal opinion. The whole context was producing conflict. The courtroom, the initial assessment of the client when the pregnancy was reported, and her professional 'success' all indicated different ascriptions of value.

Theme 8

The ascriptions of value to a challenging object may be permanently context specific, variable and inconclusive.

These views were expressed, and possibly held, by the same person, even though they were mutually contradictory.

Theme 14

It is possible to hold mutually contradictory schemas for the same object.

Theme 15

The audience may experience conflict with self-schema and other role schemas, such as 'professional'.

The following vignette was previously used to demonstrate retrospective valuing for a previously occupied role. In this chapter it is further explored to demonstrate valuing in practice.

■ The tattooed man (2)

A student nurse met a man for the first time in a unit specialising in people who display challenging behaviour. This man had soiled and smeared himself and the nurse was helping him to have a shower to clean up. The nurse was not enjoying the task and was struggling to see the man in a positive light. He noticed that the man had 'good quality' tattoos and thought this was unusual for someone with a learning difficulty. He had seen people with a learning difficulty with tattoos that were self-inflicted, but never professionally done work.

This prompted the student to look into the man's history. He discovered that the man had been a plasterer and taxi driver who was married with children. He had tried to commit suicide by hanging. He was discovered, unconscious, by his ten-year-old child who raised the alarm. The man survived but had acquired brain injury from anoxia. Acquired brain injury was an unexpected personal history on this unit, as its purpose was to support people with a learning difficulty. His behaviour was considered challenging and so he became a resident of this special unit.

The nurse considered his response to this story as a critical incident. The student realised that the man had never previously been in an institution, having had a past very similar to his own. This similarity produced a feeling of empathy: the person with a learning difficulty was no longer 'other'. The nurse acknowledged that this made the client appear different from other clients and he admitted that he 'valued' this client more for having not always been impaired. The implication that concerned the nurse was that this necessarily meant he valued people who have always been impaired less than those who have not. He had formerly believed that he unconditionally valued people with a learning difficulty. He now wondered whether this increased empathy and valuing might lead to this client being a 'favourite'.

The building where this service is provided is a grand old house with disused stables. The service manager was planning to have the stables renovated and turned into a games room for the people who lived there. Part of the requirement for this renovation was to plaster the bare brick. The man with the brain injury had been a plasterer. The nurse suggested that this man might be given the chance to do the work himself. The man's behaviour included exaggerated swaying from side to side and looking backwards at the end of each swing. He would also make a moaning sound. He did the plastering and completed the task well; however, he continued with his swaying behaviour while plastering.

The other staff discussed this man and agreed they all saw him in a different light now he had completed the plastering job to a high standard.

This story illustrates normalisation and SRV in action but being effective in a retrospective sense. The man had become re-valued, as a result of once having had a valued role and then performing something that required skill. This man had 'once been someone better'. The tattoo had been a powerful notification of incongruence.

Theme 39

Incongruity between the roles being played by the actor is likely to activate the audience to ascribe value.

The staff response to the man's plastering was to change their view of him; he was seen more positively as a result of carrying out a 'valued role'.

The student nurse in the 'Tattooed man' story experienced a conflict between his *self-schema* and his *person* schema for this particular man. He thought that he valued people with a learning difficulty. Yet in this vignette he experienced both impatience at the man's smearing behaviour and then more positive regard when he realised how the man had once been, before the anoxia. This nurse was unhappy enough about this response to identify it as a critical incident. He did not like the ascription of value that he had made.

In this story it appears that, having once had a 'valued role', a person with a learning difficulty is more likely to be ascribed positive value subsequently – even when the new role is ascribed negative value. Two accounts from other areas of practice support this idea:

1 Carers in elderly services say, for example, that they did not realise one of the people they are caring for was once a headmistress. After this realisation, they saw her differently.

2 A person who used a wheelchair following a spinal injury stated, 'I have not always been like this, you know.'

In the first example, the actor is ascribed more positive value now because of what she was in the past (a headmistress). The second actor (in the wheelchair) appears to value himself more highly because of who he once was. It also might be the case that in making this point he is engaging in impression management. This argument is similar to one made by Race (1999).

The 'tattooed man' attempted to return to his previous life as a father and husband after the injury but his role behaviour was assessed as 'not competent'. Judging from the reports of the incident, his performance conditions and behaviour were deemed insufficient. Regarding role conditions, he now got angry frequently and hit out at people, he was unable to earn an income and did not relate to his children. Regarding role behaviour, he did not perform any of the skills expected in order to have levels of competence assessed. He had returned to an ostensibly 'valuing' role (father), which resulted in a compounding of negative ascription of value.

The nurse's ascription of value was theory-driven, as he had no direct experience of the man's performance as a parent. The role behaviour he was able to observe was that of plasterer and he carried out plastering to a good standard.

The initial observation of the tattoos came from the schema incongruence. The point at which expectations were set was when the nurse started cleaning the smeared faeces. It can be argued that this behaviour has a strong social representation with negative value ascribed. For example, it sometimes features in prison demonstrations. Support staff, when asked to help clear up, often dislike someone who smears. This behaviour seems to attract the negative attribution that the person is 'deliberately' smearing; they can 'help themselves' but choose not to. The effect on the nurse in the story was possibly that extremely low expectations were set for the *person* schema for this man. It is possible that very low expectations form an incongruence with simply having once occupied the role position of *parent*; no performance is necessary.

A major theme in this chapter is the agenda of the audience. One's role in relation to the actor, one's predisposition and one's expectations all affect the value ascribed. This vignette suggests another factor – the context of the other actors being ascribed value. This client was one of several 'devalued' people in a group, and the nurse had a professional relationship with each member. One client stood apart from the rest: because he was more like the audience he was ascribed more positive value than the others. Furthermore he was ascribed positive value for simply holding the position rather than performance. Against a group of peers who were married and were parents he might be ascribed negative value because he was no longer able to carry out the role. Against the first group he was 'better' than the expectations of the members; against the second he would not be 'as good'.

Theme 5

Different contexts may produce different ascriptions of value for the same behaviour by the same actor to the same audience.

The nurse's inquiry started with an observation on congruence: the man's tattoos were 'too good' for someone with a learning difficulty. This illustrates the subtlety and complexity of presentation as described by impression management, particularly the idea of unintended impression management suggested by Tedeschi & Rosenfeld (1981). The man's primary impression management was created by the congruence between his behaviour and the institution in which he was supported. This is consistent with the labelling implied in normalisation. His secondary impression was created by the tattoos, and the incongruence between the primary and secondary impression prompted the nurse to create meaning actively. The nurse's attribution to the man then became more positive; and the implied favouritism caused sufficient anxiety for the nurse to present it to me as a critical incident.

This outcome is not exactly as impression management might predict. Typically, 'not being able to help it' leads to the object avoiding blame. In this case, the man had previously attempted to take his own life, which is an act of commission. It might be expected that such an act would lead to a negative impact on his image. Yet it had the opposite effect for the nurse. This may have been because the nurse now saw the man as someone similar to himself. It appears that this reduction in the man's 'otherness' was the critical factor.

Another possible explanation was the impact this had on the nurse's impression management. At that time he was a student nurse who made a point of describing himself as 'just an ordinary working lad' who saw the course as a 'hoop' he needed to jump through in order to qualify. He took it upon himself to read the theory (Wolfensberger) and write an account of the incident. This work became the basis for a class, with the student taking a central role. This had an impact on his impression management. He created a favourable impression on those with the power to award marks for his work. He was also seen as an 'academic' among his peers. He was perhaps the only member of the group to have a grasp of Wolfensberger's theories. He stated that he now saw himself in a more positive light. In this way, the function of the client for the nurse was similar to the 'Surprising mother' story.

Another impression management implication for the 'tattooed man' was that he had become 'surplus'. His wife and family had broken off all contact now that he could no longer meet the performance requirements of *husband*, *father* or *provider*.

Theme 32

The role taken by the audience in relation to the actor will influence the value ascribed.

The student ascription of value was very positive, whereas the wife and family's ascription was extremely negative.

The 'Tattooed man' story offers an interesting comparison with the people who have a learning difficulty described by Edgerton (1967). Many of these people tried to disguise their history, as they perceived the fact of having lived in an asylum as an unmanageable stigma. Some individuals invented a 'normal' personal history. In the 'Tattooed man' vignette, the nurse discovered that the man had a history that included not having a learning difficulty. This had a positive consequence for the value attributed to him. It suggests that a significant barrier to ascribing positive value to a person with a learning difficulty is their history.

■ The eyes have it

A woman in her forties has autism. She has above-average intelligence and holds down a good job. She says the main problem in her life is that she wants an intimate relationship with a man but she repeatedly gets rejected, sometimes within minutes of first meeting. She finds it very difficult to form relationships of any kind. She has the classic autistic characteristics of poor ability to read non-verbal language and lack of theory of mind (the ability to anticipate how another person will experience an event).

She asked a professional worker to spend an evening with her in order to practise her 'chat-up' skills, and to get feedback on how well she had performed. Overall the performance was poor. She spoke at great length about small details, did not listen very well, broke 'typical' limits of subject matter and became distracted very easily by things going on around her. The worker did, however, feed back that her eye contact was surprisingly good, given that people with autism frequently either avoid eye contact or stare.

She was pleased to get this feedback and said that only a year previously she had typically given an unbroken stare. She had realised that this put men off so she sat in a pub on a regular basis with a notebook and stopwatch. She observed how others made eye contact and worked out the rules. She told the care worker that, while having this conversation with him, she was consciously making eye contact decisions, and by the end of the evening she would be emotionally exhausted from the effort.

Groups of student nurses have been set the task of working out the rules of eye contact. They reported finding the task very difficult, and the act of thinking about the rules broke down their transactions. They found it very difficult to focus on the task of making conversation.

This woman does not have schemas for many social events. Specifically she has no schema for *forming a relationship with a man*, despite many years of trying to get it right. This is another example of the role position having different ascriptions of value from the performance. The role conditions are apparently met: she is a woman of the right age, 'well presented', in the right place for meeting people. Yet it is clear that her role behaviour does not meet the standards required. Many people with autism get exploited, particularly women who may often be sexually exploited. A tendency to believe (literally) what one has been told leaves people open to exploitation. Some people with autism are not able to judge friendship levels and so a casual acquaintance might be perceived as a 'best friend'. This particular woman has seldom been exploited, despite being inappropriately sexual at times. It is therefore reasonable to assume that there is something intimidating about her 'relationship' behaviour.

A significant problem for this woman is that she finds it very hard to manage her impression in a congruent, consistent and coherent manner, which leads men to ascribe negative value to her.

Theme 35

If the actor does not meet role expectations it is likely that ascription of value will be activated in the audience.

Theme 39

Incongruity between the roles being played by the actor is likely to activate the audience to ascribe value.

Her calculated impression is more rehearsed than it would be for most people, but the problem is with her secondary impression. A rule of impression management is that it requires insight into the rules of social behaviour; as a consequence of her autism, this woman struggles to gain such insight. For most people, eye contact is an unconscious secondary factor, but for this woman it has become part of her calculated impression strategy. Her difficulty in imagining the transaction from the perspective of the other, and her difficulty in understanding non-verbal cues, lead her to make serious errors every time. Successful impression management relies on the ability to make assumptions about how the performance will be perceived. The roles of *girlfriend* or *sexual partner* have high social salience. By putting herself in such roles, she becomes more likely to attract active ascription of value. But the role position is not sufficient to ensure positive evaluation. The role performance is 'wrong' and so negative evaluation is activated.

Theme 29

Role performance is more likely to be ascribed value than role position.

Congruence between expressive and verbal behaviour is required to elicit a positive ascription of value. Reduced theory of mind makes this a very difficult task for this woman. Someone had mentioned that her staring was intimidating and so she had worked out the rules. The act of carrying out this strategy took a significant part of her cognitive attention, and so she found it more difficult to focus on the content of her speech. It could be argued that her problems are an impairment effect because these characteristics are typical of someone with autism. This might therefore be an example of impairment effect, rather than socially constructed disability.

This woman's story offers an insight into the problems faced by someone with impairments in this area, even though she has the intelligence, strategy-planning skills, commitment and support to try to manage her impression. Where the person has a significant degree of learning difficulty, the motivation and strategy-planning skills might not be present, and that person will be less able to manage their own impression.

The professional worker was acting as a 'virtual' third member in the interaction, as described on p. 15. Subsequent attempts to form a relationship would be informed by the 'rules' he explained to her, and she would recall his advice when problems arose. However, initial attempts to form a relationship require 'in the moment' decisions; a 'blanket' strategy is unlikely to work. Inability to deal with deviation from rules, and inflexibility in interpretation, are two other typical characteristics of someone with autism. To make sense of the transaction, this woman would probably require the specialist to be sitting with her, giving 'moment by moment' advice. This would clearly be unworkable and would undermine her attempts to form a relationship. The effect of the third party in any transaction being a member of staff is likely to have secondary and primary impression management consequences for the person with a learning difficulty, perhaps undermining any potential positive ascription of value that might have resulted.

■ The sick man

A group of managers met to discuss the roles that their staff saw clients occupying. One manager reported that a client was seen as a nuisance. He had a hip problem and lay in bed all day, even when he had wet or soiled the bed. He was aggressive to staff who tried to 'encourage him' out of bed. The manager reported that staff did not want to work with him and they were very directing and controlling. Some staff thought that he was deliberately trying to 'wind them up'. At the meeting a fellow manager asked if the man might be in pain or depressed.

At a later meeting the first manager fed back progress. She said that the comment about the client being ill had stuck with her. She realised she had not done all she could because she had fallen partially into seeing the client's behaviour in a similar way to her staff. She had accepted the collaboratively produced social representation for this man. Resulting inquiries showed that there were some health problems that had since been dealt with. As a result the man was happier about getting out of bed.

Theme 2

New objects may be ascribed value in a collaborative way.

Theme 3

The social context of a collaboratively produced evaluation may inhibit active participation.

Following the diagnosis of ill health, the staff saw him as occupying the *sick* role rather than *nuisance* or *malingerer*. His behaviour had not changed but the staff's interpretation of that behaviour had significantly changed. He had been seen as 'awkward' but now he was seen as 'sick' and, as one member of the support staff said, 'the poor man can't help it'. They were now 'caring' rather than 'controlling'.

Theme 34

Positive attribution towards the actor increases the chance of positive ascription of value.

The man was now happy to get up to get a clean sheet but sometimes wanted to get back into bed. At other times he would stay up, but, if he wanted to stay in bed, the staff accepted it as part of his 'condition'. There were no complaints about washing him in bed if he did soil himself but did not want to get up.

When the man was seen as a *malingerer*, the following agenda applied:

- The staff felt they had a responsibility to avoid pressure sores. Litigation can result from negligence.
- They wanted to ensure he had a 'normal day', which included getting out of bed at a 'normal' time. This simplistic application of normalisation is endemic in many services for people with a learning difficulty.
- They wanted to be seen as working to the wider service 'values', including doing valued activities and having a valued role. This was a simplistic application of SRV.
- They had a duty to the other clients who might miss activities if the man stayed in bed.

After the diagnosis of ill health, the team agenda changed to:

- We have a duty to care for this man.
- His sickness will determine his routine and care.
- Staffing changes might be needed to facilitate the other clients' activities.

The change in agenda was related to the man's perceived role and resulting treatment. He had not changed.

Chapter 7 described the perhaps inadequate use of the term 'role' in Wolfensberger's description of historic roles and his later writing on SRV. Similarly, it can be argued that a diminished sense of role is being used when describing *malingerer* and *sick* as roles. As previously argued, this is not a role in the sense that it is a position with responsibilities. The parent role has a clearly identifiable position, which is defined legally and biologically: one is a parent through having children. The responsibilities are also clear, although there may be argument about the details and priorities within those responsibilities. A *malingerer*, in contrast, has no position or responsibilities. Once one occupies the role position of *parent*, one is always a parent even if one's children are removed. On the other hand, one occupies the role position of *president* only until one is voted out. Removal from the position would be instantly clear to everyone; there could be no interpretation of whether or not one was still the president. However, one would occupy the position of 'ex-president', which carries with it certain privileges.

Malingerer is not a role in any of these senses. Some might place an individual in this 'role'; others might disagree. The role in which the person is placed correlates with the value ascribed to that person. People might agree that the person was no longer a *malingerer* but this would be a subjective agreement, rather than something objective such as the president not getting sufficient votes in an election. The difference is that the person is cast in the 'role' of *malingerer* as a result of perception and ascribing value, not objective category criteria. The implications and consequences of this perceptual category are material; the category determines the treatment received by the person. We are talking about a real phenomenon even if it has no materially defining characteristic. It is also interesting to note that whereas roles in the 'proper' sense are neutral terms (although individuals may have their own ascribed value for that role), roles such as *malingerer*, *menace* and *unspeakable dread* are pejorative terms. As such, they carry explicit ascription of value that all who see the person in that 'role' would share. In contrast, ascription of value to *president* or *parent* is individual.

It appears that 'roles' in the sense of *malingerer* or *sick* may not be roles in the sociological sense but they have clear importance for ascribing value to an actor. Because they are located in audience perception rather than having unambiguous category-defining conditions, I suggest the following term: 'perceived status'. Like a role, a perceived status would carry expectations of behaviour, though less clearly defined than those for a role such as *parent*. Unlike a role, a perceived status would carry evaluative power, which would necessarily be agreed by those sharing the perception. This evaluative power is a consequence of the shared social representation of a pejorative term such as *malingerer* or *menace*. Similarly, 'perceived status' can be seen as a better term than Wolfensberger's term 'historic roles'.

The discussion so far has positioned a 'true' role such as *parent* (with clear category criteria) as opposite to perceived status, such as *malingerer* (with category criteria based on perception). *Sick* role is positioned between the two. It is possible to have a degree of objectivity in category entry criterion – for example, to have a medical diagnosis and a sick note. However, that criteria itself is judgement-based and, as such, is open to judgement. Two professionally based examples illustrate this point. Many managers might have doubted the validity of doctors' sick notes for some staff where, for example, a bad back was diagnosed for a member of staff who had just been moved to work elsewhere against their wishes. Similarly, the reader may have heard support staff question the diagnosis of illness for people with a learning difficulty. They might say, for example, 'He may fool the doctor but not me' or 'He's having us on'. In this sense, *sick* role might also be seen as 'perceived status'.

The implications of perceived status appear to be central to the process of ascribing value, linking attribution, schema and role theory.

Conclusion

These four vignettes have offered examples of 'valuing' taking place in settings that many of us who have worked in learning difficulty support services will recognise. They each demonstrate the complexities and non-static nature of ascribing value. The valuing depends upon a wide range of factors and contexts. These are listed in the appendix below.

Appendix: A summary of themes of ascribing value

The themes are divided into five categories:
- Themes concerned with the context of ascribing value
- Themes concerned with schema
- Examples of schema content
- Themes concerned with role
- Themes for ascribing value to role

Themes concerned with the context of ascribing value

1   The social context will influence the value ascribed.
2   New objects may be ascribed value in a collaborative way.
3   The social context of a collaboratively produced evaluation may inhibit active participation.
4   The context in which the ascription is made will determine the terms of reference and the discourse used to ascribe value.
5   Different contexts may produce different ascriptions of value for the same behaviour by the same actor to the same audience.
6   The audience may respond to 'permission' from a significant other to both form and express an ascription of value that is perceived as contentious.
7   Active collusion may take place where collaboratively produced negative ascriptions of value cause discomfort for the participants.
8   The ascriptions of value to a challenging object may be permanently context specific, variable and inconclusive.
9   The audience's schema may produce conflict with the social context. The audience may avoid ascribing value when the conflict is strong.

Themes concerned with schemas

10 The audience may struggle to create a schema for a new object.
11 The audience will reference new objects to a known schema, and this is likely to be data-driven.

12 Unknown objects may be referenced to a belief system.

13 Existing schemas act as a filter through which the new object will be ascribed value.

14 It is possible to hold mutually contradictory schemas for the same object.

15 The audience may experience conflict with self-schema and other role schemas, such as 'professional'.

16 The generation of a new schema may result from inner dialogue between existing schemas.

Examples of schema content

17 The object 'person with a learning difficulty' may activate categories that are ascribed negative value.

18 The schema for 'children of parent with a learning difficulty' includes 'different'.

19 The parent with a learning difficulty is seen as a problem to their child.

20 The schema for 'good parent' includes 'carrying out the tasks oneself'.

21 The schema for 'person with a learning difficulty' includes 'other'.

22 The schema for 'parents with a learning difficulty' includes 'needs help'.

23 The schema for 'parent with a learning difficulty' includes 'cannot give guidance'.

24 The schema for 'good parent' includes 'ability to form a relationship'.

25 The schema for 'good parent' is juxtaposed with the schema for 'person with a learning difficulty'. The two may be incompatible.

26 The social representation of 'good parent' and 'bad parent' has broad social salience.

27 A parent who becomes impaired after the decision to have a child will be ascribed more positive value than a parent who becomes impaired before the decision to have a child.

28 Learning difficulty is differentiated from physical impairment. Learning difficulty activates a more negative ascription of value.

Themes concerned with role

29 Role performance is more likely to be ascribed value than role position.

30 The social salience of the role is a different judgement from the ascription of positive value.

31 The value ascribed to a role will have a corresponding cultural resonance and social representation.

32 The role taken by the audience in relation to the actor will influence the value ascribed.

33 There may be a cost/benefit balance. The gaining of one role leads to the loss of another.

Themes of ascribing value to role

34 Positive attribution towards the actor increases the chance of positive ascription of value.

35 If the actor does not meet role expectations it is likely that ascription of value will be activated in the audience.

36 Where expectations are low, the audience is less inclined to ascribe negative value if the actor performs badly.

37 Where the context of the performance inhibits the actor, poor performance is less likely to attract negative ascription of value.

38 The audience is more likely to ascribe positive value to an actor who occupies a role to which they aspire.

39 Incongruity between the roles being played by the actor is likely to activate the audience to ascribe value.

The Eugenics Era and Following Instructions

> **Not all criminals are feeble-minded, but all feeble-minded persons are at least potential criminals. That every feeble-minded woman is a potential prostitute would hardly be disputed by anyone.**
>
> *(Lewis Terman, cited in Gould 1981, p. 181)*

When he said this, Lewis Terman was in Germany in the 1930s, when the Nazi attitude to people with a learning difficulty was emerging. In this statement he linked learning difficulty to the social 'problems' of criminality and prostitution. Learning difficulty itself had become a 'problem'. The policy resulting from this belief led to over 100,000 mentally ill and disabled people being killed (Noakes & Pridham 1988).

This chapter has proved very difficult to write on two counts. The first is that it delves into the hellish Nazi era when outsiders, particularly those cast in the role of *menace* or *object of unspeakable dread*, were treated with barely imaginable brutality. It can almost feel prurient to engage with accounts of such barbarism. Secondly it raises similar problems to Chapter 3, where you (the reader) are asked to look at an extreme situation and consider that it might shed light on your own current situation, and even your own practice.

Comparing an era of mass murder to current practice may stretch the limits of credibility. However, the aim is to highlight any qualitative similarities while acknowledging the gulf in the quantitative reality. In Chapter 3, for example, we compared the public display of human brains with the practice of having separate 'staff cups' as examples of the historic role of *diseased organism*. There are qualitative similarities between the two.

It is possible to view the Nazi era as an aberration that should simply be left in the past. Yet much can be learned from reflecting on the past, particularly when that past offers a perspective, due to its extreme nature. It can be argued that reflecting on such historical examples can help understanding of the position of people with a learning difficulty now. Strauss (1987) described the idea of 'theoretical sampling' when attempting to understand something. If we imagine an extreme position for whatever it is we are attempting to understand, then a theoretical sample offers an angle, a clear perspective. What was done to people with a learning difficulty between 1936 and 1945 in Germany offers the clearest example of extreme abuse in modern history.

The mother of a newborn child with Down syndrome related how: 'When [she was] first born we were told by a doctor that it would have been better if she had died at birth.' These words were actually spoken in the 1990s (previously available from the Down's Syndrome Association). It is fairly clear that this is *not* what is meant by 'valuing'. To say that a child's life is not worth living, that they are better off dead, is towards the extreme of devaluing. In the 1930s in Germany there was an orthodoxy, a 'scientific justification', for this point of view. Karl Binding, a German scholar, considered that the lives of people with a learning difficulty were inferior, to the extent that their lives were not worth living, or a 'life unworthy of life' as he put it (Binding & Hoche 1920, cited in Friedlander 1995). This was one of the 'scientific' ideas that underpinned the coming genocide. For a detailed and chilling account of this history and policy, see Friedlander (1995).

The first step was to create a hierarchy of humankind. Scientists who created this theoretical foundation based their reasoning on neo-Darwinian theories. The resulting hierarchy produced conclusions such as that drawn by the palaeontologist Edward Cope who suggested that there were four groups of lower forms: women, non-whites, Jews and all lower classes in superior races (Friedlander 1995). These 'lower classes' included 'feeble-minded people' or people who would now be labelled as having a learning difficulty. Once a group is perceived as inferior, then a justification can be offered for treating that group in a different, and usually inferior, way. This was mentioned in Chapter 3 when discussing Wolfensberger's ideas about historic roles and 'othering'.

Lewis Terman, the author of the quotation at the start of this chapter, was an eminent psychologist who created the Stanford–Binet intelligence test. This continues to be the standard test for measuring IQ. Terman clearly believed that there was a hierarchy of humankind and some individuals were of more inherent value than others. Indeed, Terman influenced other authors such as Tuchel (1984, pp. 48–9, cited in Noakes & Pridham 1988) who questioned the very humanity of people with a learning difficulty:

> **A child which is born an idiot [*sic*] has no personality. It would hardly last a year if it were not kept alive artificially. It is even less conscious of its existence than an animal. One does not remove anything from it if one snuffs it out.**

If these people have no human value, Tuchel claimed that precious resources would be wasted in supporting them (Noakes & Pridham *ibid*., p. 998):

> **…what labour, patience and resources are squandered simply in order to try and sustain worthless lives until nature – often cruelly tardy – removes the last possibility of their continuation?**

And when describing 'incurable lunatics' (*ibid*., p. 999) he said:

> **Their life is completely useless but they do not find it intolerable. They represent**

a terrible burden for their relatives as well as for society. Their death would not have the slightest impact except perhaps on the feelings of their mothers or their loyal nurses. Since they require a lot of care, they prompt the emergence of a profession which consists simply of maintaining absolutely worthless life for years and decades

He also noted the 'tremendous care devoted to creatures which are not only completely worthless but are of negative value'.

In these quotations Tuchel is describing the work that those of us who support people with a learning difficulty carry out on a daily basis. He implies that those who carry out this work are misguided.

Clearly the notion of 'burden' was significant to the early eugenicists and the Nazis. A more current example of this attitude can be seen in the words of medical staff to two parents of children with Down syndrome, again in the 1990s (previously available from the Down's Syndrome Association):

Our son was described by a Senior Physician as 'an unacceptable burden on resources medically, socially and educationally.'
Father of an 8-year-old boy

Our paediatrician has never given us anything positive to look at. She has basically told us that he will not amount to anything and be a burden to us throughout our lives. We know that this is not the case.
Mother of 18-month-old

This book has been a contemplation on the meaning of 'value'. The idea of 'value' was fundamental to the Nazi policy towards people with a learning difficulty. The decision was made to have a euthanasia programme in which certain lives could be ended. This is a particular definition of the word 'euthanasia'. To modern sensibilities it is defined as 'aiding someone to end their own life when that is what they wish to happen'. When Nazi policy was being implemented, it meant 'the taking of life whether or not the person wished this, although it was still defined as "mercy killing"'.

Noakes & Pridham (1988) suggested that the decision on whether to take life was based on a judgement about whether the person's life had value or worth. This idea of 'value' is defined in terms of use to the community. Binding (1920, p. 27, cited in Noakes & Pridham *ibid.*, p. 998) asked: 'Are there humans who have lost their human characteristics to such an extent that their continued existence has lost all value both for themselves and for society?' Other terms used at this time (Friedlander 1995) were *Ballastexistenzen* ('burdensome lives') and *unnütze Esser* ('useless eaters').

Binding went on to suggest that there was a stark contrast between the 'desirable youth' who had been killed on the battlefields of the First World War and those 'unworthy of life' whom he considered to be leading pampered unproductive lives. When considering this comparison, we should acknowledge that there is perhaps some coherence to his argument – however abhorrent it may be to us today. After all, this was an era in which nations had been expected to sacrifice a whole generation of men.

There was also the looming Second World War, in which human life seemed to lose its value, with millions of civilians killed on both sides and the development of industrial-scale killing under the Nazis. In this sense, people with a learning difficulty were not particularly singled out. They were, however, the first category of people to be systematically killed by the Nazi government. The killing processes used on Jews, Gypsies and homosexuals were first trialled on people with a learning difficulty. Significantly, when Binding defined the list of those who might be killed, he specifically excluded those who had been disabled while fighting in the First World War (Friedlander 1995). This perhaps implied a judgement that the person had once had 'value' and utility – an idea that echoes the 'Tattooed man' story in Chapter 10, in which a man with a serious brain injury was being valued because of what he had once been, and because he had once 'had value'.

It is interesting to compare the idea of 'a life with value' with the contemporary reference quoted in Chapter 3. Jim Dobbin, a Labour MP and chairman of the all-party Parliamentary pro-life group, countered David Cameron's view that a foetus known to have an impairment might be aborted at a later stage than a 'healthy' foetus could be aborted. He said:

> This is an equality issue. [David Cameron's] statement allows abortion for the disabled and this sends out a horrifying message to people with disabilities. This is telling people with disabilities that they have fewer human rights than people without disabilities. *Many people with severe disabilities have contributed greatly to humanity* [my emphasis].

Binding and Dobbin appear to be arguing from opposite positions. Binding was proposing the taking of life and Dobbin is proposing the right to life for a disabled child. Yet they use a similar criterion for 'value'. They both propose the idea of 'the usefulness or value of the person with a learning difficulty to the community' to support their point of view. Dobbin is arguing about human rights but these are not conditional. One has a human right, regardless of one's utility.

One vignette referred to in Chapter 6 also has resonance here.

▪ It's not fair (2)

A staff member was supporting a person with a learning difficulty who had accrued benefit to the point where income might be lost unless some large purchases were made. The staff member commented to her manager that she hated the fact that this person had a larger disposable income than she had. The staff member was struggling to pay her bills from an earned income, whereas the person with the learning difficulty 'had not earned their money'. She also did not like the fact that public money (benefit) was being spent as a means of reducing a bank balance, rather than for genuine need. The staff member felt guilty about these thoughts because she felt that she was being disrespectful to the person she supported.

One important factor in the staff member's evaluation of the person with a learning difficulty was that their income was unearned. This is a similar argument to Dobbin's and Binding's idea of utility. In all three cases, there is a corollary. If some people are valued because they are useful, there must be other people who are not valued because they are seen as having no utility.

The Nazi policy was underpinned by the same 'scientific' theories as social policy in the USA, which preceded it by 26 years. Indeed, the American Professor Lenz criticised his German counterparts for lagging behind in their efforts to use the 'science' of the day to achieve 'racial hygiene'. Hitler included Lenz's theories when he wrote *Mein Kampf* (Spitz 2005). The American response to these theories was to implement mass sterilisation for people with a learning difficulty as well as others who were thought to threaten racial purity. England also implemented a policy based on the same theories 20 years earlier than Germany. Thus we can see that this attitude to people with a learning difficulty was not peculiar to the Nazis. Germany initially copied English and American policy and then took it further.

People with a learning difficulty were first portrayed as a 'problem' in England when the Education Act of 1870 created the national elementary school system. Large numbers of children from 'lower classes' attended school for the first time and some were found to have difficulty in learning (Simmons 1978). The Royal Commission on the Blind, the Deaf and Dumb and Afflicted Classes (1885) identified large numbers of children who were not benefiting from school because of 'mental deficiency'. Simmons (*ibid.*) argues that this is the point when learning difficulty was re-conceptualised as a social rather than a private problem. Jones (1976) suggested that it was commonly believed at the time that urban populations would inevitably degenerate both physically and morally. A 'residuum' of people who were 'feeble and tainted' would be incapable of thriving, even in times of prosperity.

One comment made by Mary Dendy in the Royal Commission report (cited in Simmons 1978, p. 392) identified a moral panic from the time:

The first test (for mental deficiency) I think is that if a woman comes into the workhouse with an illegitimate child it should be evidence of weakness of mind: there is certainly evidence of lack of moral fibre.

163

Dendy's statement has similarities to the quotation at the start of this chapter, which came from Terman 20 years later in Germany. This notion of 'moral degeneracy' became one of the defining characteristics of mental deficiency. Being poor and having an illegitimate child were sufficient to earn the label 'moral defective'. There was great concern among eugenicists that 'the feeble-minded' bred more rapidly, with an average of 7.3 children per family (compared with 4 per 'normal' family), according to figures quoted by the Royal Commission.

The most pressing social concerns of the time thus became inextricably linked with 'mental deficiency'. Lord Hershell summed this up in 1898 (cited in Simmons *ibid.*, p. 394):

The existence of large classes of feeble-minded persons is a danger to the moral and physical welfare of society and calls for immediate attention both on the part of public authorities and charitable enterprise.

The Royal Commission report led to the 1913 Mental Deficiency Act, which authorised the forcible incarceration of people labelled 'feeble-minded'. Such incarceration and containment would supposedly reduce the risk of social harm posed by the presence of 'mentally deficient' people. The eugenicists put forward a number of arguments that soon became the main justification for 'mental retardation' legislation. These arguments emphasised the relationship between feeble-mindedness and a whole array of contemporary social problems (including poverty, crime, alcoholism, juvenile crime, unemployment and prostitution) and made three important assumptions about feeble-mindedness: that it was hereditary, that it resulted from breeding among the feeble-minded themselves and that feeble-minded women reproduced at a far greater rate than the rest of the population. The solution, according to eugenicists and others, was obvious: stop the feeble-minded from breeding.

The website 'Unlocking the past' identifies many examples of the consequences of this policy aimed at preventing people with a learning difficulty becoming parents. One story on this website was told by a man who used to live in a long-stay institution. He was remembering the weekly dances:

Jeffrey: **No you're not to dance with girls.**

Steve: **How did matron used to say it?**

Jeffrey: **You can't sit here, it's for the girls!** (*in a comic falsetto*)

Steve: **And what would happen if you did dance with the girls?**

Jeffrey: **She'd poke her bloody nose in.** (*laughing*)

Steve: **What would she do then?**

Jeffrey: **I said shut your bloody trap!** (*laughing*)

Steve: **What did she say to you?**

Jeffrey: **Any more and you'll go to Welch home!** (*laughing*)

Steve: And what was Welch home?

Jeffrey: For bad people.

Jeffrey described how men and women (they were all adults) were never allowed to dance together. This was something he regretted into his old age. When he challenged the matron about this, she threatened him with the punishment ward. Others in this oral history project have described how they could be severely punished for meeting up with a 'girl'. The hospital was divided on gender lines, and severe sanctions were applied to those who broke the rules. The main building had men at one end and women at the other. Each end had an 'airing yard' and these were called the 'boys' yard' and 'girls' yard' respectively. Even in the 1980s, when the yards were being used for car parking, an official memo was circulated which informed staff that there was to be no parking in the 'boys' yard' because maintenance work was being carried out.

This repressive attitude to sexuality was based on eugenicists' concerns. It underpinned both the Nazi euthanasia programme and the English institutionalisation and sexual segregation policy. It might therefore be seen as a historic issue, with no relevance to the present. However, it can be argued that similar thinking underpins current policy and practice. The following are relatively recent examples, some of which you may well recognise:

- In the 1990s a man with a learning difficulty was realistic enough to realise that he was unlikely to be able to form a sexual relationship with a woman who did not also have a learning difficulty. (Note that this was an example of a man with a learning difficulty not valuing women with a learning difficulty.) He asked to be supported in buying sex from a sex worker. In Holland there are safe, well-controlled establishments where sex can be bought and there are specialist disability sex workers. The service supporting this man refused his request, despite the fact that it is not illegal to buy sex – even in this country. Interestingly, social role valorisation was used as a justification for this refusal; paid sex was not seen as 'valued sex'.

- A couple with learning difficulty met at a day centre. They wished to have a sexual relationship but complained that they had nowhere private to go. Support staff did not allow them to spend time alone in a bedroom and so it was not just a question of finding private space but also of losing their minder!

- People with a learning difficulty frequently need support to access their doctor. How might they access contraception when they always have a minder? There is a similar problem with accessing sex education.

- A vignette entitled 'It shouldn't be allowed' (which appeared in Chapter 6) described how a support service management team decided to create a policy to help staff support people with a learning difficulty to express their sexuality. At the time there was a broadly accepted rights agenda in support services but it was also acknowledged that sexuality for people with a learning difficulty was potentially a difficult area. The managers asked staff to tell them what problems they had faced and what they would therefore like to see included in the policy. The only responses received by the managers from the staff were along the lines of 'it shouldn't happen, it is disgusting'.

- It appears that people with a learning difficulty had a better chance of having a sex life at the long-stay institutions where staff tended to turn a blind eye to 'sex in the bushes' (see the 'Unlocking the past' website for such accounts). Is this one way in which life has got worse for some people who have been resettled from the long-stay institutions into the community?

These issues echo some of those raised in 'You couldn't make it up' in Chapter 6 (see p. 77). To return to the central question in this book, it might be argued that by supporting a person with a learning difficulty to express their sexuality we are valuing them as complete human beings.

Following the rules

This section considers what happens when carers work under conditions that become extreme. The following three paragraphs summarise the story told in Friedlander (1995). In Nazi Germany, the actual killing process used for people with a learning difficulty had a particularly chilling dimension, in that it was experimental. As this was the first attempt to kill such large numbers of people, the Nazis put great effort into finding the most efficient methods. Injections of lethal doses of barbiturates had been used in the hospitals. The relative merits of death by injection and carbon monoxide poisoning were now decided by experimentation. Injection was proved to be slower than gassing. Indeed, the patients who had been injected were then gassed because the injection process was too slow.

Other methods were also tried, including transporting patients in vans in which the exhaust fumes were fed back inside, where the patients were held. In one particularly horrific but bizarre 'experiment', some patients were put into a small concrete building, which was then dynamited. This was seen as too inefficient because the area was strewn with body parts and proved difficult to clear up. In Russia and Poland, thousands of people with a learning difficulty were executed by shooting.

It is sobering to realise that the medical professions were involved at all stages of this mass killing. They were party to the 'science' that underpinned the process and its administration, as there was a formal agreement that a physician had to operate the equipment when gassing took place. Medical science adopted the eugenics position with little dissent. Staff even marked the occasion when a particularly macabre milestone was reached (Friedlander 1995, p. 110):

The staff at Hadamar arranged for a celebration when the number of patients killed there reached 10,000. On the order of the physicians, the entire staff

> assembled at the basement crematorium to participate in the burning of the ten thousandth victim. A naked corpse lay on a stretcher, covered with flowers. The supervisor Bunger made a speech and a staff member dressed up as a cleric performed a ceremony. Every staff member received a bottle of beer.

The staff who joined in this celebration included nurses, doctors and other care staff. Friedlander reports that some staff did object to the general policy and many were retired earlier. However, the majority went along with it and some gained significant career advancement by doing so.

It can be difficult to understand how medical and care staff could have participated in an activity that seems so wrong to those of us with the good fortune to work in the late twentieth and early twenty-first century. However, it is probably safe to assume that the individual staff were mostly just like us but happened to be born in a different era.

Friedlander (1995) suggested that doctors considered that the selection of people with a learning difficulty for 'euthanasia' was a medical decision. He cites Dr Friedrich Mennecke who said, 'It was not my duty to shorten the lives of the insane person, it was my duty to act as a medical expert' (US Military Tribunal, Transcript of the Proceedings in Case 1, p. 1922). As suggested below, the later abortion time allowed for an unborn child with a learning difficulty is a current example of a medical decision to terminate life. In this sense, the doctors of that time faced qualitatively similar decisions to those faced by doctors today.

Similarly, nurses are involved in such decision-making. Atherton (2011) cites Lagerwey (1999) who suggested that to perceive nurses in the Nazi era as any different or more 'evil' than contemporary nurses is to 'other' them. (The process of 'othering' people with a learning difficulty was described in Chapter 3.)

The following account is taken from the testimony of a nurse at the Nuremberg trials. (This account was also used in Chapter 1 to illustrate service values, see p. 7.) She had knowingly given lethal doses of sedative to people with a learning difficulty during the euthanasia period (Ebbinghaus 1987, p. 239, cited in Benedict & Kuhla 1999):

> When giving the dissolved medicine, I proceeded with a lot of compassion. I had told patients that they would have to take a cure… I took them lovingly and stroked them when I gave the medicine. If, for example, a patient did not empty the entire cup because it was too bitter, I talked to her nicely, telling her that she had already drunk so much that she should drink the rest, otherwise her cure couldn't be finished. Some could be convinced to empty the cup completely. In other cases, I gave the medicine by the spoonful. Like I already told you, our procedure depended on the condition of the patients. Old women, for example, who had to be fed couldn't drink on their own so it wasn't possible to give them the medicine by the spoonful. They were not to be tortured more

> **than necessary and I thought it would be better to give them an injection. In this connection, I would like to say that, like me, Luise E. [Erdmann], Margarete Ratajczak, and Erna E. thought that the patients were not to be tortured more than necessary.**

The nurse describing these events was charged with killing 150 patients. This bald fact would appear to be a perfect example of *not* valuing people with a learning difficulty. And yet she claims to have administered the medicine:

- With respect to individual need
- Behaving lovingly and reassuringly
- Minimising discomfort
- Talking nicely to the person

This list would not look out of place in a contemporary person-centred plan. The idea that this was a 'mercy killing', perhaps resembling the definition of euthanasia, might seem like an oxymoron to current sensibilities. However, it is worth considering that Jewish people with a learning difficulty were initially to be denied such a mercy killing (Friedlander 1995). This suggests that it was seen as a desirable thing and 'too good for a Jew'!

A desirable thing done with compassion can be seen as 'valuing'. The one phrase in the nurse's account that seems oddly out of place is 'the patients were not to be tortured more than necessary'. The corollary to this is that a nurse who appeared to be acting with some humanity did consider that some level of torture *was* 'necessary'. This may seem bizarre but what if the words 'be tortured' are replaced by something at the other end of the continuum, such as 'face costs'? For example, it is possible to consider the following things a person with a learning difficulty might face in this light:

- Be expected to face a thing that they find intolerable in a 'flooding' programme (when they are exposed to a phobia, for example)
- Face a reduction in their activities at a time of cuts; a senior manager was heard to say 'no more nice' when such cuts were being announced
- Be denied health treatment for reasons that have been quoted throughout this book and exposed in the Michaels Report (DOH 2008)

Another nurse involved in the Nazi euthanasia programme stated (*ibid.*):

> **Through the behavior of Dr Wernicke I realized that incurable patients were to be released by giving them Veronal [barbiturate acid] or another medicine.**

The idea of 'release' suggests an act of kindness. The nurse quoted previously had apparently acted with 'kindness'. Can we therefore argue that in a society where it is decreed that people with a learning difficulty are to be killed, individuals can carry out that task in a kindly way? Can it be further said that a nurse behaving in this way is 'valuing' the person with a learning difficulty by acting in a 'kindly' manner? Is it possible to act in a 'valuing' way in a policy context that is probably as devaluing as it is possible to be?

The events described above occurred in the 1940s but the following story happened relatively recently.

■ The cat-suit

In the 1980s a woman with a learning difficulty had anorexia. She would lift her top and look at her stomach and say it was too fat. She was referred to a specialist behavioural unit. A multidisciplinary team decided that her care plan should include the stipulation that she should be made to wear a cat-suit so that she couldn't lift her top.

The woman hated the cat-suit but staff overpowered her every day and made her put it on. This involved three staff members, one to put the suit on and two to hold her still, and she always got very distressed. A newly qualified staff nurse hated being involved with this process and doubted whether it could be either effective or morally justified. He was very uncomfortable with this level of coercion. However, the consultant psychiatrist, psychologist and ward manager had agreed on the plan so he assumed that they must be better informed. It seemed somehow consistent with the (then ubiquitous) behavioural theories. Perhaps the end would justify the means? And yet it still felt so wrong.

After a period of time it became apparent that this intervention was making things worse and the woman refused to leave her bedroom. The cat-suit was abandoned. The staff nurse's judgement had been correct; the intervention had been wrong and yet he had participated in enforcing it.

Many of us who work in services supporting people with a learning difficulty will recognise this type of situation: being expected to follow a care plan when it does not seem to be appropriate. In this particular case, the staff nurse had not been qualified for long, and experienced senior professionals had devised the care plan. The situation was also very complex. This young girl was facing serious health problems, perhaps even death, from her anorexia. Could it be argued that the ends justified the means? Perhaps it was necessary to work against her wishes and autonomy in order to achieve a benefit that she might not be able to appreciate? It is possible to define her 'forced dressing' as assault? Can this type of coercion ever be deemed appropriate and are there any circumstances in which it could be described as 'valuing'?

It is worth reflecting on the behaviour and feelings of the nurse who administered the lethal injection and the nurse who forced the woman to put on the cat-suit. The nurse giving the lethal injection appeared to believe that the ending of the person's life was morally justified and she carried out the duty with compassion. The nurse who forced on the cat-suit did not believe that his actions were justifiable but still did it on a daily basis while remaining full of doubt. Was the nurse who administered the injection therefore acting in a more 'valuing' way than the nurse forcing the woman to wear the cat-suit?

This comment was made recently by a nurse who worked in a long-stay institution in the 1970s and 1980s:

I feel so guilty when I look back at what went on in the hospital. I never hit people or anything like that but I did sometimes turn a blind eye. I think I am a good person but at the hospital it was good people caught up in bad times.

The following vignette is from current practice.

■ The cookery class

A 65-year-old woman with a learning difficulty attends a cookery course two days a week at the local FE college. She did not ask to learn cookery but at her care meeting the courses available were discussed by the care team and cookery was chosen as the most appropriate. She did agree to go on the course but she always tends to agree with staff. She has learned that the best way to keep out of trouble is to agree with staff. On the mornings that she is due to attend, she will sometimes say she has a headache to try to get out of it.

The team manager knows that the woman does not really wish to go to the lesson. However, at a previous supervision her own manager noted that some of 'her' clients did not have very full timetables. This gave the team manager a reason to persist with the cookery classes for the 65-year-old woman.

One factor that links the staff nurse in the 'Cat-suit' story, the team leader in 'The cookery class' and the nurse administering the lethal dose of medicine is that they were all following orders and meeting the expectations of their superiors. 'I was only following orders' is a common excuse when most perpetrators of atrocities are bought to task. Those of us who 'carry out orders' in more benign times are the lucky ones.

As a consequence of this excuse being offered by so many at the Nuremberg trials, a psychologist called Stanley Milgram devised a classic experiment to see if Americans were any different from the Germans who had appeared so ready to follow orders during the Holocaust. This piece of research has profound implications for behaviour in organisations.

Participants in Milgram's experiment believed that they were involved in an experiment to understand punishment and learning. The punishment was an electric shock, which the participants were asked to deliver to the 'learners' in the experiment. The learners were in fact actors who feigned the appropriate response to being given an electric shock as punishment. No shock was actually being given, but the participants believed that they were indeed pressing the lever to give the shock. Milgram was in fact conducting an experiment in conformity and how far people follow instructions when they contradict their personal belief systems. In his account (Milgram 1965, p. 128), Milgram drew the following conclusion:

> **The majority of subjects, however, comply fully with the experimenter's commands, despite the acute discomfort they often experience in connection with shocking the victim. Typically these obedient subjects report that they do not wish to hurt the victim, but they feel obligated to follow the orders of the experimenter. On questioning they often state that it would have been 'better' not to have shocked the victim at the highest voltage levels.**

The following is an extract from an interview (*ibid.*) in which the researcher asked why one participant carried on delivering the electric shocks when he found it so uncomfortable:

> I don't like what happened to that fellow in there [the victim]. He's been hollering and we had to keep giving him shocks. I didn't like that one bit. I mean he wanted to get out but he [the experimenter] just kept going, he kept throwing 450 volts. I didn't like that.
>
> *Who was actually pushing the switch?* I was, but he kept insisting. I told him 'No,' but he said you got to keep going. I told him it's time we stopped when we get up to 195 or 210 volts.
>
> *Why didn't you just stop?* He wouldn't let me. I wanted to stop. I kept insisting to stop, but he said 'No.' … I figured the voltage we were giving him was quite a bit. I wanted to stop but he [the experimenter] kept insisting not to stop.

The two nurses and the team leader in the stories above might all have felt that they could lose their jobs and the nurse in Germany may have faced worse sanctions. In the Milgram experiment, the participants were volunteers who were being given a token payment. The experimenter who gave the instructions to administer shocks had no real authority over the participants. The individuals were instructed to give painful electric shocks to a stranger and those individuals complied. Milgram carried out further experiments and came to the conclusion that gender, age and nationality made little difference; most people would follow instructions to hurt another person, even where they were very unhappy about doing so.

The story of Adolf Eichmann illustrates what can happen when someone follows instructions at a time when extreme policies are being implemented. Eichmann was initially responsible for the expulsion of Jewish people from Germany. As the state moved from expulsion to killing, his job description changed. This eventually resulted in him being responsible for the transporting of people to the concentration camps. He proved to be excellent at his job and he continued with his duties, even after being ordered to stop as the Allies advanced. He started out as an administrator of considerable ability. However, he absorbed the anti-semitic attitudes of the time and become more directly involved in the killing itself.

Eichmann made himself indispensable to the Nazi Party. His own ambition became more important than the group of people who were suffering for his success. Men like him helped to institutionalise mass murder, and the process became increasingly banal and routine (Cesarani 2006, p. 157, cited in Adams & Balfour 2009, p. 53):

> **Eichmann's attitude towards the Jews had assumed a cold inhumanity… [He] managed Genocide in the way that the director of a multi-national corporation manages production and distribution of product: calibrating the supply of raw material to the capacity of plant, monitoring output and quality controls and assuring prompt delivery.**

And similarly (BBC 5):

> **What makes his crimes so chilling is that they were not preordained by any evident pathology or inbuilt racism. Eichmann learned to hate, and to hate in a controlled and impersonal way. He applied business methods to the handling of human beings who, once they had been dehumanised, could be treated no differently from cargoes of kerosene. In his mind there was little difference between setting up a petrol station or a death camp.**

Eichmann himself was little more than a cog in a monstrous machine – an ambitious man who approached his work in an ethical vacuum, following orders extremely efficiently. He proved to be capable of organising a programme of genocide that has become the epitome of evil in modern thinking. Yet he appears to have been a fairly ordinary man.

On the other hand, at the time of the eugenics movement in England, a retired teacher called Margaret Macdowall wrote a book entitled *Simple Beginnings in the Training of Mentally Defective Children*. This book actually does not sound too out-of-step with modern sensibilities, though one has to make obvious allowances for the language used at the time (Macdowall 1930, p. xvi):

> **I have been asked to write of my work in training young imbecile children. I am making the attempt in the humble hope that some of these little ones, who,**

from failure of power and desire to express themselves, are thought unable to appreciate that reverential sympathy which is their birthright, may be better understood.

'Reverential sympathy' could be seen as the 1930 equivalent of 'valuing'. What is more, according to Macdowall that 'reverential sympathy' is a 'birthright'; not an option but a right. Macdowall stated that the effort required to help these children was justified, and argued against those who said it was not worth the effort and resources required (Macdowall 1930, p. xvi). She wrote (*ibid*., p. 1):

Knowing as I do, from many years of thought and study, that no human being is meant to inhabit the world without attaining its maximum of faculty possible under earthly conditions, even though support from without must be lifelong, I want to strive to make clear that mental training and help for these invalids means beauty and life i.e. spiritual and vital developments, while the mere care of the body alone must mean stagnation, if nothing worse.

'Attaining the maximum of faculty possible' might easily translate as 'being enabled to achieve their full potential'. The notion that such support means attaining 'spiritual ... development' pre-dated Maslow's hierarchy of needs, with 'self-actualisation' at the apex (Maslow 1943).

Macdowall held these apparently 'valuing' views about the correct way to work with children with a learning difficulty. She had been asked to write a book about her experiences because others suggested to her that standards were slipping in care and education. She also wrote (Macdowall *ibid*., p. xvii):

In 1913, after the passing of the Mental Deficiency Act, I decided to retire and live with only a few children in the recesses of the country. I felt I could not work under inspection of those who possibly might be unsympathetic.

She appeared to lack trust in the legislation of the time and those charged with the responsibility of monitoring its implementation. This would suggest that she is an example of the minority in Milgram's experiment. She was one of the few people who proved capable of acting according to a personal ethical code, rather than simply doing as they were told.

In the following story, two men who lived in a long-stay institution in the 1950s described someone who also had the courage of her own convictions.

■ Tea and toast

Getting up in the morning was horrible. Sometimes mattresses were roughly tipped and the children fell out onto the floor. At other times they were dragged roughly out of bed. At that time there was a particular female nurse who used to bring the children toast and tea in bed. She used to say 'enjoy your breakfast lads'.

This appears to be another example of someone who went against the standard practice of the time and worked according to her own inner sense of decency; she knew what she considered the right thing to do. Both Macdowall and the nurse in 'Tea and toast' appeared to value people with a learning difficulty at a time when typical standards of treatment might not have been particularly valuing. They were able to define standards of valuing for themselves.

A possible future perspective on today?

We now understand that there were genuine concerns about the wellbeing of the nation at the time of the eugenics movement. On top of this, many scientists believed that there was a hierarchy of humanity and the 'lower echelons' would breed more rapidly. The fallout from the First World War and the cost of reparations in Germany opened the way for an extreme political reaction. Certain categories of people were made into scapegoats and were seen as responsible for the problems.

From the safe vantage point of 2012, we can observe with knowing horror the wartime descent into barbarism and the genocide of people with a learning difficulty. We live and work in a time when many previously targeted groups may be seen as more included. Black, gay and disabled people have all benefited from the growth of civil rights in our society. Pinker (2011) argues that we live in safer times and are less likely to suffer violence than in any other historical period. It is perhaps worth bearing in mind that he actually includes the Nazi era in these 'safer times' but he points to a reduction in violence towards 'othered groups' that has been continuing since the seventeenth century.

This all suggests that we live in a period when people with a learning difficulty would be likely to be valued. Is this the case? We could reflect on what scholars from the future might make of the following facts, again with the benefit of hindsight:

- In the current political era in Britain, disability benefits are being cut. The idea of disability benefit cheats has emerged in the press. We do, of course, face an economic crisis but it is worth remembering that this was also true in the era of eugenics and the Nazis.

- At the beginning of the period in which people were 'resettled' from long-stay hospitals, many had the status of tenants with the legal protection that this offers. This is not usually the case now. People also had their benefits as income. Now people are more likely to receive their income as 'pocket money', once costs have been deducted. In other words people with a learning difficulty have lost control of their income and have less legal protection than they had at the beginning of the resettlement process.

- In the private sector, people with a learning difficulty are a source of profit for non-disabled others. This may lead to them becoming chattels when the business is sold. Interestingly, this is one definition of value.

- People with a learning difficulty are being denied equal access to healthcare.

- People with a learning difficulty are unlikely to have:
  - Jobs
  - Relationships
  - Children
- The law currently discriminates against an unborn child with a disability.
- People with a learning difficulty are subject to hate crime and there is evidence that they do not get full protection from the state.

How Might We Value People with a Learning Difficulty?

This book has drawn on stories from practice, policy, the media and history to explore the concept of 'valuing'. It has attempted to unravel the idea and to consider the question 'What do we mean by valuing people with a learning disability?' Various theories have been utilised in an attempt to understand the process of 'valuing'. The term 'learning disability' was changed to 'learning difficulty' as a result of a discussion that considered the social model of disability in Chapter 8.

The short answer to this question is 'it depends'. Valuing is an active cognitive process, which varies and is influenced by context. This concluding chapter is presented in five sections:

1 Personal reflection

2 Personal interaction with people with a learning difficulty

3 Personal action

4 The nature of support offered

5 The wider picture

1 Personal reflection

The fact is that we all have natural cognitive structures and processes that contain inbuilt obstacles to the true valuing of people with a learning difficulty. Statements such as 'I am a non-judgemental professional' or 'I am a non-discriminatory practitioner' actually don't make any sense. Most people naturally put things into categories and make judgements. To do so is not evil, unintelligent or politically questionable; it is simply a fact of human cognitive life.

We all have an inner drive to save cognitive energy as much as possible; in this sense 'cruising on autopilot' actually enables us to cope and make sense of the world on a day-to-day basis. Indeed it may be the case that people with autism have problems in taking such cognitive short cuts and this may help to explain why they might struggle to make sense of a complex and ambiguous reality. If we are truly to attempt to be anti-discriminatory practitioners, we (as individuals) need to understand the extent to which we *do* discriminate.

Similarly, if we wish to be non-judgemental then it is necessary to understand the extent to which we *do* actually judge. In other words, in order to value a group of people, we first need to be truthful about the extent to which we de-value them, and this requires deep reflection. Then, of course, we need to change our behaviour accordingly. The theories described in this book suggest that we should do the following:

- Become conscious of our own schemas in an attempt to become less judgemental. Avoid lazy self-schemas such as 'I am non-judgemental'. Similarly, we must become conscious of any person schema we hold for a person with a learning difficulty. Most of us probably have little awareness that we might hold such a person schema. If we do, it will almost certainly be based on deep-rooted and unconscious understanding. As professionals, we will hold a significant number of event schemas such as *interviews/ assessments*, *person-centred plan* and *support in public*. We must reconsider any role schema such as *client*, *person with a learning difficulty* or *nurse*. Through becoming conscious of our personal schemas, we can start to reformulate more valuing alternatives.

- Become conscious of any social representations we hold. In particular, it is likely that our opinion of certain people with a learning difficulty will be formed by the social representations formed by the teams to which we belong. Similarly, we need to acknowledge our own prejudices and stereotypes. A key point here may be to avoid deluding ourselves that we do not actually hold any stereotypes; we *all* do.

- Become aware of any bigger personal values, such as political and religious beliefs, and consider any conflicts with valuing. For example, does our political ideology include a judgement about people who live off benefits? If this is the case, then inevitably a shadow will be cast over the way in which we value the people we support if they live on benefits. It is unlikely that our cognitive psychology would allow us to 'fence off' people with a learning difficulty from this general rule. The resulting perceptual conflict needs to be made conscious and should be deeply considered. In this case 'I value people with a learning difficulty' is in conflict with 'I value people who earn their living above those who live on benefit'. Similarly, we might consider the implications if we, for example, respect people of high intelligence, admire people who are highly skilled or enjoy the company of socially skilled people. In each of these examples, the personal value has a corollary that might lead to people with a learning difficulty being de-valued.

- Be conscious of any negative attribution we hold for people with a learning difficulty in general and the individuals with whom we work in particular. The first response to challenging behaviour should be 'I'll assume this person has a completely valid reason for behaving like this'. Start from a position of seeing the person's behaviour as functional, rather than attempt to change them.

- Be honest enough to admit the power differential between yourself and the person with a learning difficulty. Typically the person with a learning difficulty will have lower social status, economic standing, intellect, linguistic ability, health status, support networks and legal protection. This profoundly affects the balance of your relationship. We must not assume that we have the power to 'punish' adults with a learning difficulty. For example, it cannot be claimed that we value a person if we deny them anything that is their right We need to acknowledge the fact that we do not have the legitimate power to punish them.

A useful commitment we can all make is: 'I hold both valuing and devaluing cognitive representations of people with a learning difficulty. I will attempt to reduce the impact of any devaluing representations that drive my behaviour.'

2 Personal interaction with people with a learning difficulty

What we do as practitioners can indicate valuing or devaluing. It has been argued in this book that valuing resides in both thought and action. Because of this, it is possible to hold a devaluing attitude but at the same time strive to behave in a valuing way. For example, I have always struggled to cognitively value people who have committed sexual offences but I hope that my actions when working with offenders will have been experienced as valuing. The following examples of interpersonal interaction with people with a learning difficulty would indicate valuing:

- Consider the relative value we ascribe to 'friend' and 'client'. We are likely to value 'friend' more highly, yet typically we probably ascribe the role of 'client' to a person with a learning difficulty. Do we value people more if we see them as friends and not just as clients? It is interesting to reflect on the argument that to be 'professional' is to place a boundary on relationships. There is no room to develop this argument here but we might consider what sort of boundary is most useful to the person with a learning difficulty; what would they choose?

- Consider the person with a learning difficulty worthy of sharing the same cutlery, crockery and toilets.

- Be happy to share space with a person with a learning difficulty. This might be a restaurant, theatre, street, hospital ward or jacuzzi.

- Consider the person with a learning difficulty worthy of the same dreams and aspirations as ourselves. To do this requires us to avoid the common trap of thinking that something is excellent, but only because the person has a learning difficulty. If someone has moved into accommodation where they have a private bedroom then that is a good first step. What about a sex life, owning property, having a life partner or dying with enough personal possessions to need a will?

- Be conscious of the significantly lower power status experienced by the person with a learning difficulty. This requires a tentative approach and active letting go of power that we, as professionals, hold over those we purport to support. An example is the 'contract' that people with challenging behaviour might sign as part of a person-centred plan. This, of course, has no legal status as a 'contract'. To have this status the law would demand evidence that the person who signed had not done so under duress. The power differential between the person and the body of people managing the plan probably means that such a contract is always signed under duress. Personally, I believe such 'contracts' are on a similar level to 'protection' offered by the Mafia!
- Learn to truly listen. This often means saying nothing – for long periods. And waiting. In this waiting time we should actively engage and attend. Silent mindfulness is often the key These things do not always come easily to a professional with a schedule to meet.
- Learn to truly communicate. This requires a thorough understanding of the person's linguistic development and the point to which it has progressed. To attempt to communicate at a level beyond this point is to actively disable the person, which would clearly be a case of not valuing them. Similarly, we need to be conscious of the way we use power in language and learn how to avoid these traps. Once conscious of the rules, it is necessary to carefully construct language in a way that will be understood. In order to do this, it is necessary to be aware of the roles in, and rules of, discourse and to then use one's power to facilitate more equal communication. Again it can be argued that to not learn and implement these rules is to devalue the person with a learning difficulty.
- Consider what we do as professionals to be a duty (and not a gift) to people with a learning difficulty.
- Adopt the principles of caution and reflection and collaboration and accommodation. Working in a valuing way may require a more tentative approach than is typical.
- Be wary of using humour. It is positive to engage with humour with people with a learning difficulty but only if they share and understand the joke. Any humour beyond their understanding will be devaluing of that person.

3 Personal action

In order to value people with a learning difficulty, it is also necessary to consider the wider influence of our behaviour and consequent actions:

- Challenge any bad practice and report any abuse. Be prepared to 'whistle-blow'. In cases where people with a learning difficulty have been abused, there have frequently been practitioners present who witnessed the abuse but had said nothing.
- Act with moral courage by doing the right thing, rather than the prescribed thing – if the prescribed thing seems unethical.

- Take any opportunity to challenge the schemas of others if they devalue people with a learning difficulty. Similarly, the team's social representation of the person with a learning difficulty can be devaluing. It can be difficult, for example, to challenge a team's attribution of 'laziness' to a person by suggesting that the person might actually be unwell.

- Be conscious of our impact, as staff members, on the impression others form about the people we support. This might include our dress, manner of speech and general behaviour. Are we providing the sort of support that the person would choose if they were truly empowered to do so?

- Be aware that the way we structure our support may actually help to construct that person's disability. We may be part of the problem.

- Try to avoid using a collective description. But if we must, then adopt the terminology preferred by the people we support. At present, this is 'learning difficulty' and not 'learning disability'.

- Be conscious that we may have more awareness of the person's primary and secondary impression than the person themselves. We should advise accordingly. But this must, of course, be done in a tentative manner in order to avoid steering the person away from doing what they wish to do. This requires (on the part of the practitioner) a deep understanding of some of the rules of impression management.

- Consider the impact of political change on the most vulnerable people in society when we cast our votes at national and local elections. People with a learning difficulty are seldom enabled to vote.

4 The nature of support offered

Any service that claims to value the people it supports would do the following:

- Manage a person-centred plan (PCP) in a way that maximises power for the person by asking pertinent questions. How much time is allocated to truly discover that person's wishes? Who has set the questions for the assessment? Who sets the agenda at the meeting? Who directs the process of the meeting? Why are we having a meeting at all when a meeting may well disable the person? Whose needs is the structure and process of the person-centred plan designed to meet? It is easy to fall into the trap of categorising people according to a stereotype, such as 'elderly', or to prioritise a service label such as 'challenging behaviour'.

- Free people from the tyranny of 'tickbox' services. How much of the person's PCP and broader life experiences are dictated by service targets?

- Enable people with a learning difficulty to express their sexuality.

- Support people to have valued roles. We might consider the impact of occupying that role for the person with a learning difficulty.

- Support people to develop some 'use' in their lives. What are their lives for? This is harsh language but the lives of many people with a learning difficulty can be seen as having no utility or purpose. They may be viewed as 'surplus' and their lives may appear to be wasted.

- Ensure that people with a learning difficulty have their full range of rights recognised.

- Support the person to manage their impression in order to make a positive impact on the way that others see them. This matters at both primary and secondary levels of impression. The way the service is designed and delivered will have a profound effect upon that impression.

- Enable the person to manage the details of their presentation, including their characteristics and behaviours, in a way that will enable them to be more highly valued by others. But this should be carefully balanced with the need to respect the person's right to make their own choices – they may choose to do something 'devaluing'.

- Ensure that the person has the best health possible, which requires proper access to healthcare services.

- Manage the environment in a way that enables the person. The minimum requirement is to ensure that the person is not disabled by the way the services are structured.

- Create service structures that support people with a learning difficulty to be able to speak up and be heard. Would it be possible for the person to ask for and achieve radical change in service design? Can they change their support staff? Can they change where they live? Can they truly choose the people with whom they live?

- Do people with a learning difficulty spend all their living, work and leisure time with other people with a learning difficulty? This level of segregation can be just as isolating as the old long-stay institutions.

- Services cannot be seen as valuing if they allow people with a learning difficulty to be punished or be denied their rights.

5 The wider picture

The preceding four sections all make suggestions that are within the power of practitioners and their agencies. This section considers the features of a wider society that might claim to value people with a learning difficulty. There is a limit to what individuals can do to affect this wider picture beyond careful use of a vote and becoming more politicised.

- People with a learning difficulty need to be seen as tenants in their own homes and not treated as if they were part of the fixtures and fittings of a business. If the care business is sold, are the people 'sold' with it? People should not be viewed as chattels; it is instructive to remember that historically women were men's chattels and slaves were the chattels of plantation owners. Today, treating people with a learning difficulty as possessions in this way is likely to be defined as the epitome of devaluing.

- If people are tenants in their own homes, it is not appropriate to consider a spare bedroom as 'a vacancy'. If people are valued, they can choose who moves in as a co-tenant or choose to pay more rent and leave the bedroom empty.
- All health services should be as accessible to a person with a learning difficulty as they are to a middle-class white man.
- Abortion law must not discriminate against the unborn child with a disability.
- People with a learning difficulty need to have direct representation in councils and in parliament.
- People with a learning difficulty have to be properly protected from hate crime. (Of course in Utopia there would be no hate crime!)
- The media should include a representative number of people with a learning difficulty.
- In recent times we have seen the required qualifications for learning difficulty support staff downgraded from professional qualifications to NVQ. The required learning suggested by this book cannot be covered by NVQ. At the same time we have seen the gradual erosion of pay and conditions offered by many employers of support staff. It can be argued that we cannot be seen as valuing people with a learning difficulty if those supporting them have degraded qualifications, pay and conditions.
- The examples of devaluing raised in this book should eventually become an intriguing historic relic, as bizarre as eugenics arguments appear now (to most of us at least). At that point, people may say 'Why on earth did anyone have to write that? It is obvious.'

This book set out to ask the question: 'What do we mean by valuing people?' It concludes with the question: 'What needs to happen to ensure valuing of people with a learning difficulty?' When all the points listed in the above five sections are in place, then we can say – as individuals, as a service and as a society – that we truly value people with a learning difficulty.

References

Adams, G.B. & Balfour, D.L. (2009). *Unmasking Administrative Evil*. New York, USA: M.E. Sharp Inc.

Allen, P. (2009). 'Mental deficiency institutions: have the obituaries been fair and balanced?' in Jukes, M. (ed). *Learning Disability Nursing Practice*. London: Quay Books.

Ashcroft, A., Jervis, N. & Roberts, C. (1999). A theory of mind (TOM) and people with learning disabilities: The effects of a training package. *Journal of Applied Research in Intellectual Disabilities*. **12** (1) 58–68.

Atherton, H. & Crickmore, D. (2011). (eds). *Learning Disabilities: Towards Inclusion*. Churchill Livingstone/Elsevier.

Atkinson, D. (2005). 'Narratives and people with learning disabilities' in Grant, G., Goward, P., Richardson, M. & Ramcharan, P. (eds). *Learning Disability: A Life Cycle Approach to Valuing People*. Maidenhead: Open University Press. 7–27.

Atkinson, D. & Walmsley, J. (2000). 'Oral history and the history of learning disability' in Bornat, J., Perks, R., Thompson, P. & Walmsley, J. (eds). *Oral History, Health and Welfare*. London: Routledge. 181–204.

Atkinson, D. & Williams F. (1990). *'Know me as I am': An Anthology of Prose, Poetry and Art by People with Learning Difficulties*. Hodder and Stoughton in association with the Open University and Mencap.

Audioblox (accessed 23 November 2011) http://www.audiblox2000.com/auditory-memory.htm

Augoustinos, M. & Walker, I. (1995). *Social Cognition. An Integrated Introduction*. London: Sage.

Bank-Mikkelson, N. (1980). 'Denmark' in R.J. Flyn and K.E. Nitsch (eds). *Normalisation, Social Integration and Community Services*. Texas, USA: Pro Ed.

Barga, N.K. (1996). Students with learning disabilities in education: Managing a disability. *Journal of Learning Disabilities*. **29** (4), 413–21.

Barnes C., Mercer G. & Shakespeare T. (1999). *Exploring Disability: A Sociological Introduction*. Cambridge: Polity Press.

Baron-Cohen, S. (1995). *Mind Blindness: An Essay on Autism and Theory of Mind*. Cambridge: MIT Press.

BBC 1 (accessed 15 November 2010) http://news.bbc.co.uk/1/hi/uk/7203232.stm

BBC 2 (accessed 20 November 2010) http://news.bbc.co.uk/1/hi/8222689.stm

BBC 3 Panorama. *Undercover Care: The Abuse Exposed* (broadcast 31 May 2011).

BBC 4 (accessed 15 November 2011) http://www.bbc.co.uk/history/worldwars/genocide/eichmann_01.shtml

BBC 5 (accessed 26 November 2011) http://www.bbc.co.uk/history/worldwars/genocide/eichmann_01.shtml

Bell, D.M, McKay, C. & Phillips K.J. (2001). Overcoming the barriers to voting experienced by people with learning disabilities. *British Journal of Learning Disabilities*. **29** (4) 122–27.

Benedict, S.B. & Kuhla, J. (1999). Nurses' participation in the Nazi euthanasia programme. *Western Journal of Nursing Research*. **21** (2) 246–63.

Biddle, B.J. (1986). Recent developments in role theory. *Annual Review of Sociology*. **12**, 67–92.

Biddle, B. J. & Thomas, E. J. (1979). 'Basic concepts for classifying the phenomena of role' in Biddle, B.J. & Thomas, E.J. (eds). *Role Theory: Concepts and Research*. Huntington, New York, USA: Robert E. Krieger.

Billig, M. (1987). *Arguing and Thinking: A Rhetorical Approach to Social Psychology*. Cambridge: Cambridge University Press.

Binding, K. & Hoche, A. (1920). *Die Freigabe der Verichtung Lebensunwerten Lebens*. Leipzig, Germany: Verlag vox Felix Meiner.

Birren, J. & Deutchman, D. (1991). *Guiding Autobiography Groups for Older Adults*. London: John Hopkins University Press.

Bolton, G. (2006). Narrative Writing: Reflective enquiry into professional practice. *Educational Action Research*. **14** (2) 202–18.

Booth, T. & Booth, W. (1994). *Parenting Under Pressure, Mothers and Fathers with Learning Difficulties*. Buckingham, Philadelphia, USA: Open University Press.

Braginsky, B. (1981). 'On being surplus: Its relationship to impression management and mental patienthood' in Tedeschi, J. (1981). *Impression Management and Social Psychological Research*. New York, USA: Academic Press.

185

Braginsky, D. & Braginsky, B. (1971). *Hansels and Gretels: Studies of Children in Institutions for the Mentally Retarded*. New York, USA: Holt, Reinhart & Winston.

Briton, J. (1979). Normalization: What of and what for? *Australian Journal of Retardation*. **5** (6) 224–49.

Brown H. & Smith H. (1992). *Normalisation: A Reader for the Nineties*. London: Routledge.

Burchardt, T. (2004). Capabilities and disability: the capabilities framework and the social model of disability. *Disability & Society*. **19** (7) 735–51.

Burton, M. & Chapman, M. (2004). Problems of EBP in community based services. *Journal of Learning Disabilities*. **8** (1) 56–70.

Burton, M. & Kagan, C. (2006). Decoding Valuing People. *Disability & Society*. **21** (4) 299–313.

Castlebeck (accessed 21 September 2011) http://www.castlebeck.com/index.php

Cesarani, D. (2006). *Becoming Eichmann: Rethinking the Life, Crimes, and Trial of a 'Desk Murderer'*. Essex: Da Capo Press.

Chappell, A.L., Goodley, D. & Lawthom, R. (2001). Making connections: the relevance of the social model of disability for people with learning difficulties. *British Journal of Learning Disabilities*. **29** (2) 45–50.

Child development (accessed 1 December 2011) http://childdevelopmentinfo.com/child-development/language_development.shtml

Cohen, S. (1980). *Folk Devils and Moral Panics: The Creation of Mods and Rockers*. New York, USA: St Martin's Press.

Collins (1994). *Collins English Dictionary*. Glasgow: Harper Collins Publishers.

Conservative Home website (accessed 9 October 2010) http://conservativehome.blogs.com/torydiary/sanctity_of_human_life/

Cusimano, A. (2010). *Learning Disabilities: There is a Cure*. Pennsylvania, USA: Achieve Publications.

Dagnan, D. & Cairns, M. (2005). Staff judgements of responsibility for the challenging behaviour of adults with intellectual disabilities. *Journal of Intellectual Disability Research*. **49** (1) 95–101.

Dagnan, D., Trower, P. & Smith, R. (1998). Care staff responses to people with learning disabilities and challenging behaviour: A cognitive-emotional analysis. *British Journal of Clinical Psychology*. **37** (1) 59–68.

Dagnan, D. & Weston, C. (2006). Physical intervention with people with intellectual disabilities: The influence of cognitive and emotional variables. *Journal of Applied Research in Intellectual Disabilities*. **19** (2) 219–22.

Dennison, A. & Mee, S. (2011). 'Personal narrative and life story' in Atherton, H. & Crickmore, D. (eds). *Learning Disabilities: Towards Inclusion*. Churchill Livingstone/Elsevier.

De Rosa. A.S. (1987). 'The social representation of mental illness in children and adults' in Doise, W. & Moscovici, S. (eds). *Current Issues in European Social Psychology* (Vol. 2). Cambridge: Cambridge University Press.

Devine, P.G. (1989). Stereotypes and prejudice: Their automatic and controlled components. *Journal of Personality and Social Psychology*. **56** (1) 5–18.

Department of Health and Social Services (1971). 'Better Services for the Mentally Handicapped'. Cm 4683. London: HMSO.

Department of Health and Social Services (1973). 'Local Authority Building Note no. 2'. London: HMSO.

Department of Health (2001). 'Valuing People: A new strategy for learning disability for the 21st century'. Cm 5086. London: HMSO.

Department of Health (2008). 'Healthcare for All: Report of the independent inquiry into access to healthcare for people with learning disabilities'. (accessed 21 September 2011) http://www.dh.gov.uk/en/Publicationsandstatistics/Publications/PublicationsPolicyAndGuidance/DH_099255

Department of Health (2009). 'Valuing People Now: A new three-year strategy for people with learning disabilities'. London: HMSO.

Dietrich, S., Beck, M., Bujantugs, B., Kenzine, D., Matschinger, H. & Angermeyer, M.C. (May 2004). The relationship between public causal beliefs and social distance toward mentally ill people. *Australian and New Zealand Journal of Psychiatry*. **38** (5) 348–54.

Dougherty, L. & Lister, S. (2004). *The Royal Marsden Hospital Manual of Clinical Nursing Procedures*. (6th ed). Oxford: Marsden.

Down, J.L.H. (1867). Observations on an Ethnic Classification of idiots. *The Journal of Mental Science* http://home.vicnet.net.au/~dealcc/Downs.htm

Down's Syndrome Association. http://www.downs-syndrome.org.uk/

Duffy S. (2003). *The Keys to Citizenship: A Guide to Getting Good Support for People with Learning Disabilities*. Birkenhead: Paradigm Consultancy and Development Agency Ltd.

Duncan, B.L. (1976). Differential social perception and attribution of intergroup violence: Testing the lower limits of stereotyping of blacks. *Journal of Personality and Social Psychology*. **34** (4) 590–98.

Ebbinghaus, A. (1987). *Opfer und Taterinnen*. Germany: Delphi Politik.

Edgerton, R.B. (1967). *The Cloak of Competence: Stigma in the Lives of the Mentally Retarded*. London: University of California Press.

Edublox (accessed 29 December 2011) http://www.learninginfo.org/auditory-memory.htm

Equality and Human Rights Commission (2011). 'Hidden in plain sight'. Inquiry into disability-related harassment. http://www.equalityhumanrights.com/dhfi

Fido, R. & Potts, M. (1989). It's not true what was written! Experiences of life in a mental handicap institution. *Oral History*. **17** (2) 31–35.

Fiske, S.T. & Taylor, S.E. (1991). *Social Cognition*. (2nd ed). New York, USA: McGraw Hill.

Finkelstein, V. (accessed 4 April 2012) http://www.independentliving.org/docs1/finkelstein.html

Fitzgerald, M.H. & Paterson, K. (1995). The hidden disability dilemma for the preservation of self. *Journal of Occupational Science, Australia*. **2** (1) 13–21.

Follows, R.A. (1995). *Language Use and its Effects on Empowerment for Adults with Learning Disabilities*. (MA thesis). University of Lancaster. Unpublished.

French, P. (2002). What is the evidence on evidence based nursing? An epistemological concern. *Journal of Advanced Nursing*. **37** (3) 250–57.

French, S. (1993). 'Disability, impairment or something in between?' in Swain, J., Finkelstein, V., French, S. & Oliver, M. *Disabling Barriers – Enabling Environments*. London: Sage Publications.

Friedlander, H. (1995). *The Origins of Nazi Genocide: From Euthanasia to the Final Solution*. Chapel Hill and London: The University of North Carolina Press.

Fiske, S.T. & Neuberg, S.L. (1990). 'A continuum of impression formation, from category-based to individuating processes: Influences of information and motivation on attention and interpretation' in Zenna M.P. (ed). *Advances in experimental social psychology*. (Vol 23). New York, USA: Academic Press 1–74.

Fiske, S. T. & Taylor, S. E. (1991). *Social Cognition*. (2nd ed). New York, USA: McGraw Hill.

Fitzgerald, M.H. & Paterson, K.A. (1995). The hidden disability dilemma for the preservation of self. *Journal of Occupational Science*. **2** (5) 13–21.

Forgas, J. P. (1985). Person prototypes and cultural salience: The role of cognitive and cultural factors in impression formation. *British Journal of Social Psychology*. **24** (1) 3–17.

Freedland, J. (14 May 2011). 'Safe house'. *Guardian*. (accessed 1 December 2011) www.guardian.co.uk/world/2011/may/14/holocaust-survivors-centre-freedland

Frith, U. (2003). *Autism: Explaining the Enigma*. Oxford: Blackwell.

Garfinkel, H. (1967). *Studies in Ethnomethodology*. New York, USA: Doubleday.

Gates, B. (1997). *Learning Disabilities*. London: Churchill Livingstone/Elsevier.

Gates, B. & Atherton, H. (2001). The challenge of evidence-based practice for learning disabilities. *British Journal of Nursing*. **10** (8) 517–22.

Gibbons, F.X. & Kassin, S.M. (1987). Information Consistency and Perceptual Set: Overcoming the Mental Retardation Schema. *Journal of Applied Social Psychology*. **17** (9) 810–27.

Gill, C.J. (1998). What are the problems of having a 'Hidden Disability'? *Post-Polio News, 1*. http://www.ppsg.ie/newsletter06.htm (accessed 26 July 2011)

Ginsberg, E.K. (1996). *Passing and the Fictions of Identity*. Durham, North Carolina, USA: Duke University Press.

Goffman, E. (1959). *The Presentation of Self in Everyday Life*. New York, USA: Doubleday.

Goffman, E. (1964). *Stigma*. Englewood Cliffs, New Jersey, USA: Prentice Hall.

Goffman E. (1969). *The Presentation of Self in Everyday Life*. Penguin.

Goldacre, B. (9 October 2010). 'A genetic cause for ADHD won't necessarily reduce the stigma attached'. *Guardian*.

Goodley, D. (2001). Learning difficulties, the social model of disability and impairment: challenging epistemologies. *Disability and Society*. **16** (2) 207–31.

Gould, S.J. (1981). *The Mismeasure of Man*. New York, USA: W.W. Norton.

Grey, C. (2010). *The New Social Story Book*. Arlington, Texas. USA: Future Horizons.

Guardian (accessed 1 December 2011) www.guardian.co.uk/world/2011/may/14/holocaust-survivors-centre-freedland

Hamilton, D.L. & Sherman, J.W. (1994). 'Stereotypes' in Wyer, R.S, Jr & Srull T.K. (eds). *Handbook of Social Cognition*. (Vol 2, 2nd ed). Hillsdale, New Jersey, USA: Erlbaum.

Healthcare Commission (2006). 'Joint investigation into the provision of services for people with learning disabilities at Cornwall Partnership NHS Trust'. (accessed 21 September 2011) http://www.cqc.org.uk/_db/_documents/cornwall_investigation_report.pdf

Healthcare Commission (2007). 'Investigation into the service for people with learning disabilities provided by Sutton and Merton Primary Care Trust'. (accessed 21 September 2011) http://www.cqc.org.uk/_db/_documents/Sutton_and_Merton_inv_sum_Tag.pdf

Heath, C. & Heath, D. (2007). *Made to Stick: Why Some Ideas Take Hold and Others Come Unstuck*. London: Random House Books.

Heider, F. (1958). *The Psychology of Interpersonal Relations*. New York, USA: Wiley.

HFE Bill (accessed 12 October 2010) http://www.dh.gov.uk/en/Publicationsandstatistics/Legislation/Actsandbills/DH_080211

Home Office (1968). 'Report of the Committee on Local Authority and Allied Personal Social Services'. (The Seebohm Report) Cm 3703, London: HMSO.

Howe Report (1969). 'Report of the Committee of Inquiry into Allegations of Ill-Treatment of Patients and other Irregularities at the Ely Hospital, Cardiff'. (Chairman: Geoffrey Howe). London: HMSO.

Hunt, N. (1967). *The World of Nigel Hunt*. Beaconsfield: Darwen Finlayson.

ICF (accessed 4 April 2012) http://www.disabilitaincifre.it/documenti/ICF_18.pdf

Independent (accessed 16 November 2010) http://www.independent.co.uk/opinion/commentators/deborah-orr/deborah-orr-we-must-protect-disabled-people-against-this-wave-of-barbaric-and-hateful-crimes-775617.html

Institute of Parenting (accessed 29 December 2011) http://childdevelopmentinfo.com/child-development/language_development.shtml

Jay Committee (1979). 'Report of the Committee of Enquiry into Mental Handicap Nursing and Care'. Cm 7468–1 London: HMSO.

Johns, C. (2000). *Becoming a Reflective Practitioner*. Oxford: Blackwell Science.

Jones, E.E. & Davies, K.E. (1965). 'From acts to dispositions: The attribution process in person perception' in L. Berkowitz (ed). *Advances in Experimental Social Psychology*. (Vol. 2). New York, USA: Academic Press. 79–94.

Jones, G.S. (1976). *Outcast London: A Study in the Relationship between Classes in Victorian Society*. Penguin.

Jukes, M. (2009). 'Striving towards ordinariness within a regulatory system' in Jukes, M. (ed). *Learning Disability Nursing Practice*. London: Quay Books. 39–74.

Katz, I. & Hass, R.G. (1988). Racial ambivalence and american value conflict: Correlation and priming studies of dual cognitive structures. *Journal of Personality and Social Psychology*. **55** (6) 893–905.

King's Fund Centre (1980). *An Ordinary Life. Comprehensive Locally-based Residential Services for Mentally Handicapped People*. London: King's Fund Centre.

Klotz, J. (2004). Sociocultural study of intellectual disability: moving beyond labelling and social constructionist perspectives. *British Journal of Learning Disabilities*. **32** (2) 93–104.

Lagerwey, M. (1999) Nursing ethics at Hadamar. *Qualitative Health Research*. **9** (6) 759–72.

Langdon, P.E., Clare, I.C.H. & Murphy, G.H. (2010). (accessed 1 December 2011) LD Online http://www.ldonline.org/article/6390/

Langdon, P.E., Clare, C.H.I. & Murphy, G. (2010). Measuring social desirability amongst men with intellectual disabilities: The psychometric properties of the Self- and Other-Deception Questionnaire – Intellectual Disabilities. *Research in Developmental Disabilities*. **31** (6) 1601–08.

Lemay, A.L (1999). 'Roles, identities, and expectations: Positive contributions to normalisation and social role valorization' in Flynn, R.J. & Lemay, A.L. (eds). *A Quarter Century of Normalization and Social Role Valorization*. Ottawa, Ontario, Canada: University of Ottawa Press.

Littlejohn, R. (25 September 1997). 'Once you got arrested, now you get a grant'. *Daily Mail*. http://www.highbeam.com/doc/1G1-110761743.html

Lukes, S. (2005). *Power: A Radical Review*. Basingstoke: Palgrave Macmillan.

Macdowell, M. (1930). *Simple Beginnings in the Training of Mentally Defective Children*. (3rd ed). London: Law and Local Government Publications Ltd.

Maslow, A.H. (1943). A theory of human motivation. *Psychological Review*. **50**, 70–96.

Mee, S. (2005). *Can Social Role Valorization Predict the Outcome of Social Interaction? A Study into the Process of Ascribing Value*. Lancaster (PhD thesis, unpublished).

Mee, S. (2010). You're not to dance with the girls: oral history, changing perception and practice. *Journal of Intellectual Disabilities*. **14** (1) 33–42.

Mee, S. (2012). It gets me upset talking about the Royal Albert: collaborative analysis of the ethics of an oral history project. *Educational Action Research*. (Due for publication December 2012)

Mencap (2007). 'Death by indifference' (accessed 21 September 2011) http://www.mencap.org.uk/sites/default/files/documents/2008-03/DBIreport.pdf

Meyer, W.U., Reisenzein, R. & Schutzwohl, A. (1997). Towards a process analysis of emotions: The case of surprise. *Motivation and Emotion*. **21** (3) 251–74.

Milgram, S. (1965) Liberating effects of group pressure. *Journal of Personality and Social Psychology*. **1** (2) 127–34.

Mollow, A. (2004). Identity politics and disability studies: A critique of recent theory. *Michigan Quarterly Review*. **43** (3) 269–96.

Morris, J. (1991). *Pride against Prejudice: Transforming Attitudes to Disability*. London: The Women's Press.

Moscovici, S. (1984). 'The phenomenon of social representation' in Farr, R.M. & Moscovici, S. (eds). *Social Representations*. Cambridge: Cambridge University Press.

Moscovici, S. (1988). Notes towards a description of social representations. *European Journal of Social Psychology*. **18** (3) 211–50.

Neumann, O. (1984). 'Automatic processing: A review of recent findings and a plea for an old theory' in Prinz, W. & Sanders, A.F. (eds). *Cognition and Motor Processes*. Berlin, Germany: Springer. 255–93.

Nirje, B. (1969). 'The normalisation principle and its human management implications' in Kugel, R.B. & Wolfensberger, W. (eds). *Changing Patterns in Residential Services for the Mentally Retarded*. Washington DC, USA: Presidential Committee on Mental Retardation.

189

Nursing and Midwifery Council (2004). *The NMC Code of Professional Conduct: Standards for Conduct, Performance and Ethics.* London: NMC.

Noakes, J. & Pridham, G. (1988). *Nazism: A History in Documents and Eyewitness Accounts 1919–1945.* (Vol. 2). New York, USA: Schocken Books.

Northway, R., Hutchinson, C. & Kingdom, A. (2006). *Shaping the Future: A Vision for Learning Disability Nursing.* UK learning disability consultant nurse network.

O'Brien, J. (1980). 'The principle of normalization: A foundation for effective services' in Gardner, J.F., Long, L., Nichols, R. & Iagulli, D.M. (eds). *Programme Issues in Development Disabilities.* Baltimore, Maryland, USA: Brookes Publishing.

O'Brien, J. (1985). *Normalization Training Through PASS 3: Team Leader Manual.* Decatur, Georgia, USA: Responsive Systems Associates.

O'Brien, J. (1987). 'A guide to lifestyle planning: Using the activities catalogue to integrate services and natural support systems' in Wilcox, B.W & Bellamy, G.T. (eds). *The Activities Catalogue: An Alternative Curriculum for Youth and Adults With Severe Disabilities.* Baltimore, Maryland, USA: Brookes Publishing.

O'Brien, J. & Tyne, A. (1981). *The Principle of Normalisation: A Foundation for Effective Services.* London: CMH.

Oliver, M.J. (1993). 'Re-defining disability' in Swain, J., Finkelstein, V., French, S. & Oliver, M. (eds). *Disabling Barriers – Enabling Environments.* London: Sage Publications.

Oliver M.J. (1996). *Understanding Disability: From Theory to Practice.* Hampshire and London: Macmillan Press.

Orr, D. (30 January 2008). 'We must protect disabled people against this wave of barbaric and hateful crimes'. *Independent* (accessed 16 November 2010) http://www.independent.co.uk/opinion/commentators/deborah-orr/deborah-orr-we-must-protect-disabled-people-against-this-wave-of-barbaric-and-hateful-crimes-775617.html

Paulhus, D.L. (1984) Two-component models of social desirability responding. *Journal of Personality and Social Psychology.* **46** (3) 598–609.

Paulhus, D.L. (1986). 'Self-deception and impression management in test responses' in Angleitner, A. & Wiggins, J.S. (eds). *Personality Assessment via Questionnaire.* New York, USA: Springer-Verlag. 43–165.

People First (accessed 22 November 2010) http://www.peoplefirstltd.com/why-learning-difficulty.php

Perrin, B. & Nirje, B. (1985). Setting the record straight; A critique of some frequent misconceptions of the normalization principle. *Australian and New Zealand Journal of Development Disabilities.* **11** (2) 69–74.

Pinker, S. (2011). *The Better Angels of Our Nature: The Decline of Violence in History and Its Causes.* London: Penguin.

Quarmby, K. (2011). *Scapegoat: How We Are Failing Disabled People.* London: Portobello Books.

Race, D.G. (1999). *Social Role Valorisation and the English Experience.* London: Whiting and Birch.

Race, R., Boxall, K. & Carson, I. (2005). Towards a dialogue for practice: reconciling Social Role Valorization and the Social Model of Disability. *Disability & Society.* **20** (5) 507–21.

Rapley, M. (1995). Black swans: conversation analysis of interviews with people with learning disabilities. *Clinical Psychology Forum* (Issue 84). 17.

Read, J. & Harre, N. (2001). The role of biological and genetic causal beliefs in the stigmatisation of 'mental patients'. *Journal of Mental Health.* **10** (2) 223–35.

Redley, M. (2008). Citizens with learning disabilities and the right to vote. *Disability & Society.* **23** (4) 375–84.

Reeder, G.D. & Brewer, M.B. (1979). A schematic model of dispositional attribution in interpersonal perception. *Psychological Review.* **86** (1) 61–79.

Richardson, M. (2011). 'Values based support' in Atherton, H. & Crickmore, D. (eds). *Learning Disabilities: Towards Inclusion.* Churchill Livingstone/Elsevier.

Rosch, E. (1975). Cognitive reference points. *Cognitive Psychology.* **7** (4) 532–47.

Rose, D. & Rose, J. (2005). Staff in services for people with intellectual disabilities: the impact of stress on attributions of challenging behaviour. *Journal of Intellectual Disability Research.* **49** (11) 827–38.

Royal Albert (accessed 30 November 2011)
http://www.unlockingthepast.org.uk/plugins/file_manager/files/1937_Synopsis.pdf

Rueda, R. & Mehan, H. (1986). Metacognition and passing: Strategic interactions in the lives of students with learning disabilities. *Anthropology & Education Quarterly*. **17** (3) 145–65.

Rumelhart, D.E. & Ortony, A. (1977). 'The representation of knowledge in memory' in Anderson, R.C., Spiro, R.J. & Montague, W.E. (eds). *Schooling and the Acquisition of Knowledge*. Hillsdale, New Jersey, USA: Erlbaum. 99–135.

Rumelhart, D.E. & Norman, D.A. (1978). 'Accretion, tuning, and restructuring: Three modes of learning' in Cotton, J.W. & Klatzky, R. (eds). *Semantic Factors in Cognition*. Hillsdale, New Jersey, USA: Erlbaum. 37–53.

Ryan, J. & Thomas, F. (1981). *The Politics of Mental Handicap*. Harmondsworth: Penguin.

Sagar, H. & Schofield, A. (1980). Racial and behavioural cues in black and white children's perceptions of ambiguously aggressive acts. *Journal of Personality and Social Psychology*. **39** (4) 590–98.

Schank, R. & Abelson, P. (1977). *Scripts, Plans, Goals, and Understanding: An Inquiry into Human Knowledge Structures*. Hillsdale, New Jersey, USA: Erlbaum.

Schneider, D.J. (1981). 'Tactical self presentation: Towards a broader conception' in Tedeschi, J. (ed). *Impression Management and Social Psychological Research*. New York, USA: Academic Press.

Schutzwohl, A. (1998). Surprise and Schema Strength. *Journal of Experimental Psychology: Learning, Memory, and Cognition*. **24** (5) 1182–99.

Scull, A. (1977). *Decarceration: Community Treatment and the Deviant: A Radical View*. Englewood Cliffs, New Jersey, USA: Prentice Hall.

Shifrer, D., Chandra, M. & Callahan, R. (2011). Disproportionality and learning disabilities: Parsing apart race, socioeconomic status, and language. *Journal of Learning Disability*. **44** (3) 246–55.

Silverman, D. (2001). *Interpreting Qualitative Data: Methods for Analyzing Talk, Text and Interaction*. (2nd ed). London: Sage.

Simmons, Harvey, G. (1978). Explaining social policy: The Mental Deficiency Act of 1913. *Journal of Social History*. **11** (3) 387–404.

Spitz, V. (2005). *Doctors from Hell: The Horrific Account of Nazi Experiments on Humans*. Boulder, Colorado, USA: Sentient.

Stanley, L. (1993). *On auto/biography in sociology. Sociology*. **27** (1) 41–52.

Strauss A.L. (1987). *Qualitative Analysis for Social Scientists*. Cambridge: Cambridge University Press.

Swain, J., French, S., Barnes, C., & Thomas, C. (eds). (2004). *Disabling Barriers – Enabling Environments*. London: Sage.

Taylor, S.E. & Crocker, J. (1981). 'Schematic bases of social information processing' in Higgins, E.T., Herman, C.P. & Zanna, M.P. (eds), *Social Cognition: The Ontario Symposium*. (Vol. 1). Hillsdale, New Jersey, USA: Erlbaum.

Tedeschi, J. (1981). *Impression Management and Social Psychological Research*. New York, USA: Academic Press.

Tedeschi, J. & Reiss, R. (1981). 'Identity, the phenomenal self and laboratory research' in Tedeschi, J. (ed). *Impression Management and Social Psychological Research*. New York, USA: Academic Press.

Tedeschi, J. & Rosenfeld, A. (1981). 'Self presentation and the phenomenal self' in Tedeschi, J. (ed). *Impression Management and Social Psychological Research*. New York, USA: Academic Press.

Thomas, C. (1999). *Female Forms: Experiencing and Understanding Disability*. Buckingham, Philadelphia, USA: Open University Press.

Thomas, C. (2004). 'Representing disability' in Swain, J., French, S., Barnes, C., & Thomas, C. (eds). *Disabling Barriers – Enabling Environments*. London: Sage.

Thomas, S. & Wolfensberger, W. (1999). 'An overview of social role valorisation' in Flynn, R.J. & Lemay, R.A. *A Quarter Century of Normalisation and Social Role Valorisation: Evolution and Impact*. Syracuse, New York, USA: Syracuse University, Training Institute for Human Service.

Torgesen, J. (1980). Conceptual and educational implications of the use of efficient task strategies by learning disabled children. *Journal of Learning Disabilities*. **13** (7) 19–26.

191

Trower, P., Casey, A. & Dryden, W. (1988). *Cognitive Behaviour Counselling in Action*. London: Sage.

Tuchel, J. (1984). *Kein Recht auf Leben. Beitrage und Dokumente zur Entrechtung und Vernichtung 'Lebensunwerten Lebens' im Nationalsozialismus*. Berlin, Germany.

Turkington, C. & Harris, J. (2006). *The Encyclopedia of Learning Disabilities*. New York, USA: Bookworks.

United Nations (1971). *Declaration of the General and Specific Rights of the Mentally Retarded*. Geneva, Switzerland: UN.

Unlocking the past (accessed 30 November 2011)
http://www.unlockingthepast.org.uk/plugins/file_manager/files/sm_test_01.html

Valeras, A.B. (2010). 'We don't have a box': Understanding hidden disability identity utilizing narrative research methodology. *Disability Studies Quarterly*. **30** (3) http://dsq-sds.org/article/view/1267/1297

Walker, I. & Read, J. (2002). The differential effectiveness of psychosocial and biogenetic causal explanations in reducing negative attitudes toward 'mental illness'. *Psychiatry*. **65** (4) 313–25.

Weigel, L., Langdon, P.E., Collins, S. & O'Brien, Y. (2006). Challenging behaviour and learning disabilities: The relationship between expressed emotion and staff attributions. *British Journal of Clinical Psychology*. **45** (2) 205–16.

Weiner B. (1985). An attributional theory of achievement, motivation and emotion. *Psychological Review* **92**. (4) 547–73.

Weiner B. (1986). *An Attributional Theory of Motivation and Emotion*. Berlin, Germany: Springer-Verlag.

Wetherell, W., Taylor, S. & Yates, S. (2001). *Discourse as Data: A Guide for Analysis*. London: Sage.

Wetherell, W., Taylor, S. & Yates, S. (2001b). *Discourse Theory and Practice: A Reader*. London: Sage.

Wolfensberger, W. (1972). *Normalisation: The Principle of Normalisation in Human Services*. Toronto, Canada: National Institute on Mental Retardation.

Wolfensberger, W. (1980). 'The definitions of normalisation: Update, problems, disagreements and misunderstandings' in , R.J.Flynn & Nitsch, K.E. (eds). *Normalisation, Social Integration and Community Service*. Baltimore, Maryland, USA: University Park Press.

Wolfensberger, W. (1983). Social Role Valorisation: A proposed new term for the principle of normalisation. *Mental Retardation*. **21** (6) 234–39.

Wolfensberger, W (1984). 'Holocaust II'. *Journal of Learning Disabilities*. **17** (7) 439–40.

Wolfensberger, W. (1994). The growing threat to the lives of handicapped people in the context of modernistic values. *Disability and Society*. **9** (3) 395–413.

Wolfensberger, W. (1995). Social Role Valorisation is too conservative. No, it is too radical. *Disability and Society*. **10** (3) 365–68.

Wolfensberger, W. (1998). *A Brief Introduction to Social Role Valorisation as a High Order Concept for Addressing the Plight of Socially Devalued People, and for Structuring Human Services* (3rd ed., rev.) Syracuse, New York, USA: Syracuse University, Training Institute for Human Service.

Wolfensberger, W. (2001). The story of the 'Cruickshank Chairs' at Syracuse University: A contribution to the history of the brain injury construct. *Mental Retardation*. **39** (6) 472–81.

Wolfensberger, W. & Glen, L. (1975). *Program Analysis of Service Systems, a Method for the Qualitative Evaluation of Human Services*. (3rd ed). Vol. 1 Handbook. Toronto, Canada: National Institute on Mental Retardation. Reprinted 1978.

Wolfensberger, W. & Thomas, S. (1983). *PASSING (Program Analysis of Service Systems Implementing Normalisation Goals)*. Normalisation Criteria Ratings Manual (2nd ed). Toronto, Canada: National Institute on Mental Retardation.

Wolfensberger, W. & Thomas, S. (1994). Obstacles in the professional human service culture to implementation of social role valorisation and community integration of clients. *Care in Place*. **1** (1) 53–56.

Wolfensberger, W. (1995). An 'if this, then that' formulation of decisions related to social role valorization as a better way of interpreting it to people. *Mental Retardation*. **33** (3) 163–69.

Wood, P. (1980). *International Classification of Impairments, Disabilities and Handicaps*. Geneva, Switzerland: World Health Organisation.

World Health Organisation (2001) (accessed 4 April 2012) http://www.disabilitaincifre.it/documenti/ICF_18.pdf

Index